Rethinking Welfare

Rethinking Welfare

Bill Jordan

Basil Blackwell

Copyright © Bill Jordan 1987

First published 1987

Basil Blackwell Ltd
108 Cowley Road, Oxford, OX4 1JF, UK

Basil Blackwell Inc.
432 Park Avenue South, Suite 1503
New York, NY 10016, USA

British Library Cataloguing in Publication Data
Jordan, Bill, 1941–
   Rethinking Welfare.
   1. Social service   2. Public welfare
   I. Title
   361   HV40

   ISBN 0–631–15347–0
   ISBN 0–631–15348–9 Pbk

Library of Congress Cataloging in Publication Data
Jordan, Bill, 1941–
   Rethinking welfare.

   Includes index.
   1. Social policy. 2. Public welfare. 3. Social service.
   4. Equality. 5. Welfare state. I. Title.
HV31.J66   1987   361.6′1   86–26385
ISBN 0–631–15347–0
ISBN 0–631–15348–9 (pbk.)

Typeset in 10 on 11½ pt Ehrhardt
by Opus, Oxford
Printed in Great Britain by Billing & Sons Ltd, Worcester

Contents

Acknowledgements

I have benefited from some very helpful criticisms and comments on early drafts of this book from Iain Hampsher-Monk, Michael Hill, Peter Ashby, Keith Hart, Ray Pahl, John May and Jean Packman. I am very grateful for these, and hope the final product is better than the versions they saw. As with my other recent books, I received help from Alex Allan, both through her superb typing, and through discussions which were at least as valuable as any with the people mentioned above. As the book was being finished, she left Exeter to go to Oxford, and to produce her own thoughts rather than typing mine. Her new role is far more appropriate, but my colleagues and I will miss her greatly. Final assistance with amendments was nobly given by Samantha Youll, Sue Ridler and Marian Gowen.

1

The Future of Welfare

In the course of any day, we move several times between spheres of life that are equally crucial for our wellbeing. In the domestic sphere, we give and receive affection and encouragement; we also do essential services for each other. From our jobs we get pay, pensions, perks and prospects. From the commercial sphere, we buy most of the goods that sustain our daily lives. From the state we get education, health care, parts of our income and possibly housing. Anyone who spends the whole day in the state sphere of welfare is probably in prison or hospital – though he or she may be living alone in a council house on social security, and be unable to afford to go out to the shops.

The difference between advanced and simple societies lies partly in the separation of these spheres. In simple societies these aspects of welfare would all be part of the customary, face-to-face social relationships of communal living. We have divided them off into apparently divergent systems, which seem to use entirely different principles for distributing wellbeing. In the domestic sphere, most of us seem to be instinctively co-operative – we usually try to contribute to family life according to our abilities, and to treat members according to their needs. In the commercial sphere (as both producers and consumers), most of us appear instinctively rivalrous, competing for scarce resources, accumulating wealth and striving for advantage – even if it is for the advantage of our trade union in relation to others. In the state sphere, we are mostly passive contributors or beneficiaries – grateful or grumbling, but playing little part in the provision of services.

So entrenched is the separation between these spheres that few books try to analyse how they all contribute to welfare. It is certainly difficult to measure and compare the contributions of the different sectors, especially the domestic sphere, where people do a great many services for each other on an unpaid basis. As a result, Richard Titmuss's pioneering essay on the social division of welfare,[1] though widely acknowledged, has not been satisfactorily followed up. Books about welfare are usually concerned with the state's social services.

But in real life we *must* make such comparisons, or we could not make decisions. We *have* to choose between alternative courses of action which involve inputs and outputs from all these spheres. For instance, one person might be deciding whether to stay on the dole or take a job at a wage that is below the benefit level. Another might be deciding whether to stay with her husband or to move out and claim supplementary benefit. A third might be debating whether to go to the doctor about a symptom or simply to the chemist, to buy a brand-name remedy. A fourth might be wondering whether she can go on looking after her disabled elderly mother, and if not whether to try for local authority or private residential care. A fifth might be unsure whether to ask a neighbour to look after her children while she is in hospital, or whether to request that they go into local authority care; and a sixth might be trying to choose whether to send his children to state or private schools.[2]

What is more, governments shift the boundaries between the spheres of welfare, and do so quite deliberately. The creation of welfare states was largely an attempt to make the social services a part of everyone's life, rather than a sphere that dealt exclusively with social casualties. More recently, market-minded governments have been trying to shift the boundaries in the opposite direction, making activities that were the exclusive sphere of the state open to competition from the commercial sector. Tax and benefit cuts are intended to shift income towards the rich, with possible consequences for stimulating commercial activity and hence employment. Community care programmes are meant to move people out of health service institutions and into 'ordinary' life – either with families, or in private or local authority residential care. The relaxation of Sunday trading laws would move some sabbatical activities from the domestic sphere into the commercial one.

So I shall try in this book to develop a framework for looking at all these sources of welfare, and for examining the implications for public policy of such a framework. In the first part I shall consider the relationship between personal and social welfare, and the principles by which welfare is distributed in the various spheres. In the second part I shall look at some of the major socioeconomic changes that are taking place in advanced countries of the Western world, and their implications for welfare. In the third part I shall look at a number of issues for the social services in the light of these changes, and at the principles derived from the first part of my analysis.

As far as possible, I want to make my framework one that applies to all the advanced capitalist countries, but inevitably I shall tend to use examples mainly from Western Europe and, in the final section, particularly from Britain. International comparisons are as important as comparisons between the spheres within society, because my intention is to break out of stereotypical assumptions about what constitutes welfare or how it can be provided. But this in turn involves a tension between two sets of factors. On the one hand, it is clear that the socioeconomic changes that have most affected the boundaries of welfare in the advanced capitalist countries –

employment and unemployment, earnings and social security, the 'fiscal crisis of the state' – are all *international*, and stem from major changes in the international location of production, division of labour and patterns of trade. On the other hand, traditional analyses of welfare (in terms of state social services) are deeply bound up with ideas about *national* economic management and the nation-state. As a background to the analysis that follows in the rest of this book, it is the latter issue that I shall discuss in this opening chapter.

Nation-States and Social Welfare

In spite of some convergence between the advanced capitalist countries since the Second World War, there are still enormous differences between them in the balance between their spheres of welfare. The most obvious contrast is in terms of the proportion of GNP spent on state social protection schemes, from Sweden (33 per cent) to Japan (10 per cent).[3] These differences in turn conceal others over the balance *between* state services, with the United States spending a higher proportion of GNP on state education than any other country except the Netherlands, but having only 2 per cent of its housing stock publicly owned (compared with about 30 per cent in Britain).[4] Yet these contrasts are very crude, because they tell us little about the eventual distribution of spending power, or about how some countries which devote a high proportion of GNP to social services (like Austria and Germany) still contrive to end up with a relatively unequal distribution of final incomes (compared with Sweden or the Netherlands);[5] whereas others, with low spending on social services (like Japan and Australia), end up with a relatively equal final distribution (compared with the United States, Britain or France).[6]

Nevertheless, with the partial exceptions of the United States, Japan and Australia, the public sector generally, and the social services in particular, have come to be seen as the most important providers of welfare in advanced capitalist countries (while the state is seen as virtually the sole arbiter of welfare in the Eastern bloc). This was certainly not always the case; nor was the liberal market approach to welfare always the only alternative to state provision. The trade unions in many European countries fought long and hard for the right to provide their own welfare benefits for their members out of union dues,[7] and in Britain the Friendly Societies were equally tenacious in their attempts to keep services on a mutual contributory basis. The syndicalist tradition of socialism emphasized the solidarity of producers, and workers' control as a source of welfare; while anarchism, far from seeing the state as a major source of welfare, wanted to abolish it altogether. So why has the emphasis on state social welfare become so universal?

The answers to this question seem to lie in the period between the wars and immediately after the Second World War. International recession, the contraction of world trade and mass unemployment all pointed to a need for national economic management and a greater state involvement in social life. In the 1930s the apparent success of totalitarian regimes – the Nazis 'solved' the problem of 6 million unemployed people in Germany in a few years, while Stalin accomplished a more rapid process of industrialization and urbanization in Russia than had been achieved anywhere else – challenged liberal democratic governments to discover new ways to run their societies. The war itself drew states further than ever before into the direction of economic and social activities. Keynesian economics seemed to offer a method of national economic management for the postwar period that was consistent with liberal democratic traditions.

The result was a whole series of postwar political 'settlements' in Western Europe, collectively referred to as the 'social democratic compromise'. The terms on which trade unions and social democratic parties entered the state as partners in national economic management were enormously varied – they will be analysed in greater detail in chapter 6. The common theme was that labour movements, representing organized industrial workers, lent their support to new social institutions (including social services) which were supposed to guarantee full employment, a share in growing prosperity and the satisfaction of certain basic needs.

With hindsight, we can see that the success of these new systems depended more on the peculiar economic circumstances of the times – the new American-led world order, political stability, reconstruction programmes, Marshall aid, the dominance of large national enterprises, the national industrial self-sufficiency generated by the war, plentiful and flexible supplies of labour, the application of a new wave of technological innovation, the growth of demand for consumer durables and so on – than on their institutions or techniques. The unprecedented sustained growth of national income all over Western Europe for the 25 years after the war was credited to the new methods of national economic management, especially by the labour leaderships who shared in this process. If it did nothing else, the postwar era thoroughly incorporated organized labour and the social democratic political parties into the institutional framework of the nation-state. Whereas before the First World War organized labour presented itself primarily as an international (pacifist) force, after the Second World War it took on the guise of a partner in national economic management. Although the political trappings of this process were less evident in the United States and Japan, the economic underpinnings were similar.

The paradoxical outcome of all this is that social democratic parties and trade unions have become so identified with the machinery of national economic management that they no longer represent an alternative, critical force. Once outside the state and suspicious of all its institutions, now they look to the state to consolidate their apparent gains from the postwar period. For the European labour movements, the welfare of their main constituents – the working class – seems inextricably tied up with the mechanisms of the modern capitalist state, even when it can no longer deliver the same results.

By contrast, market-minded political parties are able to take a far broader view of welfare, since they regard state provision as only one relevant sphere. The radicalism of the new political right lies in its scope for dismantling state machinery, privatizing state enterprises or cutting social services – forms of public asset-stripping that are much easier to accomplish under modern economic conditions than the planning of national targets that was once the pride of social democratic governments.

One new factor that has upset the balance of national forces on which the postwar settlement depended is the emergence of international enterprises, which transcend national boundaries. Unlike large national companies, multinational corporations do not depend on co-operation with any particular national state for their success. They can select their production sites and markets on a global calculation of advantage; and while state taxes, subsidies, regulations and restrictions are all relevant considerations, all nation-states are forced to compete for the favours they offer by way of investment and employment.[8]

So instead of being essential partners in the management of the national economy, organized labour is reduced to being a potential productive partner for international capital. National success (in terms of growth and employment rates) depends on productivity and efficiency at the plant level, not on planning and co-ordination by the state. Market-minded governments (like Margaret Thatcher's) have been able to drop labour from their economic councils and actually use international economic forces to bring the trade union movement to heel, deliberately opening up large parts of industry to a flood of overseas competition, and waiting for the inefficient and unlucky companies to be washed away.

This is not to say that the managed economy of the postwar era is no longer possible. A few countries have been successful in the use of corporate methods of economic management, and have also kept down unemployment and sustained their social services. What these countries – Sweden, Austria, Norway – have in common is that they are small, homogeneous and rich, with efficient industrial sectors and a strong continuity of (mainly social democratic) governments. Their success still inspires social democrats and trade unionists in other European countries, even where none of these conditions exists.

Because the same political and economic conditions gave rise both to the incorporation of organized labour into the state and the creation of modern social services, it is not surprising that the political theory and practice of national economic management is so closely associated with the view of welfare as residing chiefly in the public sector. But the other reason for this close association is the hostility of market-minded governments to the public sector in general, and to social services in particular.

The Public Sector and the Market

It has been a declared policy of market-minded governments to reduce state spending, and especially spending on social welfare. As a result, market-minded policies have cut the living standards of poorer people, and especially those who depend most on state benefits and services. At the same time, as part of an attempt to create a more dynamic and enterprise-orientated system, they have redistributed resources in favour of the rich, mainly through tax cuts.

By far the most thoroughgoing instance of these policies, and an example for market-minded governments elsewhere in the advanced capitalist world, has been the United States.[9] Of course, under Ronald Reagan policy has consisted not in cutting public spending but in transferring it from social welfare to armaments, but the example is no less forceful for this. In the United States the more recent and *ad hoc* nature of most social welfare programmes, the weakness of organized labour and the greater dominance of the enterprise ethos all made cuts in this form of spending much easier to accomplish.

The United States now stands as a model for market-minded European governments of the kind of society they might aspire to create, and as a warning to European labour movements. It is a dualized society, with one labour market providing high salaries for professional people and those qualified in advanced technologies, and high wages for the stronger section of organized labour, and a second labour market paying low wages to a casualized and fragmented workforce consisting mainly of unskilled, short-term or part-time employees, many of whom are women, blacks or recent immigrants from Latin America.[10] The social services are being rapidly adapted to this two-sector economy, subsidizing low wages or paying 'workfare' – public assistance made conditional on some form of compulsory employment.

In the face of this threat, it is not surprising that the stance of European labour movements is mainly defensive, trying to protect the public sector and the social services as the bastions of working-class welfare. They can justifiably argue that market-minded policies have – except in the United States – reinforced unemployment, and that they have universally worsened the plight of the poorest groups in society. What are less convincing are their claims that a return to national economic management based on an expanded public sector would contribute to more sustained growth and a significant reduction in unemployment. While state institutions may to some extent protect workers and welfare beneficiaries in uncompetitive economies from the worst consequences of international capitalist development, they can no more harness the forces of this development to national prosperity than they could catch the Holy Ghost in a paper bag. Without the power to plan and direct national industrial investment and output, their programmes can deliver only limited advantages to their working-class constituencies. The experiences of the Mitterrand regime in France from 1981 to 1986 illustrate this lesson.

Meanwhile, the purposes of the very state social services that they seek to defend are being transformed by a combination of socioeconomic change and market-minded government policy. While it may still be true in Sweden that the welfare state gives social rights of citizenship to all, and guarantees an equal autonomous status to working-class citizens, in Britain (to quote the opposite case) the social services are increasingly becoming the instruments of exclusion from economic and social participation. One sector of British society – the poorest – is being trapped by a combination of high unemployment, low wages and a depressed public housing system; means-tested benefits tie their incomes to the poverty line, whether they are in work or out of it.[11] The very people who most depend on state social welfare services are least likely to be in regular employment, to be members of trade unions or to play any active part in organized political life. The welfare state in Britain is coming to be an instrument of division rather than solidarity, and better-paid, regular, organized workers are being drawn into the market sector, with their interests as ratepayers and taxpayers opposed to the excluded, casualized sector of welfare beneficiaries.

Fair Shares of Welfare

The postwar welfare state was claimed as more than a political settlement; its strongest advocates argued that it had a moral basis in social justice. The new, universal social rights of citizenship that it provided were hailed as setting standards of fairness between equal members of the same community, and radically modifying class divisions.[12]

But the standards incorporated into the social services were derived from the institutions of postwar industrialized capitalism. For instance, ideas of what was a 'fair reward' for labour were the product of struggles between employers and trade unions, and of unions' greater or lesser success in organizing workers in their trade or sector. Unions with market power, which could eliminate the threat of casual, cut-rate or blackleg competition, were then able to establish closed shops, apprentice schemes, promotion and pay structures favourable to their members. Wide differentials in pay and conditions, which were largely a reflection of this interplay between market forces and organizational power, were justified as 'fair' by vague reference to skills, and to notions of a 'labour theory of value'. Fairness was therefore a very complex social construct, whose assumptions were derived from the history and institutions of the labour movement, and from power relations within it.

We can see this in the roles and rules of the social services themselves. For example, the regulations governing sickness and unemployment benefits are still designed as much to eliminate 'unfair' competition from claimants of these benefits with people in work as they are with claimants' welfare in mind. Trade unions, which played their part in the administration of social security systems, acquiesced in (or demanded) standard rates of benefit which were well below average earnings, and earnings-related supplements for those with higher pay. Controls over claimants' behaviour, and especially over their opportunities to do part-time or casual work, were an important part of ensuring that they could not become a rival, disorganized workforce, or a source of cheap labour for employers. Married women were included mainly as dependants on men, on the assumption that they would be housewives, or secondary earners.

It is therefore not surprising that these institutionalized definitions of fairness should be challenged by the social and economic changes that have swept through advanced capitalist societies. It may have been fair to base rewards on union power while the overall strength of organized labour seemed to be growing, while industrial employment as a proportion of all paid work was expanding and while there was full employment (for men at least); it is not so clearly fair at a time of mass unemployment, a shrinking industrial workforce and falling trade union membership. It must have seemed fair to treat married women as home-based dependants while the historical trend was towards their withdrawal from the labour market with increasing prosperity, but not now that they are taking paid work in growing numbers. An uncritical consensus on fair shares, over pay and over the welfare state, can no longer be assumed.

These changes have gone so far that they confront the labour movement – especially in less successful industrial economies like Britain – with a very awkward dilemma. A dual labour market, with a shrinking organized sector and a growing casualized, fragmented one, fed by married women and the unemployed, means that union power is reduced, and there is a choice between two overall strategies, neatly summarized by John Goldthorpe:

> From the standpoint of the unions, the first concern must be that of how best they can secure their labour-market power against the threats that dualism can pose. And what would in this respect seem crucial is which of two very different strategies national union movements aim to pursue: that is, whether they strive to uphold class orientation, which must entail as far as possible opposing dualism – for example, by seeking legislation which can check employers' attempts to generate it and by regarding secondary workers, even if non-union members, as

still forming part of the unions' constituency; or whether, on the other hand, they in effect accept dualism and fall back on the defence of the specific sectional interests of their enrolled members, in the hope that these interests may then be as much protected as undermined by dualism through the 'shock absorber' function the secondary work-force performs.[13]

Goldthorpe goes on to suggest that the first strategy is extremely difficult to accomplish and the second is more likely to prevail, especially in circumstances of economic adversity. What can be expected from the second approach is 'the fundamental division and effective depoliticisation of the working class, with the concomitant disappearance of any organised challenge to the capitalist order in the name of economic democracy and social equality'.[14]

But these changes pose problems not only for labour movements. If dualism erodes acceptance of the standards of fairness institutionalized in the welfare state, it can lead to the breakdown of respect for state regulations in general. Research is beginning to indicate signs that those excluded from the organized labour market and from membership of trade unions develop attitudes towards income tax and social security benefits which are at odds not merely with union norms but also with official rules. In particular, for people who cannot get jobs with a traditional structure of employment protection, pay and promotion, short-term 'cash jobs' (whether they are claiming, working or self-employed) provide the only available way of cushioning themselves against adversity and uncertainty.[15] Although individual employers may gain from this, it represents 'unfair competition' with other firms as well as with organized labour, and threatens to turn the labour market into a Hobbesian jungle.

Aims of This Book

The main aim of this book is to reopen the debate about welfare shares, and particularly to do so in terms of fairness. While there is general agreement that the consensus that underpinned the welfare state has broken down, there have been few attempts to rethink the principles of welfare distribution in practical or policy terms. Though there has been increasing interest in questions of justice in political philosophy in recent years, fewer efforts have been made to apply these new ideas to the details of social policy in the light of economic change.

My first concern will be to find a framework that allows questions about individuals' personal welfare to be discussed along with those about the welfare of others, and of the community as a whole. This involves an analysis of the various sources of personal welfare, and the values according to which we share welfare among ourselves in everyday relationships. It also involves considering whether the ideas about fair shares that we apply informally, in small-scale transactions, can be used in debates about shares of welfare in wider society. This is the agenda of the first part of the book.

My second concern is how social change has affected the systems through which the various forms of welfare are distributed. By mapping these changes and their effects, I hope to apply the framework developed in part one to the new social and economic configurations of advanced capitalist societies which will be described in part two.

My third concern is to consider in greater detail what the implications of a new approach to welfare shares – taking account of all the spheres in which wellbeing is distributed – might be for policy within the social services. My aim is to develop a wider understanding of social policy which allows the analysis of informal and commercial aspects of welfare to be better meshed with accounts of the operation of state systems of provision.

My overall objective is to try to unlock the debate about the future of welfare from the trap of arguments about the managed economy and the scale of public spending – to restore it instead to its proper place, as a question about wellbeing in every sphere of social and economic life. I shall argue that we all deal in welfare issues all the time; my aim is to clarify how we deal with them now, and how we might deal with them better in future.

Notes

1 R. M. Titmuss, 'The Social Division of Welfare', in *Essays on the Welfare State*, Allen & Unwin, 1958.
2 Peter Taylor-Gooby, 'Privatisation, Power and the Welfare State', *Sociology*, vol. 20, no. 2, May 1986, pp. 228–46, has published the results of a large-scale survey of attitudes towards state and commercial services for health, education, housing and pensions. Although commercial provision was seen as superior to state services on almost every count, levels of satisfaction with state services were high, and dissatisfaction was expressed slightly more in terms of inadequate resources than lack of consumer control. Hence respondents favoured more spending on state services *and* more scope for private welfare provision, and would be prepared to pay for these – they were not perceived as mutually exclusive alternatives.
3 Eurostat, *Review 1973–82*, Statistical Office of the European Communities, 1984, table 3.5.2, p. 134. The Netherlands' proportion of spending is roughly the same as Sweden's, and that of the United States is about 13 per cent.
4 Joan Higgins, *States of Welfare: Comparative Analysis of Social Policy*, Basil Blackwell and Martin Robertson, 1981. The United States also spends very low proportions on state health provision compared with European countries, and especially Sweden (see Ian Gough, *The Political Economy of the Welfare State*, Macmillan, 1979, table 5.2, p. 79). But whereas private commercial schemes predominate in health in the United States, occupational ones are the major

source in Japan – 99 per cent of all employees in companies with over 5,000 workers get health insurance, and 93 per cent live in company houses (Higgins, *States of Welfare*, p. 143). The UK in 1980 devoted the lowest proportion of its GNP to all social welfare expenditure of the European Community countries (21.4 per cent, compared with Ireland's 21.9 per cent and the Netherlands' 30.7 per cent), but at that time a relatively high proportion of this went on housing compared with the other European countries (see Robert Walker, 'Resources, Welfare Expenditure and Poverty in the European Countries', in R. Walker, R. Lawson and P. Townsend (eds), *Responses to Poverty: Lessons from Europe*, Heinemann, 1984, table 2.12, p. 47; and Eurostat, *Review 1973–82*, table 2.2.11, p. 78).

5 G. Esping-Andersen and W. Korpi, 'Social Policy as Class Politics in Post-War Capitalism: Scandinavia, Austria and Germany', in J. H. Goldthorpe (ed.), *Order and Conflict in Contemporary Capitalism*, Oxford University Press, 1984.

6 Francis C. Castles, *The Working Class and Welfare: Reflections on the Political Development of the Welfare State in Australia and New Zealand, 1890–1980*, Allen & Unwin, 1986.

7 Noel Whiteside, 'Industrial Labour, Unemployment and the Growth of Social Insurance, 1900–1930', paper for the International Economic History Conference, Budapest, August 1982. See also J. Alber, 'Government Responses to the Challenge of Unemployment: The Development of Unemployment Insurance in Europe', in P. Flora and A. Heidenheimer (eds), *The Development of Welfare States in Europe and America*, Transaction Books, 1981.

8 There is a good deal of dispute about the extent to which transnational companies disrupt or destroy the potential for national economic management. The original argument for their disruptive effects (and the proposal to use selective nationalization as a countermeasure) was set out by Stuart Holland in *The Socialist Challenge*, Quartet Books, 1975. Recent restatements of these problems are contained in C. Offe, *Disorganised Capitalism: Contemporary Transformations of Work and Politics*, Polity Press, 1985, and R. Murray, 'Why Britain Can't Work in the Shadow of Keynes', *Guardian*, 28 October 1985. For the argument that success or failure in manufacturing has little to do with transnational companies' power, see Jim Tomlinson, 'The Rise and Decline of National Economic Management with Special Reference to Britain and Sweden', paper for the ESRC Symposium on Socio-Economic Change in the West, Cambridge, 1986.

9 In Britain, by contrast, outside the field of housing, where very substantial cuts have been made, Margaret Thatcher's Conservative government has not achieved a cut in overall spending on state social services. If spending in 1978–9 is taken as the base-line, housing expenditure fell by 69 per cent up to 1984–5 but overall spending was down less than 1 per cent, with a rise of 27 per cent in expenditure on social security and 15 per cent on health and personal social services (Taylor-Gooby, 'Privatisation, Power and the Welfare State', table 1, p. 229). Conversely, the growth of expenditure on commercial welfare provision was rapid in Britain in the 1970s, and was scarcely accelerated by Conservative policies (ibid., table 2, p. 230).

10 See for instance E. Ginzberg, 'The Jobs Problem', *Scientific American*, January 1977, pp. 20–43, and E. Ginzberg, 'The Mechanization of Work', *Scientific American*, September 1982, pp. 39–47; R. Edwards, M. Reich and R. Gordon,

Segmented Work, Divided Workers, Historical Transformation of Labour in the United States, Cambridge University Press, 1982. For dual labour markets in European countries see F. Wilkinson (ed.), *The Dynamics of Labour Market Segmentation*, Academic Press, 1981, and S. Berger and M. J. Piore, *Dualism and Discontinuity in Industrial Societies*, Cambridge University Press, 1980.

11 See for instance CES Ltd, *The Outer Estates of Britain: Preliminary Comparison of Four Estates*, CES, Paper 23, 1984, and report in *Guardian*, 24 October 1984. See also Bill Jordan, *The State: Authority and Autonomy*, Basil Blackwell, 1985, ch. 13.

12 See for instance T. H. Marshall, *Citizenship and Social Class*, Cambridge University Press, 1950.

13 J. H. Goldthorpe, 'The End of Convergence: Corporatist and Dualist Tendencies in Modern Western Societies', in B. Roberts, R. Finnegan and D. Gallie (eds), *New Approaches to Economic Life: Economic Restructuring, Unemployment and the Social Division of Labour*, Manchester University Press, 1985, p. 149.

14 Ibid., p. 150.

15 See for example Robert Turner, Anne-Marie Bostyn and Daniel Wright, 'The Work Ethic in a Scottish Town with Declining Employment', in Roberts et al., *New Approaches to Economic Life*, ch. 26. In a pilot study in Exeter on 'Labour Market Decisions in Low Income Households' (Simon James, Bill Jordan and Helen Kay, 1986, unpublished) we found that, out of 14 households, members of 6 volunteered that they did 'cash jobs' that were undeclared to tax and benefit authorities. Of these, 3 were self-employed, 2 were building workers, and one was a woman doing part-time cleaning. Only one of these talked of doing undeclared work while *unemployed* – the rest all did extra work which was not declared for *tax* purposes.

Part One

Fairness and Welfare

2

Personal Welfare

What do we mean when we talk about *our* welfare? For a generation after the Second World War, this question was seldom discussed. It was recognized that some of us gave more emphasis to the contribution of individual effort and family cohesiveness, and others to that of state social services, but there appeared to be general agreement that everyone's welfare depended on some balance between these elements. In Western Europe especially, political debates were about their relative importance, and political differences were a matter of emphasis.

Now the question has become an urgent one. In present political conflicts about welfare, the protagonists share few common assumptions about aims or means. Nothing is taken for granted, and spheres of state provision or private freedom that once seemed inviolable are being explored, sometimes invaded, plundered and re-partitioned. So I shall start with an examination of how we think about our own welfare, and that of our families and friends, to see whether there are any universal assumptions or principles, and any way in which our welfare can be compared with that of others.

Recently I asked a group of 30 new students on a postgraduate social work course to tell each other (in pairs) what had contributed most to their welfare in the past three years. Having started the exercise, several stopped to ask me whether they should interpret welfare in 'the broadest sense – as equivalent to "wellbeing"'. I encouraged them to interpret it any way they wanted. Afterwards, when I had written up a list of their contributions on the blackboard, a number described a process of working from the 'material' to the 'more profound and intangible' factors. The first one mentioned was 'financial security', but this had different meanings for various members of the group. Those who had been unemployed saw financial security in terms of establishing their entitlement to DHSS benefits; those who had been in regular employment saw it in terms of retaining their standard of living. Then came housing, with again a contrast between those who had managed to secure adequate accommodation and those who had improved their standards, or even bought their own home. Friends, partners and family were important, providing love, support, stability, encouragement and stimulation.

Employment had made a number of contrasting contributions to students' welfare. Only a few had achieved any measure of job security, and not all had sought to achieve a higher income. Of those who had, one had stayed longer than he wanted in a well-paid job in order to be able to afford to train to be a social worker, a much lower-paid post. Those who had experienced unemployment emphasized that their jobs had provided an opportunity to contribute to society, to participate, and to demonstrate commitment. Others stressed the achievement of an identity through work, the satisfaction of the work itself, and the sense of having embarked on a career. Training was seen in terms of both career prospects and the fulfilment of a *life-plan*.

Several students felt that the development of their own personal resources had contributed to their welfare, because it had given them greater confidence. They spoke particularly of the development of a certain kind of ability to sustain their life-plans according to their principles, even in adverse circumstances, and against the opposition of others. When asked to describe this in a word, they chose 'autonomy'.

Leisure, travel and 'fun' were all seen as significant contributions to welfare, not simply as recreation, but also as adventure and a means to self-discovery. Whereas other goods or activities made for the security that was one ingredient in welfare, travel in particular was seen as providing the 'constructive insecurity' necessary for some forms of development associated with autonomy.

Finally, the students mentioned their connections with wider movements or smaller associations. Religious faith was important for some, though there were those who mentioned *loss* of faith as a contribution to welfare, as well as those who had found faith. Joining political movements (including the women's movement) was another significant factor; others mentioned community groups or specialized voluntary associations.

It could be argued that this group was unrepresentative. After all, they had in common the choice of a career that required elements of altruism, a special interest in people and concern for social problems. They were youngish (aged 22–45) and educationally privileged (all had degrees). Yet their answers were interesting precisely because they revealed the diversity of factors affecting individual perceptions of welfare. Apart from employment (where social workers might be expected to be slightly less materialistic than some other professions), their answers reveal an interpretation of welfare which, I would suggest, is typical of people in the modern developed societies of the West, and perhaps also of the more prosperous Eastern European states.

This view of welfare is individual and subjective. It values goods and activities not according to a monetary or conventional measure (their price in the market or their place in public esteem), but according to how they serve the individual's scheme for his or her life. Even though we live in a society where commercial values and marketed commodities have invaded every sphere of living, welfare is still seen as measurable only in terms of personal choice, by reference to long-term plans and conscious principles.

Equally, there is scarcely any mention of the social services of the welfare state, except by those students who had been unemployed for long periods, and by the very few who had been seriously ill, and who therefore mentioned access to health care as contributing to their welfare (others mentioned the enjoyment of *good* health, but this was rather different). Does this imply that the welfare state is irrelevant to the welfare of 'normal', healthy and relatively successful citizens, and is concerned only with a deprived, disabled or deviant minority?

Welfare, Projects and Commitments

What that exercise seemed to show was that welfare meant different things to different people. People chose a variety of goods, relationships and activities as contributing to their welfare, and the same things had entirely different significances between individuals. Travel, for instance, was purely recreational to some, but an important element in self-development for others.

Does this mean that we cannot generalize about welfare? Does it imply that we cannot compare one person's welfare with another's? Does it suggest that we cannot judge whether a particular action – such as transferring something from A to B – improves B's welfare more than it decreases A's?

I shall argue that it implies none of these things; that we can indeed generalize, compare and even measure. But it does mean that in any discussion of anyone's welfare we have to take account of what I shall call people's 'projects' and 'commitments'.

Projects are long-term plans that people make for their lives. They are not necessarily very specific or detailed, nor do they always involve a timetable that sets out the stages at which the parts of the project will be completed. They are purposes that people pursue over time; most people have several, and generally they are loosely linked together, though at any point they may conflict with each other.[1] Choosing a project for one's life necessarily involves giving up other possible projects. For instance, higher education, vocational training and a professional career are all projects, and any specific degree, training or career excludes others – but a person might have to choose between (for example) doing a PhD or training course immediately after his or her first degree.

Most people seem to have a very general overall *life-plan*, made up of a number of projects, some quite specific (such as wanting to do up an old house, make a beautiful garden or run a marathon) and others much more vague (such as to make a better contribution to society, be creative or develop one's spiritual faculties). Sometimes people's projects all feed into a unified purpose (to be rich or powerful), but – outside television drama series – this seems to be comparatively rare. Equally, it is rare for people not to be able to articulate *some* overall purpose, since it is from such a purpose that we construct our identities, and attach meanings to decisions and actions.[2]

It is important to distinguish between projects and *preferences*. Most consumer surveys (including political polls) measure the specific choices people are making or intend to make – Brand X or Brand Y, Conservative or Labour. This is perfectly valid as a way of predicting demand or voting patterns, but it is limited in its significance for welfare. Projects influence decisions that are seen as significant – either positively or negatively – for the purposes with which they are associated. Preferences are tactical or short-term choices, whereas projects are long-term and require strategic decisions. Hence preferences can really be explained only in terms of projects and life-plans.

Commitments are patterns or consistencies in relationships. They arise from kinship, from affection, from attraction, from shared membership of groups and from roles in organizations and communities. Some commitments are perceived mainly as responsibilities, such as those that arise from having dependants, or from roles such as guardian, tutor or counsellor. Others are seen as more egalitarian and reciprocal, such as friend, lover, neighbour, workmate or comrade – but these too imply duties, such as lending a sympathetic ear, helping out in emergencies and so on. Commitment to certain values, such as Christianity, socialism or ecology, also implies (usually) membership of some kind of organization, choice of some actions and rejection of others, and even the selection of certain projects at the expense of others which are seen as inconsistent with these values.

People can and do change their projects and commitments. They abandon ambitions, drop friends, leave families. They acknowledge mistakes, or simply move on. What was seen as a major contribution to welfare at one time is re-evaluated as an unnecessary burden. But other projects and commitments emerge to take their place because, even though we sometimes painfully experience that what was once meaningful and valued can become empty, it seems almost impossible for anyone to live for any length of time without granting significance and value to something. For instance, the most apparently alienated and fragmented personalities in mental hospitals appear often to make fierce attachments to discarded objects, or to repeated routines, rituals or phrases.[3]

The subjective view of welfare that I am proposing implies that people assess their own welfare in relation to their projects and commitments, and make choices in pursuit of their welfare with these in mind. In choosing one course of action over another, they show that they assess the state of affairs brought about by that action to be more conducive to their welfare than that which would result from the other action. They may later come to think that they were wrong, but at the time their choice was governed by their view of their welfare requirements.

However, the subjective view does not imply that people are concerned only with their own welfare. What it does strongly indicate is a certain way of going about the business of improving the welfare of others. If others' welfare can be understood only in terms of their projects and commitments, it suggests that we can meaningfully contribute to the welfare of those who arouse our concern only by finding out about their life-plans and learning ways of helping them to fulfil their projects and commitments.

It also implies that we need to take these things into account in any attempt to compare one person's welfare with another's, and to settle disputes about welfare shares.

Co-operation and Comparisons of Welfare

How do we deal with someone's complaint that he or she is worse off than someone else – that the level of personal welfare he or she is achieving is less than that of another? In everyday life this kind of complaint is most likely to arise where both people are members of the same family, group or association, and where one is complaining that the other is getting more benefit from membership of that collectivity. This is because, in everyday life, comparisons are most likely to be meaningful – in the sense that there is something that can be done about them – where two or more people are co-operating in some form of association for their mutual benefit. Hence the complaint is likely to be that one person is 'getting more out of it' than another.

Let's start from the simplest form of co-operative association, a partnership between two people, and with the commonest form of partnership, a couple living together. Any such partnership normally consists of routine exchanges of services (cooking, cleaning, shopping, driving, gardening, decorating, etc.) and sharing of resources (space, household goods, income and so on), according to regular and routine patterns, which change rather little. But it also consists of very flexible responses to day-to-day circumstances, where partners can quickly adjust to their pattern of behaviour to changes such as sickness, stress or a special demand on the energies of one of them from outside. These changes are usually made on the basis of discussion – of renegotiation (for the time being) of some of the routines of everyday life.

The assumption behind any form of co-operation is that it creates a mutual benefit that could not otherwise arise, though it is also a commitment that creates mutual duties. So there is always a potential question in any partnership concerning whether the burdens of mutual responsibility are fairly divided and whether both parties are fairly enabled to pursue their own chosen individual projects. This question is seldom posed in precisely this form in real life; but I would argue that there is no reason *in principle* why any couple should not be able to make a systematic investigation of their relationship in terms of the comparative welfare that both derive from it.

Suppose that a devoted couple wanted to make sure that neither was taking advantage of the other's goodwill and generosity, and that both were benefiting equally from their shared life together. Suppose also (because it makes the comparison much easier) that they were both middle-aged, middle-class, comfortably off and employed in interesting jobs. They might start by reviewing all the tasks they did in the household, including child care or attention given to elderly relatives, and they might actually log up the time spent on these, to make sure neither was doing more than the other. Then they might make sure that the way they used shared resources such as transport, space and money was equally beneficial. This would not necessarily mean that they shared these on a strict half-and-half basis. For instance, they might take turns to use a specially valuable space in the house, or to use the surplus from their income for a special individual project, or to use the car. They might even decide to take turns to go part-time at work, to use the extra opportunity this gave them to complete a special project, or do a training course. Finally, they might trade in a whole list of 'diswelfares' of their relationship – annoying habits, irritating omissions, thoughtless oversights, careless actions – which they could agree to correct for each other on a one-for-one basis.

I use this example to show that, where there is a co-operative partnership for mutual benefit, systematic comparisons of welfare which take account of individual projects are certainly possible theoretically, and may indeed take place in some partnerships. The form they would take is a detailed negotiation of how the roles and resources that are shared can allow a fair partition of the benefits and burdens of co-operation, and enable each partner to pursue individual as well as joint projects equally advantageously.

But to return to the complaint about inequality in welfare, it is much more likely that the kinds of re-negotiations I have described would arise because one of the partners felt relatively deprived or exploited in the relationship. Whereas the devoted couple were imagined as carrying out a systematic review of their partnership, ordinary couples tend to have *ad hoc* discussions (or rows) arising from particular moans or grievances and leading to marginal shifts in who does what, when or how, or who gets how much. While this form of negotiation seems less edifying than my imaginary one, a series of rows over a period of time may accomplish considerable change in the balance of a relationship, through frequent marginal shifts in benefits and responsibilities.

What I have tried to describe is a process of 'give and take' aimed at comparing and perhaps redistributing welfare in co-operative associations. But we should recognize that a complaint about being worse off than someone else within such an association may call for much more fundamental changes than the ones I have considered. It may indeed be a challenge to the basic terms of that association – the roles of the members, the 'currency' of the benefits distributed and so on. Thus, for instance, a wife complaining that she gets less out of the marriage than her husband may be asking for a marginal adjustment of their relationship (fewer chores, more spare time), or she may be pointing out a fundamental inequality in their roles, where she does not enjoy the same freedom or opportunities for individual projects as he does because of the basic division of responsibilities between them. The kind of re-negotiation that the latter complaint demands is far more radical and problematic. That there is scope for give and take in relationships is evidenced by the very high proportion of people who live within partnerships of one kind or another in our society; that it is difficult to re-negotiate the terms of partnerships is witnessed by a divorce rate equivalent to one in three marriages in some advanced countries, and a probably higher rate of breakdown in other forms of pair relationships.

Scope for Give and Take

The hypothetical example of the ideal middle-aged, middle-class couple gives rise to a suspicion that the kind of negotiation I have described may depend on certain special conditions, such as a degree of material comfort, or even prosperity. Perhaps it depends on shared ideas about equality and freedom between partners, or on both having equal access to outside opportunities for self-development. Perhaps it applies only to a very narrow field of partnerships (heterosexual or gay) between adults, and cannot encompass more than the exclusive pair and their immediate dependants.

It is important here to distinguish between a hypothetical example of systematic comparison and readjustment, and real-life examples of negotiation. In real life, give and take is mostly an *ad hoc* matter, and a response to day-to-day changes in circumstances. Not only families, but also small groups and associations, have the dual character of providing a certain predictable security (through routine exchanges), but also a range of spontaneous variable, personal responses to specific situations. People adapt their behaviour to quite small changes in others' moods, luck, health and so on; hence they are often able to negotiate in a give-and-take way without explicit bargaining or agreement, but just by the way they speak, the way they look or by very small changes in their behaviour which may not even be consciously acknowledged.

But people are also capable of fairly large and radical shifts in roles, involving major changes in personal projects, and in the allocation of shared resources and responsibilities. Usually this occurs as a result of a crisis – a serious illness, death, divorce, loss of a job or some other unexpected change in life's pattern. So sometimes these adaptations are provoked by adversity, rather than being the consequence of advantages or prosperity; and they may well extend beyond the confines of a couple relationship.

The following example is based on real people, though for reasons of anonymity it has been adapted.

Example

Rita Johnson was 19 and her mother Beryl was 48 when her brother John (aged 17) had an acute schizophrenic breakdown. Rita was training as a pharmacist and her mother worked as a part-time supervisor in a shop. John was admitted to psychiatric hospital for six months, but then was considered fit to be discharged home, if he received low-key, non-intrusive, non-critical care and help with daily life (a normal requirement for people recovering from serious schizophrenic episodes). The only follow-up medical attention he would receive would be monthly visits from a community psychiatric nurse, who would inject him with long-acting medication. The family lived in a very remote cottage, where they had moved some five years previously; Mr Johnson was a farm worker, who deserted them soon after the move, and had disappeared.

Beryl and Rita discussed their situation. They were determined to have John at home, but recognized that this would mean a change in their life-style. Ideally they would both work part-time, sharing the care tasks between them; however, their combined part-time earnings would not sustain the family, nor would each be able to afford to have her own car, and there was no public transport to either workplace. Alternatively, they could *both* give up work and draw benefits, sharing the care between them, but they both felt that this would be unduly isolating and would probably cause stress and conflict.

So they decided that Beryl would become a full-time worker (she had the opportunity of promotion to manageress), as her earnings were a good deal higher than her daughter's, and Rita would draw supplementary benefit and care for John and the home. It was understood between them that Rita would probably stay at home until Beryl retired, which meant that she would not marry until she was over 30.

Ten years on, John is much better and leads a more normal life – he participates quite fully in social groups, though he still gives little practical help in the house, and has no prospect of employment. Rita is still at home and unemployed, because transport problems preclude any part-time employment, though she is active in arts and crafts, and earns a little extra money from selling her products. Beryl is about to retire, and Rita will then be free to start a life away from home.

Re-negotiations of this kind, arising from serious illness or disability, are increasingly necessary as households adapt to meet the needs of elderly people with progressive physical handicaps. But another common cause of re-negotiations is divorce. Here, couples who split up have to reach agreements over their roles as parents to their children, and over sharing out resources, in the unpromising new situation brought about by the breakup of a relationship. Yet nowadays an increasing proportion of couples do reach such agreements on a non-adversarial, negotiated basis; and even the state's agencies for settling issues about fairness and welfare in divorce are increasingly turning to methods of conciliation (helping parties to reach agreed solutions) rather than arbitration between conflicting claims.

The example of divorce shows that give-and-take negotiation about welfare does not necessarily require a shared life together or agreement about fundamental values. What it does require is a degree of basic trust over one area of common concern (in this case, parenting of children), and a recognition that the parties can gain by co-operation. This basic trust is not a matter of seeing the other person as altruistic, or seeing no conflicts of interest; but it does require a belief that the other person will abide by agreements and will not disown them opportunistically for the sake of short-term advantage. Mutual gain from co-operation does not necessarily imply shared projects, but it does often imply the sacrifice of *competitive* advantage in the name of reciprocal benefit over a defined sphere of activities or roles.

Personal Welfare and Co-operation

It would be useful at this point to gather together my arguments about personal welfare and co-operation, because they are very important for the rest of the book. I have suggested that each individual seeks his or her wellbeing through personal projects and commitments. But these involve co-operative relationships with others, where the parties to the association create benefits in terms of personal welfare which would not exist if they remained in isolation. These benefits are *shared* between the associates, because they are mutual, and often involve roles that are complementary, and resources that are jointly used.

The very notion of sharing implies some standard of *fairness*. If two or more people share anything, it is always appropriate to ask by what criterion the shares are allotted, and particularly to require an explanation in terms of what makes them 'fair'. If someone says, 'This is your share', it would always make sense to ask, 'How is that fair?' and would never be good enough for him to reply 'Because I say so' or 'I don't have to explain', unless he was authorized in some way (in terms of fairness) to do the sharing. The very concept of sharing therefore implies that some explanation of what is fair can be offered (even if it is only 'the luck of the draw').

Clearly, this does not mean that shares must be equal. There may be unequal shares in terms of the original agreement to co-operate (and hence a *right* to a larger share), in terms of greater effort or contribution (and hence *deserving* a larger share) or in terms of greater need (*requiring* a larger share).

These different criteria of fairness will be discussed in chapter 4. Nor does it mean that there will always be easy agreement on what are fair shares, or that people will always *get* fair shares from co-operation. But it does mean that *fairness will always be an issue raised by co-operation*, even at the smallest-scale level of social relationships. The negotiations involving comparisons of welfare in co-operative partnerships are therefore concerned with fairness, and with adapting roles and routines to allow a fairer distribution of the benefits and burdens of co-operation.

To summarize:

1 individuals seek their own wellbeing according to personal plans, through projects and commitments;
2 they co-operate with others to produce benefits, the sum of which is greater than the welfare they could produce by their individual, isolated efforts;
3 all co-operation entails a sharing of benefits and burdens;
4 all sharing entails a notion of fairness, in terms of which shares can be compared and explained;
5 standards of fairness are used in the negotiations through which individuals adjust their roles in co-operation, as well as their shares of the benefits.

Give and Take in the Social Services

The discussion so far seems very remote from the issues and methods of the state social services. Their concern for social welfare appears to be much more formal, impersonal and bureaucratic. They are used to give out standard rations of state assistance of various kinds to meet certain needs. They do not appear to take account of people's projects or commitments, or to be interested in their subjective views of their own welfare, or to be willing to negotiate with them.

But this is not entirely the case. The personal social services are – or should be – very much concerned with the types of detailed comparison of, and negotiations about, welfare which I have described. It is characteristic of the personal social services that they are used to deliver those forms of state provision that require very sensitive assessments of need, and a special sort of trust and goodwill about the way in which they are delivered. Hence the social workers and care assistants who make assessments and provide services are encouraged to do this in *personal* and not impersonal ways, paying close attention to the individual meanings their clients attach to the choices they are making, and giving generous offers of time to discuss the significance of choices to be made within a relationship of understanding and encouragement.

As an example, we could take decisions about the placement of children in care. The British Children Act of 1975[4] imposed a duty on local authorities to ascertain the wishes and feelings of children in care in relation to any possibility of adoption; and to do the same more broadly in relation to decisions and plans about the child's life in care (or the chance of returning to his or her parents), as far as is practicable. The local authority is required by law to give due consideration to these wishes and feelings, having regard to the age and understanding of the child.

This amounts to a recognition (for the first time in British law) that children – even at quite a young age – already have commitments, and may even have projects. They usually have feelings of loyalty towards their natural parents, and sometimes affection even towards parents who have abused them. They already have an embryonic sense of their own identity, as part of a wider family and community, and some expectations and hopes for their future, which are likely to be clearer the older they are when they come into care. In other words, the child already has a subjective view of his or her own welfare, against which anyone else's decision must be set.

The law does not require social workers to make decisions in line with the child's view, but only to ascertain it and give it due consideration, as part of the local authority's general duty to exercise its powers in relation to the child so as to promote his or her welfare.[5] The child's view can be overridden by the social worker, whose powers allow her to impose a longer-term perspective. For instance, children often hold on to the hope of returning to rejecting parents, and many also prefer the neutrality of a residential home to the substitution of an alien family.[6] Social workers often try – sometimes unsuccessfully – to get children to accept the advantages of substitute parents (foster or adoptive); in a few cases they may encourage children to return to their natural parents against their wills (Maria Colwell was one of these).[7]

It could well be argued that in these instances the social worker is acting in much the same way as parents do towards children of their own. After all, parents often override the immediate wishes of their children; better-off parents, for example, often send unwilling children to boarding schools. In this respect care-givers in the family usually have power to impose their definitions of welfare needs on their dependants, whether they are children, disabled adults or frail elderly people. These definitions of welfare are usually heavily imbued with ideological and cultural values of what is good for such people, which rationalize the gulf between the care-giver's perception of their needs and their subjective view of their wants.

If there is this close parallel between the powers and motives of social workers who deal with children, disabled and elderly people and those of their family care-givers, then it would seem that the personal social services largely substitute officials for family members at times of important decision-making in the lives of dependent people. The job of a social worker in these situations becomes one of substituting for family members who are absent, unable or unwilling to look after the client's welfare, and to do so as much in the spirit of a good parent, son or daughter as possible – to arrange care or some other provision for them by colleagues in the department, or whoever else can best provide it. It is noteworthy that one statutory power – to apply for the detention of mentally ill people in hospital against their wills – can be exercised by social workers or the person's nearest relative.[8]

Give and Take in Wider Society

It is a far cry from recognizing that there is a basis for comparison and redistribution of welfare between individuals in personal relationships (or even in personal social services) to applying the same framework to wider society. Yet in the most general sense there may be some grounds for a claim that give and take must underlie every form of human society, from the least developed to the most advanced, because without it society would simply break down.

We all know that social life – and especially the economic sphere – is characterized by both co-operation and competition (conflict). From some perspectives conflict and competition seem the dominant modes of interaction, and they are certainly the ones stressed alike by Marxism, neoclassical economics and the kind of social Darwinism that was popular among late nineteenth-century sociologists in Britain. Conflict between classes and groups is emphasized in Marxism, and competition between individuals and groups (enterprises, interests), in neoclassical economics and in social Darwinism.

Yet if these modes of interaction did predominate, we would expect societies to look rather different from the way they actually appear. If there were no basic trust between individuals and groups, it would be very difficult to achieve even rudimentary organization, let alone complex social and economic systems. Any form of co-operative activity assumes that mutual benefits will be greater than the gain any single party can make by unilateral withdrawal. But in theory, there are always opportunities in any joint project for 'free-riding' – for individuals to get the benefits of mutuality without pulling their weight, or indeed without making any contribution at all. So, however much all may benefit from co-operation, cheats always stand to benefit most, and in theory this should eventually lead to ever-increasing withdrawals from any organized enterprise, and hence to an atomized competitive society of conflicting individuals.[9]

In practice, however, this does not seem to happen, and one possible explanation has recently been provided by games theory and computer simulation. The political scientist Robert Axelrod invited his colleagues throughout the United States to enter computer programs to compete in a game called 'The Prisoner's Dilemma', in which participants engaged in a long series of moves which could involve co-operation or attempts to gain (or frustrate) competitive advantage.[10] The most successful strategy over a series of trials was 'Tit for Tat', which started with a move of trust and co-operation, retaliated at once to attempted exploitation, but then responded immediately with reciprocity to moves of co-operation. This simple strategy of instant but minimal defence and instant forgiveness at the first sign of contrition was much more productive than more sophisticated attempts to gain competitive advantage – mainly because cheats tend to frustrate and eventually destroy each other, whereas co-operators tend to build benign networks. This game helps explain why co-operation seems to predominate in all social systems, and why even in battle far fewer people kill each other than would be possible (or indeed seem probable).[11]

Similarly, in the animal kingdom it seems that reciprocal services for mutual benefit are exchanged not merely by members of the same species, but also by different species for each other. Those that are able to develop co-operative strategies for mutual protection from predators or adverse conditions seem to gain considerable advantages over species that rely on competition alone for survival. Symbiotic relationships between animals and plants are also common, so that biological interdependence and reciprocity does not depend on similarity, but can occur between members of different kingdoms.

It was the intuitive perception of some kind of normative order in societies that led even the most individualistic of the early political philosophers to insist that a moral code underlay all social systems. So, for instance, Hobbes argued that, even though people's individual psychologies inclined them to try to gain competitive advantage over each other, the natural laws of ethics required them to live in peace and harmony, and the state merely enforced these laws for mutual benefit.[12] By contrast, Locke thought that God had created a world of natural abundance in which people could live freely as equals as long as they obeyed its moral laws, and that political society was a consequence of artificial (man-made) conditions which required more formal regulation.[13] But both Hobbes and Locke contrasted nightmare 'states of war', where society had broken down into conflicting, amoral groups and individuals, and where no social organization was possible, with orderly co-operaton under some form of give-and-take principles.[14]

The Limits of Co-operation

Given that both co-operation and conflict are characteristics of all social systems, is it possible to generalize about the factors that lead to a predominance of one mode over the other? Can we predict in any reliable way when people are likely to perceive the mutual advantages of co-operative relations, and when they will seek competitive advantage? Is this a matter of individual day-to-day calculation, of ideological commitment, of experienced social solidarity or of something else?

We know that all systems of social relationships involve the handling of a series of complex notions of sameness and difference between individuals and groups. People distinguish themselves from others – by their individual characteristics, their roles and their allegiance to kinship and social groupings – while at the same time acknowledging membership and commitment to common families, clans, associations or causes. I have an uncle who is a councillor in Zimbabwe, a cousin who is a teacher in Australia and a nephew who is a student in France; but there would be a number of political issues on which we could agree, as well as some over which we would differ. My immediate colleagues at work share little common ground on social policy priorities, but all would be fiercely loyal to each other if our course came under threat. Notions of sameness and difference are not undimensional but cross-cutting, and the complexity of differential group membership and affiliations increases with economic development and social mobility.

In complex, developed societies, co-operation between individuals and groups may take place in one sphere of social or economic life while at the same time competition is occurring in another. But the basis of co-operation is always similar, whether it is small-scale and informal or large-scale and organized. This is the perception that there is some public good (a co-operatively created welfare product) in terms of which what people have in common (their collective identity as members of the same family, neighbourhood, union, association or country) is more important than their differences.[15] Once this common collective welfare good is identified, co-operation overrides individual calculation of costs and benefits, at least in the short run. Instead, individuals work together on the basis of trust, responding co-operatively to each other, even in the face of short-term personal disadvantage. This involves relying on each other's willingness to reciprocate, and to stick by the terms of co-operation, even if their individual circumstances alter. It underlies the organization of small voluntary groups, and of whole societies.

Those public goods that are shared by all members of society are usually provided through the state, which organizes both their provision and whatever co-operation is necessary to ensure it. For example, defence involves the collection of taxes, the deployment of armed forces and decisions about when national interests are at stake. In democratic countries successful defence policies require for their basis at least a majority perception that mutual protection rather than sectional interest is being served, that costs are reasonable and fairly shared, and that realistic, prudent aims are being pursued. Within the rules of democracy, the perception by a majority that all or any of these did not apply to defence policy might lead to a change of government. But the perception by the citizens of one region that their security and protection lay more in membership of another state than in their present one would represent a breach of the 'social contract' on which their citizenship was founded: it would signify a breakdown of the trust underpinning nationality as a collective identity.

With every sphere of inclusiveness (large and small) that defines a co-operative membership, there is also a process of exclusion. In the case of citizenship, exclusion entails lack of rights to the benefits of membership, and may also (in times of war) entail loss of liberty or persecution. By certain actions individuals may also be taken to have excluded themselves from society or from certain rights of membership.[16] So, for instance, treason is taken as being the most serious breach of membership, and other criminal offences involve losing some of the rights and liberties of citizenship.

Standards of fairness in the distribution of welfare reflect important perceptions of collective identities, in society as a whole and within social groups. For example, the perception of black people as 'immigrants' leads to their being seen as less deserving of social services than the indigenous population. In some countries migrant workers do not have full citizenship rights; in others, even though black people may have formal citizenship, they are denied many of the advantages of membership of the community through the attitudes and actions of the white majority. Or again, groups with a strong occupational identity, such as miners and printers, form fierce group loyalties and strong labour organizations; but these act to exclude not merely 'scabs' and 'traitors' but also the interests of other trade unions and of non-unionized workers. In other cases, a stereotypical role identity in one system of co-operation (such as women's identity as wives, mothers and care-givers) is carried over into men's perceptions of their role in the labour market and wider society, so that women are not treated as equal workers and citizens.

In all these situations, radicalism consists in challenging the social categories by which people are included in or excluded from the rights and benefits of co-operation, and the definitions of fairness that stem from membership of these categories. The radical challenge consists in portraying the exclusion of blacks, women or the poor from full participation in economic, social or political life as unfair and discriminatory, and in drawing attention to the assumptions among those who exclude them about what makes them 'different' rather than the same as (and equal with) themselves.

Conclusions

I have argued that individuals frame decisions about their personal welfare in terms of their projects and commitments, compare and share welfare with others through negotiation, and co-operate according to perceptions of fairness through give and take. But they also exclude others from certain types of co-operative association, deal differently with people they classify as members of their own families, groups, unions, classes or nations from the way they deal with others, and hence use discriminatory standards of fairness in their wider social relations.

The contentious part of my analysis so far is the emphasis that I have given to informal processes of co-operation and negotiation in the sharing of welfare goods. What I have said implies that welfare distribution is in some sense subject to general moral rules of conduct,[17] even though these are applied differentially as between members and non-members of social groups, and according to differential assumptions about the nature of roles within memberships. A more orthodox view in the social sciences is that the various spheres of welfare distribution, far from being subject to one set of common moral rules, are either quite separate and non-comparable, or else subject to the dominance of the economic sphere. According to this view, reciprocity and mutuality of the kind I have described is possible only in simple, stable, small communities with shared values and face-to-face relationships.[18] The social sciences were developed out of the distinctions first between political science and ethics, and then between these and economics, psychology, sociology and so on. All of these depended to some degree on the perception of society as a series of transactions between individuals bound together through formal roles, of which the economic and political were the most important.[19] It is to this view that I shall turn in the next chapter.

Notes

1 See for instance, Albert Weale, *Political Theory and Social Policy*, Macmillan, 1983, pp. 24–9. Weale's account of projects is a development and improvement on the notion of a 'plan of life', found in David Miller, *Social Justice*, Clarendon Press, 1976, pp. 133–43, and John Rawls, *A Theory of Justice*, Clarendon Press, 1972, pp. 407–16. Miller, for instance, suggests that most workers share rather simple plans of life which consist of holding a steady job, and bringing in enough income to support their homes and families (p. 139). This really describes the patterns of people's lives as seen from the outside, largely excluding their individual aspirations, and hence their projects. To discover the subjective elements in welfare would require the more prolonged and detailed discussion, which the students discovered took place after they had dealt with common material needs. Weale's notion of projects is deficient because it excludes commitments (see p. 000 below), which both limit individual projects (in that they require time and energy for their maintenance and development) and form the basis for family, group and community projects, which are shared with others.
2 For example, Michael Polanyi and Harry Prosch, *Meaning*, University of Chicago Press, 1975, argue that the very acts of understanding and knowing require personal skill and judgement which alone give facts and events significance to us.

Hence all knowledge is *personal* and not universal. 'Having recognised personal participation as the universal principle of knowing, and having determined the structure of this knowing, we are now able to see that the personal participation through which we reach our evaluation of human actions as the actions of sentient, intelligent, and morally responsible beings is a legitimate instance of scientific knowing . . . *All* knowing is personal knowing – participation through indwelling' (p. 44). People are thus inevitably *involved* in what they see and do, and communicate only through shared commitments to common meanings – and to the meaningfulness of events, objects, relationships, etc. Hence it is impossible to maintain, except for very short periods, a nihilistic perspective, such as that the whole universe is random, meaningless or absurd. 'We might justifiably claim, therefore, that everything we know is *full* of meaning, is not absurd at all, although we can sometimes fail to grasp these meainings and fall into absurdities' (p. 179).

Similarly David Miller (*Social Justice*, p. 133) suggests, in relation to 'plans of life', that 'I take it that a person has to have such a plan, for a person's *identity* is established by the aims and activities which constitute his plan of life, and without such an identity he could hardly be regarded as a person in the full sense, rather as an organisation of a certain type which was potentially a p ·on.' Of course this helps to show why we should not regard very generalized pi . .s of life, such as those Miller attributes to 'most workers', as satisfactory definitions of life-plans, since they would not give individual identities, but rather would make them indistinguishable from each other.

3 Irving Goffman, *Asylums*, Penguin, 1963.
4 Children Act, 1975, section 18.
5 Ibid.
6 See for instance Barbara Kahan, *Growing up in Care: Ten People Talking*, Basil Blackwell, 1979, who gives a long account by a child herself of an unsuccessful fostering placement and her longing to be returned to a children's home. See also Raissa Page and G. A. Clark (eds), *Who Cares? People in Care Speak Out*, National Children's Bureau, 1977, for other examples of children who preferred the neutrality of children's homes.
7 Jean Packman, *The Child's Generation: Child Care Policy from Curtis to Houghton*, Basil Blackwell and Martin Robertson, 1975.
8 Mental Health Act, 1982, section 13(4).
9 The problem is clearly set out in Mancur Olson's theory of collective action (M. Olson, *The Logic of Collective Action*, Harvard University Press, 1965). The rational individual's best option is to take a 'free ride' on the efforts of others without contributing himself to the production of a public good, because his own contribution would make no difference to the quantity or quality of the good in a large community; but this leads, via the rational choices of individuals, to the good not being produced. See also Claus Offe, 'Democracy *versus* the Welfare State? Structural Foundations of a Neo-Conservative Argument', paper presented to a Conference on Poverty, Charity and Welfare, New Orleans, February 1986.
10 Robert Axelrod, *The Evolution of Co-operation*, Basic Books, 1984.
11 During the first two years of the First World War, the soldiers of both sides in the trenches evolved a complex system of signals to each other to indicate that they

were *not* shooting to kill, though they would retaliate immediately if the other side took advantage of this co-operative pact. This system culminated in the famous truce of Christmas 1915, which so alarmed the generals that they had to devise new tactics to defeat inter-adversary co-operation ('Nice Guys Finish First', BBC2 TV, *Horizon*, 15 April 1986. See also Richard Dawkins, 'The Nice Way to Survive', *The Listener*, vol. 715, no. 2956, 17 April 1986.

12 Thomas Hobbes, *Leviathan* (1651), Basil Blackwell, 1966, chs X–XIII.

13 John Locke, *Two Treatises of Government* (1698), Cambridge University Press, 1967, *Second Treatise*, sections 6–50.

14 Hobbes, *Leviathan*, ch. XIII, and Locke, *Second Treatise*, sections 11 and 93.

15 For further discussion of this point see Claus Offe, 'Democracy *versus* the Welfare State?'

16 Thus for instance, in Locke's political theory, despots, usurpers, traitors and all forms of criminals were taken to have put themselves beyond the contract on which organized society was based, and therefore to have forfeited their right to life (*Second Treatise of Government*, section 93). Also, defeated enemies in times of war could legitimately be deprived of their liberty – this formed the basis of his justification of slavery (sections 184–5).

17 There is some evidence from developmental psychologists that this code, though universal, takes slightly different forms among men and women, at least in advanced capitalist societies. Studies of separate groups of boys and girls at play have suggested that boys tend to be more concerned with developing general rules for settling disputes according to *fairness*, whereas girls maintain co-operation by abandoning competitive games, for the sake of not harming their relationships – they are more concerned to include others and care for them. See Carol Gilligan, *In A Different Voice*, Harvard University Press, 1982, pp. 1–10.

18 Michael Taylor, *Community, Anarchy and Liberty*, Cambridge University Press, 1982, argues that communities exist where 'members hold in common a wide range of values and beliefs; relations between them are generally directed and many-sided; and they practise reciprocity in many areas' (p. 38). These communities, he suggests, are better vehicles for the just distribution of welfare because 'public goods are more likely to be provided, or provided in optimal amounts, by the members of *small* publics than by those of large ones' (p. 93). Such communities therefore tend to be egalitarian, and to have social controls to reduce inequalities and direct a large proportion of reciprocal help to those in greatest need. '. . . the (small stable) community is not a continuously harmonious place, in which necessarily there are no tensions, no social constraints on individual action, no occasions on which some individuals are persuaded, induced and even forced by others to do things they otherwise would not have done. . . . community makes possible the effective use of social controls which are an alternative to the concentrated force of the state. These controls, the use of which is largely shared among the community's members, may be thought of as more egalitarian than those of the state, less liable to be used for purposes not widely approved. . . .' (p. 140).

19 Liberals and Marxian socialists have both tended to mistrust traditional small communities and their methods of social control. For instance, Karl Marx and Frederick Engels regarded it as one of the greatest benefits of capitalism that it rescued individuals from 'the idiocy of rural life' (*Manifesto of the Communist Party*

(1848), in Marx and Engels, *Collected Works*, Lawrence and Wishart, 1976, vol. 6, p. 488). Similarly, Marx wrote of Indian peasant communities that they 'restrained the human mind within the smallest possible compass, making it the unresisting tool of superstition, enslaving it beneath traditional rules' (*British Rule in India*) (1857), in Karl Marx and Frederick Engels, *Collected Works*, vol. 15, Lawrence and Wishart, 1980, pp. 526–41). For a modern critique of the attempt to restore the notion of 'community' in the personal social services, see Professor Robert Pinker's dissenting appendix to the Barclay Report (Appendix B), *Social Workers: Their Role and Tasks*, Allen & Unwin, 1982, pp. 244–5. 'It is a romantic illusion to suppose that by dispersing a handful of professional social workers into the community we can miraculously revive the sleeping giants of populist altruism. The most localised system of "social" services in the history of British social policy was the Poor Law. Its relieving officers and guardians all served localities and constituencies that were sufficiently small to be intimately known. It was just this . . . that added a uniquely hurtful dimension to the experience of stigma against the recipients of poor relief.'

An exception to this general tendency in the social sciences is provided by Marcel Mauss, whose book *The Gift* was published in 1925 (M. Mauss, *The Gift: Forms and Functions of Exchange in Archaic Societies*, Cohen and West, 1954). Mauss (who was a nephew of Emile Durkheim) emphasized the often hidden co-operative processes (symbolized by the giving of gifts) through which people in advanced societies reconcile individualism with dependence on others. I am indebted to Keith Hart for pointing out the similarity between many of Mauss's ideas and my own.

3

Welfare in Society

Modern developed societies are not small, stable communities. Their members do not all meet each other face-to-face, do not share beliefs and values, cannot persuade or shame each other to do things, and do not recognize reciprocal duties. They are large, complex units, with very diverse memberships, organized around quite different principles.

Yet modern developed societies have somehow to solve the same problem as traditional clans and villages: how to reconcile the welfare of the individual with that of the community. In spite of their size and complexity, they have to create structures in which people can get by with each other. Social science has tried to account for cohesion and conflict in modern societies, after the breakdown of the old status-based order of customary agrarian communities, by identifying new systems of interlocking social roles. These systems are described as evolving out of changes in productive relations and in forms of political authority. The social sciences have therefore analysed and prescribed mainly in terms of formal systems of roles, their attendant rights and duties, or the power relations implicit in them.

There is a persistent problem in the social sciences about value and evaluation. The earliest modern political theorists (such as Hobbes and Locke) tried to link the new, more powerful states and emerging economic institutions (money, profit, interest, private property) with the moral sphere (natural laws). Locke linked labour with value, saying it provided the moral basis for property.[1] The 'labour theory of value' came in the eighteenth- and nineteenth-century British political economists' works to lose its moral connotations;[2] but Marx took the labour theory of value as his basis for denouncing the class exploitation inherent in capitalism – the covert coercion of those who created value by those who created nothing, on which both the wealth and the political authority of the bourgeoisie were built.[3] Weber analysed the emergence of value-neutral forms of rational–legal authority, characteristic of the sphere of public administration.[4]

All of these theories describe systems of relationships in which welfare is distributed and redistributed according to generalized rules among anonymous social actors. The rules themselves are seen as largely the products of impersonal social processes and – once established – as working largely automatically. We may try to evaluate the whole system by some criteria (the utilitarian one of the greatest happiness of the greatest number being the most famous example), but what we are then evaluating are the rules themselves or their outcomes, and not the actions of individual actors.

The odd thing about all these theories is how little they tell us about welfare as defined in the last chapter. They are framed in such a way as to exclude the possibility of accounts of adjustments and negotiations – give and take – of the kind I have described. They are impersonal and formal, and they say little about the projects, commitments or values which are the stuff of welfare transactions. Despite the pervasive influence of the social sciences, and their penetration into political debate and media reporting, everyday discussion obstinately clings to the moral evaluation of individuals and their actions.

I am not suggesting that the social sciences are inadequate to the task of analysing markets, political systems or the formal workings of the public services; clearly, their analyses are sophisticated and relevant. But markets, political authority and the public services are all impersonal and formal in their workings, whereas everyday life (even in these spheres) is mostly personal and informal. What's more, the relationships *between* these formal analyses have been a persistent problem to the social sciences. For instance, since the seventeenth century theorists have tried to link types of political authority with types of economic relations, but no satisfactory linkage has ever been achieved.[5] Sociology and social administration, which might have acted as bridging disciplines, have either derived their theories from one of the other two, or analysed social life and social services as if they were separate spheres.

In this chapter I want to consider the formal distribution of welfare, as it is analysed in three influential traditions. Each tradition is presented as a set of coherent and internally consistent propositions about welfare shares and the mechanisms used to determine them. The aim is to distinguish between these three mutually exclusive systems of formal distribution, and to illustrate how their views of welfare are contrasted, so as to clarify their claims, and the problems they raise. It is also to show how their notions of welfare and the way it is shared are in many respects different from those of everyday small-scale transactions.

The distributive mechanisms associated with these three systems are, respectively, the market, the authoritative state allocation of resources, and the public services. Each tradition suggests that its characteristic mechanism is best suited to reconciling individual with communal welfare by means of a system of formal roles. It is important for the purposes of this book to clarify how these mechanisms not only operate quite differently, and bring about different outcomes, but also embody *quite different concepts about what welfare is.*

However, I am faced with a problem of terminology. The traditions I am trying to analyse must (for purposes of brevity) be presented as 'ideal types' – schematic representations of the views of many authors. They also correspond very roughly to broad *political* traditions, which provide much the most convenient shorthand labels for them. However in using these I run the risk of being accused of caricaturing the views of people and parties which adopt these titles for their own (very different) views.

I should therefore state very firmly at the outset that the terms I shall use for the three traditions are convenient shorthand labels, and that the ideas set out do not apply to most people who use these names to describe their beliefs. The first tradition I shall refer to as 'liberal', though it corresponds roughly with nineteenth-century British Liberalism and some modern Conservatism.[6] The second I shall call 'socialist', though it corresponds most closely with the authoritarian state socialism developed by Lenin and his followers, and now practised as a system in Eastern Europe.[7] The third I shall call 'Fabian', though its origins can be traced back to Jeremy Bentham in Britain and to many continental authors of the eighteenth century, and its modern heirs come from a broad spectrum of opinion in the centre of European politics.[8]

The second thing to say about this analysis is that no existing society can be said to embody one of these traditions to the exclusion of the others: all contain some mixture of the three. Indeed, postwar advanced capitalist countries seemed to have discovered a stable balance between elements derived from all three traditions. The major part of their economies consisted of privately owned enterprises, which sold their products in markets. But there was also an infrastructure of state-owned industries and services, whose allocation of inputs and outputs was determined by political processes, according to non-market criteria. The social services met certain widespread social needs and provided basic health care and education. The three spheres were meshed together by organizations for national economic and social management which included employers, employees and state officials.

In the first chapter I suggested that there was now much evidence and some agreement that these formal systems did not solve modern problems of social co-operation as well as they seemed to in the immediate postwar period, and that they might be in some tension with each other. More voices are now being raised to assert the primacy of the market against the state, of productive industry against public services or of minority social needs against majority political decisions. Meanwhile, some commentators are arguing that the informal system of social relationships is adapting more quickly to socioeconomic change than the formal, and is prefiguring the breakdown of some or all of these established systems.[9]

So there are good reasons for re-examining the three traditions in this simplified form, to see how their views of welfare contrast and conflict, in order to understand these renewed tensions. It is also an opportunity to consider how well any of them accord with the small-scale sharing of welfare discussed in the second chapter.

It may well be, of course, that most people's view of welfare is based on some mixture of all these three traditions. Probably, for example, most modern British liberals are much more open to the Fabian view of welfare than were their nineteenth-century predecessors, and most modern British socialists are far more concerned about individual rights and liberties than are East European Marxists. However, what I hope to show in this chapter is that each of these traditional systems operates as a coherent whole, and that it is difficult to adapt them to each other without destroying their internal consistency. So it may be that the tensions at present experienced in modern societies result from contradictions in such compromise positions, and strong conflicting forces at work in our social systems. If so, it will be necessary to rethink the intellectual basis of the sharing of welfare in modern societies as well as the mechanism by which welfare is distributed. Liberals may have to reconsider their view of the efficacy of markets in order to accommodate an acceptable standard of equality in the terms of citizenship, and socialists may have to rethink the role of state power in securing fairness and freedom.

The Liberal Tradition

Liberal principles give prime importance to individual rights, and to the exercise of individual choices. Society is seen as composed of autonomous individuals, each with a sphere of legitimate decision-making, and each with the right to control certain resources. These resources are the individual's own attributes, capacities and skills, and his or her *property* – the things he or she rightfully owns or possesses. Society consists of all the relationships between individuals who are members of this community; it is essentially a system of voluntary co-operation, founded on informal or contractual exchanges of goods and services. The commercial market is the formal mechanism through which individuals exchange things which are theirs to buy and sell, including their labour power. The state simply superintends and regulates these voluntary exchanges.

How does this highly atomistic and apparently fragmented system reconcile individual with communal welfare? The liberal model of society can be summarized in seven assumptions, which link individual choice and welfare with the distribution of goods and services in society:

1 Each individual is the best judge of his or her own welfare.
2 Social welfare depends on the welfare of individuals.
3 If one individual's welfare increases while no one's decreases, then social welfare increases.

4 Each individual is entitled to such property as he or she acquires by lawful means.
5 The market is a system for voluntary exchange, under contract, for mutual advantage.
6 Since no one will participate in market transactions except in pursuit of his or her own welfare, the market will maximize welfare.
7 The state protects individuals from harm by defending society against external attack, by upholding their rights against theft, force and fraud, and by safeguarding the rules for commercial transactions.

So liberal principles neatly link together the formal and informal exchanges that individuals make, whether in the intimacy of the family, in unstructured neighbourhood networks or in the commercial transactions of the marketplace. What all have in common is that they are *voluntary*, the result of individual choice, that they take place within a framework of known personal rights and property rights, and that individuals can seek redress for alleged wrongs through the guardian of this social order, the state.

We can see that liberal principles conform with the view of personal welfare and informal welfare transactions that I developed in the last chapter in two important respects. In the first place, liberalism suggests a subjective view of welfare, which allows for individual projects and commitments, and for people to gather the resources they need (as property) to pursue these. In the second place, it proposes a system of exchange between people which is voluntaristic, and which allows dissimilar goods and services to be traded through a flexible medium (money).

But if markets are supposed to formalize and generalize a process of give and take, they do so in a very peculiar and distorted way. We saw in the last chapter that in personal relationships this process was closely related to the characteristics and circumstances of the social actors. Markets are designed to be completely impersonal, to eliminate these factors from exchange.[10] Furthermore, give and take took account of the resources and abilities of the actors, as well as their individual plans and commitments. Markets take no such account; indeed, they are designed to allow some people to accumulate very large stocks of resources, and to trade with people who have very few. Far from allowing such differences to be offset, markets allow for advantages to be reinforced; their anonymity protects the strong from having to give any consideration to the disadvantages of the weak.

This means that the alleged beneficial effects of market systems on the distribution of welfare are left entirely to the workings of the 'invisible hand'. Adam Smith's famous account of how the greed and selfishness of traditional landlords and the obsessive moneymaking of the urban tradespeople gave rise – through markets – to 'nearly the same distribution of the necessaries of life, which would have been made, had the earth been divided into equal portions among all its inhabitants' had nothing to do with good intentions, understanding or compassion.[11] It was the result of impersonal economic laws, which produced unexpected and unlooked-for consequences. The systematic elimination of human values from the formal economy is supposed to produce a paradoxically optimal distribution of welfare by a process which is completely different from informal give and take – one motivated by pure selfishness and gain.[12]

The paradox is even more striking in the case of property. Locke tried to account for the evolution from inclusive property (commons, woodlands) to exclusive (private) property through the invention of money, and to justify it by reference to the higher productivity of enclosed (improved) land.[13] Adam Smith and his successors acknowledged that most large landowners had acquired their property holdings by force or fraud, and that the state's property laws were largely a defence for the rich against the poor.[14] Yet vastly unequal property (including inheritance) was justified by liberals on utilitarian grounds as a necessary condition for prosperity, or for the proper functioning of markets.[15] So liberals include private property within the concept of the individual who is to be protected by the state, thus institutionalizing inequality of resources. By contrast, informal systems usually try to offset or reduce inequalities.

These special features of market exchange and private property have given the state and the informal system certain characteristic roles within the liberal tradition. The state's role is confined to activities which promote communal welfare but which might not stem from individual decisions. For instance, the state may organize or provide education, because the liberal definition of an individual generally means a person who has reached the age of maturity, and has developed his or her faculties. By this definition, children are *potential* individual citizens who are not fully developed, and not yet ready to pursue their own welfare needs; hence it is not inconsistent for the state to require them to be educated, and to provide state schools for them to receive education. Even an ultra-liberal society, the United States, developed state education earlier in the nineteenth century than Britain did, and even Britain made primary education compulsory in 1870.

Certain environmental services, such as drains and sewers, which are not profitable for any one enterprise to provide but are essential for public health, have been seen by liberals as public goods that can be secured only through state intervention; so too have certain industries and infrastructural services of strategic importance. But as economic conditions change, so may the list of spheres for state involvement. In the nineteenth century, posts and telegraphs were regarded as suitable for state management, but parts of these are now being privatized. In Britain, the Westland Helicopters scandal showed how strategic and market considerations could be given different weights even by members of a strongly neo-liberal government.

More problematic still for liberalism is the sphere of social welfare provision. No liberal regime has ever been able to shed state responsibility for the livelihood of large groups of people who are unable to make a living in the labour market or to save enough against illness, disability or old age. In principle, liberal theory would require people to insure themselves against these eventualities; in practice, there are always many who cannot or do not do so, and in any case it is highly unlikely that the most vulnerable people in a market society could find an insurance company that would offer them terms that they could afford. So there is always a hard core of people – the mentally or physically handicapped or ill, widows, orphans, single parents and so on – in need of income, housing and health services, unable to provide for themselves, and throwing themselves on the mercy of the state.

The liberal tradition is to try to limit the state's responsibilities by appealing to the principle of give and take in the informal sphere. Family and wider kin should, it argues, provide for these unfortunates, and if they cannot, then individuals should give to charities out of compassion for the rest. In other words, while insisting that the market provides the ideal formal framework for voluntary mutuality, and that individual enterprise and widespread trade are the ideal vehicles for welfare distribution, the liberal tradition still relies on informal processes to redistribute resources after market mechanisms have worked, and to do so according to very different principles from the market's own.

A crucial weakness of the liberal tradition is that it cannot explain why individuals whose concern for their own welfare motivates them to produce, exchange and accumulate should provide for their own sick or handicapped dependents, still less for those of others. Although liberals challenge state social services with the 'free rider' problem, it poses a huge problem for their own system, which assumes both a subjective definition of welfare *and* that accumulation motivates exchange. If people really believed in liberal principles, they might regard it as an insult to offer charity to strangers, believing that self-help alone actually contributed to personal welfare, and that economic failure deserved punishment.[16] This was the perfectly consistent attitude of Scrooge in Dickens's *Christmas Carol* when he was invited to contribute to a Benevolent Fund for those in need: 'Are there no prisons?' he drily enquired.[17] Modern liberal writers strongly assert the right of those asked to assist the unfortunate to help only those they know personally.[18] The Victorian Charity Organization Society gave financial assistance only where it could be shown that it would make the recipient more self-sufficient.[19]

How could a truly liberal state provide for the rest of those who cannot support themselves in a way that is consistent with its own principle? It could perhaps most easily justify making some provision for mentally handicapped people and those with disabilities from birth – though even here parents could be expected to insure against the possible costs of having a child with such an affliction. So long as these were seen as incomplete individuals, unable to form plans for their own welfare or to carry them through, and hence not as full individuals and full citizens, the state might provide services for them – though the implication would be that these would be protective services, rather than ones aimed at enabling them to participate as fully and normally as possible. Indeed, in a pure liberal society, parents of mentally and physically handicapped children might be faced with a choice (as in the nineteenth century) between bearing the full cost of caring for them themselves, or consigning them to state institutional care.

What then of the others, who could never earn enough to subsist, let alone to insure themselves and their dependants against illness and unemployment? Liberal principles seem to offer no positive reasons why anything should be done for them; presumably, they should seek the protection of stronger and more able individuals, either in families, communes or private institutions. The only possible justification for keeping them alive at all would be that the sight of them dying in the streets would be distressing for ordinary citizens, and would also constitute a public health hazard. State provision of residual services for the destitute could thus be regarded as somewhat similar to the provision of sewers and drains – which perhaps explains to some extent why the architect of the New Poor Law of 1834 was also an expert on sewerage, and an advocate of drains.[20] Of course, provision made for the sake of public health and decency would be likely to take much the same form as the Victorian Poor Law – institutions where the able-bodied were required to work for their keep and the rest were barely kept alive, in conditions intentionally no better than those of the worst off outside their walls.

Pure liberalism would therefore uphold a subjective view of welfare, and would respect individual projects and commitments; but it would give no guarantees against misfortunes, misjudgements and failures. Above all, it has never been able to offer a convincing account of how even the most industrious and virtuous person of limited ability could succeed in meeting his or her basic needs without good fortune or the patronage of someone more able. What is more, there is obviously a huge difference between the opportunities for pursuing his individual projects of a rich man (who could afford the resources to develop several at once) and a poor man (who could only earn enough for subsistence by working long hours) or a woman with no independent income and several children to care for.

Hence, while seeming to give equal autonomy for all, the liberal model of society produces great inequality, with freedom and opportunity for some, and constraint and suffering for others. Liberal principles seem therefore to invite and assume high rates of cheating, crime and subversion in the formal sphere; the relative stability of societies with strongly liberal traditions must depend heavily on the mechanisms of the informal sphere.

The Socialist Tradition

Socialist principles are concerned more with group than with individual rights. They draw attention to radical differences between the autonomy enjoyed by one class of citizens – the owners of the means of production – and the dependence of another class – those who are forced to sell their labour power by working for wages, in order to subsist. They insist that these class differences must be abolished before welfare can be maximized and equalized, and that the power of the state must be used to achieve this transformation of society.

The assumptions behind a socialist theory of welfare might be summarized as follows:

1 Each individual's welfare depends on needs which he or she is not capable of meeting by his or her efforts alone.
2 Social welfare depends on social co-operation and social solidarity.
3 Social welfare is therefore something more than, and different from the welfare of individuals.
4 Labour is the source of all value, and labour content is the true measure of everything produced for use or exchange.
5 No individual is entitled to harm or exploit any other individual; to this end, no individual is entitled to more property than he or she needs for his or her own use.
6 The state has a responsibility to protect individuals from harm and exploitation by each other, and to meet their needs.
7 The state is responsible for social welfare, by means of overseeing the establishment of systems for social co-operation and solidarity.

In socialist theory, since *individual* command over the resources required for modern methods of industrial production cannot be achieved without creating an exploitative class, the only way to abolish exploitation is to deny individuals the right to own productive resources. This entails severe restrictions on individual property rights, and hence on individual choices. Instead, the state creates the forms of economic and social organization which it deems best for meeting needs. The state ultimately has the right to control prices, wages and the distribution of all social goods, since it alone determines needs, and allocates resources to meet them. Individuals' welfare is maximized through their membership of groups and collectives and their participation in communal activities, and not through a search for competitive advantage or personal achievement.

The socialist view of welfare is much closer to the informal system in respect of co-operation and sharing than the liberal one. It conveys much more accurately the mutual interdependence of people, and the benefits of co-operative transactions (as in Robert Axelrod's computer game, and in the animal kingdom). It also reflects the informal system's concern to avoid hurt and not to take advantage of weakness, and sees equality as the most reliable principle for making sure that these evils are prevented.

The socialist tradition tries to find an alternative way of measuring costs and benefits to the market measure (money) in the distribution of welfare. In selecting labour time, it seems to choose a measure which is close to the one used in the informal sphere (human time and energy) to compare *inputs* to welfare exchanges, but not *outputs*. In everyday life we are highly selective about the people whose help we will accept, and about the forms that help should take. One person's efforts at co-operation are decidedly not as good as another's, and our judgements about who and what is helpful are highly subjective.

It is this subjectivity and choosiness that is not allowed for in the socialist tradition. The informal system of co-operation and mutual support is one that is very flexible as between wider-scale *community* solidarity (usually in adversity, and especially in the face of outside threat), and small-scale family and network exchanges of services. In this way we can choose what we give and take, and with whom – the individual and subjective elements of market exchange are combined with the solidarity of socialist communalism. The latter provides only one side of the coin; even societies with strong liberal traditions tend to adopt economic planning and authoritarian allocation of resources in times of war, reflecting the development of stronger social solidarity.

Because socialist principles lead to an 'objective theory of the good', they suggest that the state's leaders are in a better position to identify and meet welfare needs than individual people themselves.[21] They therefore lead to the provision of standardized goods and services which are designed for common human requirements, but make little allowance for individuality. Whereas the informal system of co-operation is well geared to people's idiosyncratic views of their welfare, state decisions about production and distribution tend to respond very crudely to human needs. The command economies of Eastern Europe illustrate the weakness of authoritative systems which lack the mechanisms for linking needs through monetary demand with decisions about production. Socialist systems have a built-in distrust of individual preferences (by consumers or voters) and an ideological commitment to maximize co-operation according to their own perceptions of overall communal needs, not being deflected by sectional pressures.[22]

The other major difficulty of socialist co-operation concerns the extent to which it is truly voluntary. In the informal system we do reciprocal services in direct response to individual needs, or as part of a regular pattern of exchange. But where the state determines needs and allocates resources, this process becomes completely depersonalized, and there is no obvious linkage between inputs of labour and benefits from state services. Instead, work becomes something that is owed to the state, which in turn makes certain standard guarantees of communal welfare.

This has indeed been the problem of countries that have tried to move towards a socialist system by way of state planning. As Marx saw clearly, production for need entails each member of society working to the full extent of his or her abilities, voluntarily co-operating in maximizing social welfare for all. Individual welfare coincides with communal welfare because each individual embraces co-operation, recognizes need, and wants to do his or her part. But in the transitional phase, old injustices are still at issue; workers can be persuaded to work only if they are paid the full value of their contribution. Hence the motto is not 'to each according to his need' but 'to each according to his labour'.[23] Transferring resources to the working class means taking them away from the bourgeoisie – and bourgeois resistance requires (in Marxist theory) a phase of working-class dictatorship to accomplish its purposes.

The consequences of these dilemmas are illustrated by the Eastern European countries. Even though there is little organized resistance to centrally planned socialism, there is little commitment to it either. The intelligentsia barely tolerate it, and clearly underfunction in many respects – they have 'surplus consciousness' which is not used up in their largely mechanical, programmed role in public life.[24] Even though many skilled workers, and those in heavy industry, are relatively well paid, they demonstrate little enthusiasm for their tasks, and are as instrumental in their approach to their work roles as their Western counterparts. The state's plans for production and distribution are still (nearly 70 years after the Russian Revolution) experienced as imposed, and there is little evidence that the people are internalizing productive values, or coming to experience their jobs as non-alienated work.

If welfare does not consist of voluntary (even joyful) production for social need, if instead work is more imposed, more coercive even than under capitalism, wherein does welfare lie? Many critics of Eastern Europe suggest that people there are even more consumption-orientated, even more privatized in their family lives, than in the West. The state is driven into inducing work effort and conformity by differential material rewards, by small privileges, by better housing and facilities – indeed, by all the methods of capitalism, which ignore need, and concentrate instead on industrial or political 'desert'. Welfare consists in having a good job and everything that goes with it, and in knowing the right people; and it is individual welfare, not social welfare, that matters to people.

The requirement to reward potentially disaffected workers at all levels well enough to engage their co-operation means that East European systems tend to attach social welfare services to the workplace, and to work roles.[25] Whereas liberalism tends to see social services as concerned with people who are excluded from the labour market, socialism sees them as sustaining, enhancing and extending work roles, or as rewards for work well done. Just as the early trade unions ran their own social services, and members received benefits as workers from their peers rather than from the state, so socialist social services tend to link welfare with work, even to the extent of measuring benefits in terms of work effort.

In Eastern Europe, the coercive aspects of work in state enterprises, and the limited, standardized goods and services available through the official system, have produced many paradoxical results. On the one hand there is a flourishing 'secondary' (market) economy in goods and services that are unofficially produced and exchanged for cash. It is widely argued that the official command economy would not work at all without this unofficial one to supplement it.[26] Second, there is widespread corruption – the trading in political advantage, and the resources available through political position. This generates inequalities in power and possessions which may rival those produced by market capitalism. Third, because neither individual nor group projects are encouraged or enabled, voluntary organizations, associations and interest groups are generally weak (except in Poland and among religious people), and communal activity is confined mainly to somewhat bogus state and party-led organizations with a few well-connected enthusiasts, and an apathetic mass of outsiders, who therefore increasingly invest their energies and enthusiasms in family and private life.

So this version of the socialist tradition seems to institutionalize some features of informal, voluntary co-operation at the expense of suppressing others. It seems not so much to reconcile individual with communal welfare as to drive individualism underground, producing high rates of dissidence and disaffection among intellectuals and instrumental and materialistic deviance among workers. Above all, it seems to undermine the kind of voluntary bodies, consisting of people with shared enthusiasms doing common projects, which many people regard as the hallmark of a healthy community.

The Fabian Tradition

I am using this term to include a broad spectrum of approaches which employ state agencies to remedy diswelfares or promote welfare services within advanced capitalist societies. Because the Fabian tradition is one of reacting to specific political and economic circumstances, rather than designing social institutions *a priori*, it is more difficult to give a list of consistent and coherent principles. However, any list would probably include the following:

1 Market capitalist societies produce structural inequalities and disadvantages, which fall disproportionately on working-class individuals.
2 The state is the only system capable of remedying these features of market capitalism.

3 The state can markedly reduce the diswelfares associated with capitalism by selectively taking key enterprises into public ownership, and managing them according to non-profit principles.
4 The state should regulate capitalist development so as to reduce environmental and social diswelfares.
5 The state should redistribute income so as to reduce the disadvantages of certain groups, and to equalize life chances between members of the different classes.
6 The state should provide welfare services in kind, free or at reduced cost, for certain essential needs.
7 The best way to ensure that the state performs these functions is to include working-class organizations and parties within its institutions and elites.

The first and most obvious thing to say about Fabian principles is that they look at society 'from the top down', and especially through the eyes of state officials. They assume that the malfunctions of the formal economy can be corrected by the actions of official agencies of one kind or another. They assume that experts can diagnose general faults in the social system and prescribe organizational remedies which are rational and effective. They assume that goods and services delivered in this way can be made as acceptable as those produced either by private enterprises or informally. They assume that officials can act disinterestedly, and can provide services in ways that win public support. And they assume that informal systems will not be damaged by such provision, but will supplement it.

The difficulty about the Fabian approach is that, although its diagnosis of the faults in capitalism corresponds closely with that of ordinary people (whose informal system is largely a response to these same faults), its methods of remedying them do not always mesh well with everyday life-styles. People who feel powerless, alienated and disadvantaged in the face of large-scale private enterprises do not feel less so in relation to large-scale public bureaucracies. State agencies seem to insist on a passivity among their clientele which is greater than that of those whose lives are ruled by market forces, and state officials often appear far from disinterested parties in welfare transactions, since their own livelihoods are dependent on the perpetuation of the systems they administer.

Although in principle public services are organized around a theory of give and take, with contributors also being potential beneficiaries, in practice they are often perceived by contributors as favouring certain groups, or free riders. From the beneficiaries' point of view, their conditions for eligibility often prescribe passive roles, so that they are excluded from participation in economic life, even when they are keen to contribute.

For all these reasons, even though the Fabian tradition accords with informal systems in recognizing special needs and trying to provide for them, its formal methods do not command such enthusiastic support as they once did. Further expansions of the public sector, and particularly of social services, require detailed justification to convince a sceptical electorate, including working-class people who have not always been the most obvious gainers from state social welfare services.

The dilemmas of the social services will be discussed in much more detail in the part three, and for this reason I shall not consider the Fabian tradition any further at this stage. The main point here is that paternalistically planned, bureaucratic, impersonal services with complex rational–legal entitlement conditions represent a very formalized mode of welfare provision which lacks the flexibility and reciprocity of the informal system.

Conclusions

In this chapter I have considered what the social sciences generally, and certain powerful intellectual traditions in particular, have to say about the distribution of welfare in modern advanced societies. I have examined their contributions briefly from the standpoint of their accounts of how formal systems reconcile individual with communal welfare. Both the liberal and the socialist traditions argue that the relations in which property is held, production is carried out and exchange occurs are crucial for this; the Fabian tradition argues for special state systems with principles of their own.

What all have in common is that their processes do not obviously allow for adjustments in terms of fairness, freedom or equality which were characteristic of the negotiations about welfare discussed in the last chapter. Trading in a market is *not* like sitting down to discuss one's relationship with one's partner – it is impersonal, and pays no heed to aspirations or constraints. Working in a state factory is *not* like co-operating in a small commune – neither goals nor means are under the control of the workers. Receiving a benefit from the social security office is *not* like receiving a gift from a friend – there is no reciprocity, no individualization and no warmth about it.

What these formal systems of co-operation do is to allow us to conduct transactions which are essential for both communal and individual welfare on a very large (often transnational) scale, and hence to transcend the exclusiveness of small-scale, personal transactions. Without markets there could have been no economic development; without nation-states there could have been no extensive public infrastructure or services to redistribute resources between regions or localities. The creation of formal roles allows large numbers of strangers to be included in complex co-operative systems which override their local preferences and prejudices, their personal idiosyncrasies and animosities, *and* many of their ethical scruples. We may not approve of some of the policies of our government or our employer, but only rarely does this lead us to resign our job or transfer our citizenship.

But this does not mean that formal systems are not subject to evaluation, or that membership of particular large-scale formal organizations does not have implications for membership of others. On the contrary, we use the same evaluative terminology in discussing economic or political institutions as we do for debating the morality of individual conduct and personal relationships; we also often speak as if attachment to particular political, religious or ethnic groupings excluded people from participation in certain others. Yet it is in the nature of formal systems that their rules and roles are fixed and impersonal, and are not readily susceptible to the adaptations and negotiations that allow small-scale personal relationships to be readjusted through a moral dialogue of give and take.

This use of an evaluative vocabulary that spans personal and impersonal, formal and informal, is therefore a problematic one. We need to analyse how notions of fairness, freedom, equality, need, desert, rights and so on can be used to discuss both personal and communal welfare, and how it is shared in small and large systems. We also need to consider how these systems themselves mesh with each other, and how people make decisions about co-operation and competition within very different spheres of social organization. These issues will be the subjects of the next three chapters.

Notes

1 John Locke, *Two Treatises of Government* (1698), Cambridge University Press, 1967, *Second Treatise*, sections 27–50.
2 For instance, Adam Smith's *Inquiry into the Nature and Causes of the Wealth of Nations* (1776), books I and II; David Ricardo's *Principles of Political Economy and Taxation* (1817), and John Stuart Mill's *Principles of Political Economy with some of their Applications to Social Philosophy* (1848), book 1.
3 Karl Marx, *Capital*, vol. 1 (1867), especially chs 6 and 7.
4 Max Weber, *The Theory of Social and Economic Organization* (1920), Free Press, 1947, especially ch. III, part II, section 3.
5 There are stylized 'histories' of the forms of political authority linked with particular economic relations in Hobbes, Locke, James Harrington (*Prerogative of Popular Government*, 1658) and other seventeenth-century writers. Rousseau's *A Discourse on the Origin and Foundations of Inequality among Men*, and *A Discourse on Political Economy* contain unsophisticated accounts of possible links; Adam Smith's *Wealth of Nations*, books IV and V, is an extremely sophisticated account of the relationship between commerce, productive relations and political authority. It would probably cope better than Marx's theory with the case of Japan, which moved straight from feudal-capitalism (the Tokugawa period) to state capitalism (Meiji period). See Mishio Morishima, '*The Transformation of Japanese Society from Centralized Feudalism to Dualism*', paper given to ESRC Conference on Socioeconomic Development of the West, Cambridge, April 1986.

6 Liberalism was never as pure as my ideal-type model would suggest. For instance, even such a prototypical nineteenth-century British liberal as John Stuart Mill had ideas about personal development and the emancipation of women which are not properly represented in these principles; he was also very optimistic that, given proper population control, the whole class basis of British society could be broken down, and the distinction between capital and labour abolished (*Principles of Political Economy*, book IV, ch. vii). Modern liberals are far more interested in ideas about community, participation and population control than this summary of principles would suggest.

7 Both pre-Marxian utopian socialists and the syndicalist tradition have ideas which cannot be absorbed into my rather simple and crude framework, while of course there are aspects of both Russian and Chinese communism which go well beyond this set of principles. As a view of social conflict, this tradition is certainly older than Marx. The idea of a class basis for society and of differential citizenship within a set of commercial relationships is clearly evident in Locke – see for instance 'Some Considerations on the Consequences of the Lowering of Interest, and Raising the Value of Money' in *The Works of John Locke in Four Volumes*, W. Strachan et al., 1777, vol. II, especially pp. 10–46. It entered not only into British political economy, but also into the writings of the French socialists Saint-Simon and Fourier. It seems likely that Marx was strongly influenced by the largely anonymous Ricardian socialist school (such as the author of 'The Source and Remedy of National Difficulties: A Letter to Lord John Russell' (1821), who wrote, 'It is admitted that the rents, interests or money, or profits of trade, is paid out of the labour of others. . . . Whatever may be due to the capitalist he can only receive the surplus-labour of the labourer; for the labourer must live' (p. 23); and 'Truly wealthy a nation, when the working day is 6 hours rather than 12 hours. *Wealth* is not command over surplus labour time but rather, *disposable time* outside that needed in direct productions for *every individual* and the whole of society' (p. 6; quoted by Marx in *Grundrisse: Foundations of the Critique of Political Economy (Rough Draft)*, Penguin, 1973, p. 706). Others of the same school quoted by Marx were Thomas Hodgskin and William Thompson. It was Hodgskin who wrote of 'that natural law which gives wealth to labour and labour only'. What distinguished these writers (including Owen) from many of their socialist predecessors and contemporaries was their recognition that capitalism had created potentially liberating forces of production, which freed people from the constraints of earlier communal societies, and hence that socialism should not look wistfully back to pre-capitalist social formations, but should look ahead at how more advanced productive forces might lead to transformed productive relations, and ultimately to a classless society.

8 Bentham elaborated proposals for administrative and institutional solutions to a whole range of social and environmental problems, from crime and pauperism – *Panopticon* (1791) and *Pauper Management Improved* (1798) – to suffocation in mines and manufactories, disease and mortality from putrid water, and about the custody of children – *Constitutional Code* (1843), his fullest and most uncannily accurate anticipation of the modern state's services. He was much influenced by Prussian and French theorists and public administrators. Fabians such as the Webbs and Laski acknowledged their intellectual debt to him.

9 For instance, Andre Gorz, *Farewell to the Working Class: An Essay on*

Post-Industrial Socialism (1980), Pluto, 1982, who argues that people are now more interested in the 'sphere of autonomy' outside work than in organizing to control the 'sphere of necessity' (production); Jonathan Gershuny and Ian Miles, *The New Service Economy: The Transformation of Employment in Industrial Societies*, Pinter, 1983, who suggest that 'self-servicing' may be a faster growing sector than service employment; and Ray Pahl, *Divisions of Labour*, Basil Blackwell, 1984, who argues that changes in household patterns of informal labour utilization and self-provisioning have been more dynamic than those in the formal labour market.

10 The implications of this will be discussed in more detail in chapter 4.

11 Adam Smith, *The Theory of Moral Sentiments* (1760), part IV, ch. 1. 'The Rich only select from the heap what is most precious and agreeable. They consume little more than the poor, in spite of their natural selfishness and rapacity, though they mean only their own conveniency, though the sole end which they propose from the labours of all the thousands they employ, be the satisfaction of their own vain and insatiable desires, they divide with the poor the produce of all their improvements. They are led by an invisible hand . . .'

12 See also Adam Smith, *Wealth of Nations*, book III, ch. iv, sections 10 and 17.

13 Locke, *Second Treatise*, sections 35–50.

14 Smith, *Wealth of Nations*, book V, ch. i, part b, sections 2–12.

15 See for instance Jeremy Bentham, *Principles of the Civil Code* (1790), part I, chs xi–xiv, and John Stuart Mill, *Some Considerations Concerning Representative Government*, ch. 2.

16 See for instance Robert Sugden, 'Hard Luck Stories: The Problem of the Uninsured in a Laissez-Faire Society', *Journal of Social Policy*, vol. II, no. 2, 1982, p. 215.

17 Charles Dickens, *A Christmas Carol* (1843), Chapman & Hall, 1910, p. 15.

18 F. A. Hayek, *The Constitution of Liberty*, Routledge & Kegan Paul, 1960, chs 18 and 19.

19 C. L. Mowat, *The Charity Organisation Society*, Methuen, 1961.

20 S. E. Finer, *The Life and Times of Sir Edwin Chadwick*, Methuen, 1952.

21 Albert Weale, *Political Theory and Social Policy*, Macmillan, 1983, pp. 23–4.

22 See especially F. Feher, A. Heller and G. Markus, *Dictatorship Over Needs*, Basil Blackwell, 1985; M. Vajda, *The State and Socialism*, Allison & Busby, 1981; and Rudolf Bahro, *The Alternative in Eastern Europe*, New Left Books, 1978. Bahro wrote that 'the abolition of private property in the means of production has in no way meant their immediate transformation into the property of the people. Rather, the whole society stands property-less against the state machine' (pp. 10–11). All these writers condemn the system in Eastern Europe as inferior to modern Western democracy in its distribution of welfare, mainly because the state's power leaves people so powerless, and with such little scope for (legally) implementing their own chosen projects, shared and co-operative as well as individualistic.

23 The stage at which socialism operated according to this principle was called 'the lower stage of communism' by Marx in his *Critique of the Gotha Programme*. See R. Van der Veen and P. van Parijs, 'A Capitalist Road to Communism', *Theory of Society*, March 1985.

24 Bahro, *The Alternative in Eastern Europe*, pp. 10–11.

25 G. V. Rimlinger, *Welfare Policy and Industrialisation in Europe, America and Russia*, John Wiley, 1971.

26 See for instance Feher, Heller and Markus, *Dictatorship over Needs*, pp. 99–100.

27 For a critique of the Fabian tradition see Roger Hadley and Stephen Hatch, *Social Policy and the Failure of the State: Centralised Social Services and Participatory Alternatives*, Allen & Unwin, 1981, pp. 3–5.

4

Fairness

So far I have looked at the *processes* by which people seek and share welfare, and at theories about the formal allocation of welfare in societies. Now I shall turn to the *values* that people use in claiming or comparing shares of welfare, and how they apply to formal systems in wider communities. In this chapter I shall look at the value of fairness (or justice).

It seems to me that fairness is the primary value that we appeal to in everyday life when negotiating about welfare. It is the main principle that underpins the processes of give and take which I have suggested are fundamental to all social organization, because it implies reciprocity and mutual advantage according to some measured standard. There seems to be a universal notion that 'fair's fair' (fair shares, fair dos) which corresponds with Robert Axelrod's 'tit for tat' programme in his computer game, and suggests that we should always start with co-operative moves in relation to others, and always respond co-operatively when they do so.

Fairness is a comparative value; it enables us to apply a standard to the way we share things out between us. In disputes about who gets what, negotiations, arbitrations and settlements all deal in fairness. But if all social organization is based on people's capacity to share fairly, why then are all modern societies based on the highly impersonal, generalized processes analysed in the last chapter?

The usual answer to this question involves imagining a large community in which all the natural resources (land, water and minerals) are held in common, and there is no formal organization to settle disputes about how they are to be used for the production of life's necessities. It is usually argued or assumed that:

1 commitment to sharing on the basis of fairness will be weaker in a large community than in a small one; people will organize themselves into small groups (families or clans) and share within these, but they will compete with other small groups, ultimately by use of force;
2 people will claim a larger share of resources than that which is their arithmetical dividend because it is in their interests to try to get more out of common resources than their 'fair share', partly because they see that

others are likely to do so, and partly because, even if others do not, they themselves will benefit more than the rest by doing so. This is a special case of the 'free rider' problem discussed in chapter 2; the best-known examples are the tendency of commoners to overgraze land by each putting too many animals on it, and the tendency of fishermen to overfish inshore waters. It is referred to as 'the tragedy of the commons' and leads to the assumption that this form of economic organization is either unfair or inefficient, or both;[1]

3 people will neglect some or all of those individuals who are least able to fend for themselves, because they cannot assert their needs or compete for their share of resources.

All the approaches to communal welfare discussed in the last chapter use the central power of the state to establish a formal system for allocating shares. The liberal tradition addresses itself primarily to the first problem, arguing that private property and markets allow large communities to engage in orderly exchange under fair conditions. The socialist tradition draws attention to the unfairness of capitalist productive relations and the outcomes of market exchange, and uses authoritative allocation of shares to tackle the second problem. The Fabian tradition tries to reconcile these two approaches, and to address the third problem. All three therefore claim to establish systems of social order which allow each person to receive his or her *due* (fair share).

In this chapter I shall look at what we mean, in the context of informal and formal systems of welfare shares, when we talk about what is 'due' to us. What am I claiming when I say that it is fair that I should be allowed to have this, or do that? There are three distinct claims that I may be making:

1 that I have a right to have it, or do it;
2 that I deserve to have it, or do it;
3 that I need to have it, or do it.

These are really quite different claims, though I might be making all three at once in saying that it was fair for me to have something or do something.

Rights

In ordinary life, for instance among colleagues or friends, I should claim that I had a right to have or do anything only if there were some written or unwritten *rule* about how things or actions were to be divided up between us, or if we were playing some game that was governed by rules. The language of rights is – except among the very pompous – reserved for arguing one's case (often jokingly) when there is a dispute about fairness in some field of activity which is governed by rules. For instance, if the group of people agree to share the use of a room on the basis of a rota, I might defend my presence in it, if challenged, by saying, 'I've every right to be here – it's my turn' (or alternatively, 'I'm quite *entitled* to be here . . .').

People who are on very friendly and informal terms seldom use the language of rights and entitlements in their everyday relationships; indeed, it might well be regarded as a kind of signal of an impending quarrel between people on these terms for one of them to start to say, 'You've no right to . . .', or 'I've every right to . . .'. In families, it is usually teenagers who are fighting for their independence who employ the language of rights, though women who have suddenly become aware of the narrow constraints of their marital and maternal roles also increasingly use it. The idea of the traditional power-holders in families – husbands and fathers – having *rights* to discipline, overrule or place demands on others is closely associated with a certain historical structure of family relationships, and with a largely discredited manner of exercising this power – as in the notion of 'conjugal rights'.

People make rules when they draw up an agreement, in anticipation of possible disputes; a contract is a formal agreement, specifying rights and duties, which allows either side to make a claim against the other if these are not fulfilled. Marriage is a legal contract which carries certain enforceable consequences over property, income and children, but nowadays many couples also come to specific agreements about how they will fulfil their day-to-day roles, so that there can be fairness in every aspect of their relationship with each other (as was discussed in the second chapter).

So far I have given examples of relationships, groups and associations where there are usually opportunities for individuals to discuss any rules that are to be made, to review them, and to change them from time to time. Equally common is the more formal (often larger) association, where new members have the opportunity to learn of the rules before they join, and then implicitly subscribe to them in joining. Sometimes the constitutions of organizations allow the rules to be challenged and changed by members; sometimes rules can be subtly bent and reinterpreted by ingenious individuals; sometimes the full implications of certain rules, or the way they are applied, cause individuals to leave associations, grumbling that 'The way they do things there isn't fair at all.'

What I am suggesting is that in ordinary life the idea of fairness in the distribution of welfare *according to rights or entitlements* is characteristic of an order established by rules to which people explicitly or implicitly have given their agreement. Without the individual's agreement or tacit consent, the notion of fairness in terms of rights makes little sense in an everyday context. For instance, suppose that my colleagues and I have a rule that the last person leaving the room that we all share should wash up the coffee cups, and suppose that I am talking to a complete stranger in the otherwise empty room at the end of the day: I can scarcely claim that it is fair for me to rush out of the room, and shout back to him that as he's last he has to wash up the cups!

Let us see how this idea of fairness translates from the small-scale context into wider society. One obvious difference is that we do not *join* societies in the same way as we might join voluntary associations, except perhaps when we apply for the citizenship of a country to which we have emigrated. We do not subscribe to the rules which govern communal living – either laws or customs – but simply grow up within them. Some political theorists have argued that voting implies a form of consent, but this is clearly quite different from the consent given by joining, or withheld by leaving, a voluntary association (accurately described as 'voting with one's feet').[2] Besides, most countries strictly limit the numbers of people who can join their societies or leave them, or both.

Yet the language of fairness in terms of rights is very much used in wider social, and especially economic, relations. Sometimes it refers to rights established under law; here the justification in terms of fairness is presumably that the law is the same for all, and that all are equal in the eyes of the law. Sometimes it is used in connection with contracts, and here clearly there is at least formal consent. But there are also times when we use the language of rights about economic life, and particularly about such issues as property and employment. This is much more problematic, because such notions are embedded in the whole fabric of how society is organized; it is therefore impossible to extract them from their context, and to look at *my* property rights or *your* employment rights outside this established system of relationships.

First let us look at property. What I own in the way of a house, vehicle, furniture and so on I have come by through a mixture of purchase, gift and inheritance, but probably over 95 per cent of it has been through buying things out of earnings. The Duke of Devonshire owns a great deal more than I do, and it seems likely that he inherited about the same proportion of his holdings in property as I purchased. Under the rules of our society, he has as much right to his estates as I do to my garden; but is it *fair* that either of us has what we do, especially when many people in our society have almost nothing at all, and when they certainly have not agreed to the rules by which I have acquired a comfortably sized house and garden, and the Duke of Devonshire a great estate?

The liberal account of fairness justifies the necessity of property holdings in general terms both as an expression of the subjective view of welfare (I must be allowed to acquire what I need for my projects) and as a means of maximizing communal welfare (people need property holdings to avoid the 'tragedy of the commons', to improve productive efficiency, and to provide the security for industry and trade).[3] The problem of enormous inequality in property holdings is recognized, but is usually brushed aside as an unfortunate historical legacy – there is no way of knowing whether the

Duke's ancestors acquired their estates through force and fraud, or whether the very fine bookcase that I have was made from old church pews that were pinched by my ancestor or was given to him by an enthusiastic Victorian restorer. Liberals will often concede that property might be much more fairly redistributed in *theory*, but the practical difficulties always seem to be overwhelming, especially in the case of industrial plant, most of which is now owned by giant impersonal international corporations.

Instead, liberals concentrate on the processes by which people acquire property in a market society, and argue that the important issue is that the rules governing the various markets – in labour, goods and services – should be fair. Since the essence of markets (in liberal terms) is voluntary exchange, this really amounts to saying that fairness consists in seeing that markets are as free as possible from interference and constraint. The criteria of fairness cannot meaningfully be applied to the results of market exchange (since these are the products of millions of voluntary transactions between individuals), but only to the conditions in which exchange takes place.[4]

The first effect of this approach is really to exclude all notions of fairness and rights from economic transactions. The difference between markets and more traditional and informal systems of exchange is precisely that they exclude all non-economic elements from the process. If I offer to swap something with a friend, or ask a favour of a neighbour, all kinds of non-economic issues can be brought into play. The friend can take account of my personal circumstances, my state of health and the context of our relationship; the neighbour can remember past favours I have done him, and look forward to things he may need from me. Informal exchanges of goods and services are likely to be heavily influenced by social roles; for instance, in his large-scale survey of formal and informal work, Pahl found that single parents were much more likely to get jobs done around their houses by friends, on an unpaid basis, than married couples – he even heard them say things like 'I've just come round to borrow your husband.'[5] By contrast, markets take no account of such factors as social roles, personal circumstances, differential levels of welfare and friendly (or hostile) relationships: they provide a context in which each individual is able to trade or earn totally impersonally.

In some countries, trading is still influenced (at least in traditional parts of the economy) by non-economic factors. For Westerners such behaviour as haggling (in which the trader's prosperity or penury is often brought into discussions of the price) or hustling (in which demands for payments for services have menacing overtones) or soliciting custom (by shouts to passers-by from shops) seem at first to be both intrusive and undignified. However, these are really surviving elements of the personal and negotiable factors in exchange, which Western versions of the market have excluded.[6] They embarrass us by referring (sometimes rather obscurely) to standards of fairness and of distribution in welfare which we have learned to forget when we are going about our economic business, and which we have marginalized into such activities as begging, busking, the selling of lucky charms and some vaguely menacing transactions involving surplus asphalt.

There is room for dispute about how such customary (archaic) trading patterns relate to modern Westernized markets. Can they be explained in the same rational–egoistic terms as impersonal market behaviour (that they give economic advantages under certain conditions)? Or do they represent *alternatives* to rational–egoistic economic behaviour, which co-exist with conventional modern markets, and mesh into them? For instance, a number of studies have drawn attention to the practice among certain Third World street traders in fruit and vegetables to reserve part of their supplies for favoured regular buyers at lower prices than they can get on the open market, in return for regular orders.[7] This is done on a non-contractual, trust basis, and breach of trust terminates the arrangement. The important point is perhaps not whether these customs can be explained in strictly rational–egoistic calculations, but that a system based on informal personal tit-for-tat and fairness should largely *underpin* the operation of Westernized impersonal markets. People know that they can rely on customary arrangements if the market fails them. In the earlier examples, they try to appeal to Western tourists' compassion (or nervousness) if they cannot make a living by ordinary market competition.

The second effect of the liberal system is profoundly conservative, in the sense that it encourages not only the acquisition but also the retention of property – what we have we hold. Exclusive individual property rights, which are the basis of the whole liberal system, encourage a mentality of ownership and control which is tenaciously possessive, and backed by laws which are ferocious in their punishment of those who steal or trespass. At the time of writing, a wealthy individual has just been acquitted of a murder charge in a British court, on the grounds that he mistook an undercover policeman on his estate for an intruder, and therefore beat him to death. Ironically, the policeman was investigating his slayer's alleged involvement in a gold bullion robbery.

In other cultures, people give away their property much more freely – to friends, kin, or even comparative strangers. This is particularly true of the Middle Eastern countries; it is customary to give away expensive goods, and to leave it entirely as a matter of honour and trust what is done or given in return. In Western culture, property is not as a rule redistributed by its owners in such a way as to redistribute welfare (though income may be, in the form of charity); possessive individualism, which is the hallmark of liberalism, encourages us to build up stocks of property, sometimes as a project in itself.

All this means that, although liberalism's primary definition of fairness (justice) is in terms of individual rights, the effect of its version of these rights is really to exclude any notion of redistributive fairness from day-to-day economic life. The result is that people often feel that economic transactions are unfair (and complain loudly about this), but they can never do anything about it. It is common to hear people say that they could not get a fair price, or a fair wage, and that they were forced to sell, or to work, against their will, implying that the market is neither fair nor free; but there is no mechanism by which such wrongs can be righted within the liberal order. Even people who feel obscurely guilty about their economic advantages can do little about it in the marketplace, and are reduced to making charitable contributions, which sometimes makes them feel guiltier still, since they themselves would be unwilling to receive charity. One of the few ways that the market system has found of getting round this problem is the idea of sponsorship, by which individuals and organizations can be asked to pay uneconomic prices for services, as a pseudo-market way of rewarding non-economic values.

In real life no one acts as if private property, capitalist industry or the market have anything to do with fairness. They are simply treated as efficient and convenient ways of optimizing the use of resources and price opportunities *under certain circumstances*. All of us – rich and poor – use markets when they suit our purposes, but we spend much of our lives protecting ourselves from their adverse consequences. The rich accumulate privileges and property holdings for themselves and their families; the poor try to preserve informal resources and networks, so that they have something to fall back on in adversity. Far from accepting market conditions or outcomes as fair, we act as if their only justice lies in their allowing us to hedge against them in various ways without withdrawing from them altogether.

In developing economies, people's main protection from market uncertainty is subsistence production. On the West African savannah, for instance, both pastoralists and agriculturalists sell only part of their produce on the market, and are able to survive market failures by withholding a larger proportion for consumption.[8] Even in more developed economies, townspeople have plentiful informal opportunities for gaining income[9] and also in the last resort, usually have a rural kinship network to which to retreat for subsistence. The same was true to some extent even after the industrialization of European countries – for instance, in Britain in the later nineteenth century, and elsewhere up to the Second World War.[10]

In advanced capitalist countries corporate social organizations (firms, state enterprises, trade unions) can be seen as a kind of dialectical response to markets, replacing competition with various attempts at monopoly. All these corporations provide insulation from the negative effects of market prices, while exploiting gains from market power. They protect the individuals that they incorporate (shareholders, employees, members) from the isolation and vulnerability of market competition. Corporate bodies are therefore a distinctive social form in advanced capitalism, even though the liberal tradition mainly insists on treating them in law as if they were individuals and hence subject to the same economic and social rules as individuals.

Corporate organization indicates that, despite liberal theory, markets are not seen as processes for sharing welfare according to fairness. Markets are not associations, they do not have members, and they do not share benefits in terms of rights. Markets involve exchanges between aggregates of individuals; they are open to all, including members of other nations. Corporations also can be very large, often international; but they are associations, and they do have memberships. For instance, large firms not only give employees pay, but they also often provide them with promotion prospects, a career structure, employment security, pensions, sports facilities, expense accounts, health and welfare provision and so on.

Until recently, it seemed that large corporations (private firms or state enterprises) were destined to become the dominant social forms of advanced societies. Both capitalist and socialist developed economies were increasingly characterized by large organizations, consisting of complex bureaucratic hierarchies, engaged in productive and distributive activities and meshed together through formal organizational links. Both types of society seemed indeed to be converging towards similar types of managed economy ('organized capitalism' was the Western version), in which all individuals would participate as members of national corporations (enterprises and unions), and would gain their security and status from the membership of large-scale associations. This in turn would provide the form of fairness that was missing from the market – fairness through organizational shares.

But recently several new socioeconomic trends have disturbed assumptions about an easy reconciliation between corporations and markets, and about the progressive incorporation of individuals into national associations. On the one hand, productive enterprises have got much larger and more international in scale. They often produce more than whole national economies and exchange more internally between their constituent firms in different countries than whole states trade between each other. On the other hand, in the advanced capitalist countries large productive enterprises are reducing their permanent workforces, and hence offering their corporate benefits to fewer full-time workers; this in turn has caused falling trade union membership. To some extent this is being offset by offering employees new terms of membership (for example, share ownership in some enterprises, especially in the United States), and this in turn has stimulated interest among socialists in new forms of 'social ownership' for public enterprises. But the dominant effect seems to be that fewer individuals are coming to enjoy the characteristic protection, security and prospects for advancement associated with membership of large organizations, and more are exposed to the isolation and uncertainty of the market.

It could be argued, of course, that in advanced capitalist countries state benefits and services have replaced informal productive systems as protection against vulnerability in the market. But in many ways they are an unsatisfactory substitute for informal sources, as we shall see in subsequent chapters, because they are far less flexible, and mesh less well with both the labour market and the domestic sphere. The freedom to move between the informal and formal systems and to combine them in different ways, plus the access to productive resources, were all positive features of earlier societies; by contrast, state social services tend to trap people in passivity and dependence, and to be a substitute for economic participation, rather than a supplement to it.

So let us now turn to the socialist approach. This is largely a reaction against the liberal one; it points out that the individual rights granted by liberalism, and especially the rights to accumulate large-scale property holdings and to own means of production, create a whole class of people who are permanently disadvantaged in their attempt to make a living. The members of the working class are forced to sell their labour-power as if it were a commodity, while those who buy it have many alternative means both of exploiting workers' labour to their advantage, and of pursuing projects of their own.[11]

Consequently, the socialist approach dismisses liberal notions of individual rights as bourgeois mystifications; it dispenses not only with property rights, but also largely with individual civil and political rights, and substitutes instead group rights, such as the right of workers as a class to receive the value of the fruits of their labour. Perhaps the nearest thing to an individual right which the socialist approach recognizes is the right to employment – one which is conspicuously lacking in the liberal notion of rights. But the right to employment is balanced by an obligation to *accept* the state's offer of work, and to co-operate in its schemes for meeting communal need on its terms. Similarly, even under capitalism, the group rights of trade unionists in relation to pay and conditions are upheld, but once a group decision on strike action is agreed, individuals forfeit the right to decide to continue working.

There are some close similarities in effect between the liberal and socialist versions of rights. The socialist approach, like the liberal, excludes individual and personal factors from economic transactions, because product designs, prices and wages are all determined by the political leadership. As a result, the planned economy – as much as the market – is an impersonal way of meeting needs; indeed, the needs that are recognized are a good deal more generalized, and the products more standardized, than in the market. This has the paradoxical effect that in all planned and guaranteed societies there are flourishing 'secondary economies' of privately produced goods and informally provided services, paid for in cash.[12] In many cases this secondary economy may be much more personalized and more closely related to individual and household needs than the market is in Western countries, since it often operates more like the informal (non-monetary) part of capitalist economies, with reciprocal services being exchanged through a network of known contacts.

Clearly, rights are created as a result of the rules by which both socialist and liberal regimes order their societies, though they contrast greately in their forms and implications. Both sets of principles would claim that their particular clusters of rights guarantee fairness (justice) in society, and allow the reconciliation of individual with communal welfare. What I have tried to show in this section is that the notion of fairness as established through rights which we employ in personal relationships is quite different from the one used in either liberal or socialist principles, especially in relation to economic transactions. In everyday life, we draw up the rules of any relationship, group or association with some reference to the actual interests, characteristics and abilities of the participants, allotting roles and responsibilities by negotiation and working out their implications by consent. The rights and duties so established are held to be fair mainly because they have taken account of people's views, their aspirations and their limitations, not because they conform to abstract or universal principles of justice. In both liberal and socialist societies, highly generalized rights are incorporated into economic systems which are purposefully made impersonal, and where all individual idiosyncracies are deliberately eliminated from the transactions.

Both systems can argue that their principles allow a very generalized type of fairness as between citizens by guaranteeing these rights; but both also require other systems, run according to other principles, to underpin their methods of economic allocation, if they are to meet claims to fairness which stem from the personal characteristics and abilities of citizens.

Deserts

To return to ordinary life, when I say I 'deserve' something, I can reasonably be asked to give a reason for my claim. I am then required to draw attention to some characteristic (presumably virtuous) of mine, or of my actions, which merits reward. Fairness that stems from desert consists in giving each person his or her due according to their merits. A system which was organized around deserts would be a true meritocracy – the virtuous would get everything, and the vicious nothing (except perhaps punishment).

The first thing to say about desert is that we do *not* organize our everyday life like this. In fact, we live from day to day without appealing to the principle of desert at all, unless we are remarkably priggish and boring. In ordinary relationships we use other criteria of fairness, such as the attempt to equalize welfare, which have nothing to do with desert. This is because to share welfare according to desert would mean assessing each particular action, or each individual's contribution to a group project, every time there was to be any distribution of benefits. It would mean that there were no general rules or regular roles through which welfare was shared – no standard rations of fairness. Such endless, detailed claims and counter-claims from individuals would be very time-consuming, and disputes would be difficult to settle. So instead, in informal systems it is only when one of us has done something exceptionally and unusually meritorious that an appeal to desert is made, as in: 'I've walked three miles to town and back to get everyone's shopping, so I deserve the most comfortable chair.' Conversely, it is only when someone (usually a child) has done something wrong that he or she is told that – in fairness – they should do without their usual ration of something.

It could be argued that, while desert is seldom central to sharing welfare in informal systems, it plays an important role *at the margins*. Most families, groups and associations have some sorts of rewards and punishments through which they give or withhold parts of the welfare to be distributed. I would argue that in most informal systems this aspect of welfare distribution is very marginal, and often half-joking, as in fines for swearing, various kinds of mock-punishments, or booby prizes. Most sports clubs distribute cups and other awards at the end of their seasons, but it is particularly noticeable in British working-class clubs that almost everyone wins something, even if it is only a trophy for the most own-goals or dropped catches.

So it is quite surprising to find how central a role desert – or at least, differential reward – plays in formal systems, and in the organization of wider society. We regard it as quite acceptable that some people earn much higher incomes than others, and that some forms of work (notably, the tasks done by housewives and care-givers to kin) are not paid at all. This kind of differentiation, which many of us would not tolerate for a moment in any informal group or club we belonged to, is part of the fabric of economic life; furthermore, most societies also have overt or covert systems for rewarding 'political desert'.[13]

The relationship between differential rewards and supposed desert or merit is very confused. It is certainly common to hear trade unionists and others argue that groups like teachers or nurses deserve higher pay, while businessmen often suggest that initiative and risk-taking deserve greater rewards. But it is not at all clear that this implies that teachers, nurses or business leaders are more meritorious than others. It may imply that certain rewards (salary levels) are necessary in order to attract enough people, or the right people, to do the job; but in this case we would expect certain very unpleasant or difficult jobs to be more highly rewarded, and other easier and more status-giving ones to be less so. In liberal theory, differential rewards are usually justified in terms of social utility rather than merit – that certain jobs (such as wealth creation or healing the sick) are of greater usefulness to the community as a whole, and therefore should be more highly rewarded.[14] The same principle would help to explain why an inventor who patents some mechanism which turns out to have enormous commercial potential might become very rich, whereas an equally ingenious and industrious inventor whose creations have no practical application would receive nothing at all.

The test is not merit according to any measure of virtue, but usefulness to one's fellow members of society, who are willing to pay more for skills which are more highly valued. Perhaps the only example of differential payment by *virtue* would be the practice (recently adopted by some employers at the time of writing) of paying non-smoking workers considerably more than smokers (though non-smoking may also have some social utility); a pure example of social utility payments would be piecework.

Fairness over earnings is problematic because pay is supposed to be the 'reward' for effort and skill. Reward in this sense hardly has the same meaning as when it is used to signify a recognition of merit. It is often part of the point of rewarding virtuous actions (such as bravery) that they were performed without thought of self or recompense; yet rewards for labour are inducements to work. More accurately, they are inducements to engage in particular kinds of formal, organized work, called employment, for money. Historically, people have been drawn out of informal (peasant, subsistence) production (family or communal co-operation) into formal (factory, office) work partly by coercive measures (expropriation, taxation) and partly by the inducement of pay.

Fair pay therefore is supposed to be both a fair return for effort and skill expended and a fair share of the product of formal economic co-operation. So it is somehow related both to the individual's contribution (compared with others') and to the output of the whole co-operative enterprise; but in capitalist societies it is also related to competition between enterprises in the market. Finally, fair pay is also pay which allows the worker to live, and to meet his or her needs.

Trade unions in capitalist countries display a strong ambivalence about market forces in relation to wage determination.[15] On the one hand, unions exist largely to protect their members from the poverty and insecurity that can accompany falls in demand for particular workers or skills. They use their organization, and their influence within the state (in the direction of legislation on minimum wages, employment protection, compensation for redundancy and so on), to resist adverse market forces. On the other hand, when demand for their members' services is high, they exploit this as much as possible, both to maximize the short-term advantages in terms of pay and conditions, and to negotiate arrangements which protect their long-term interests, such as closed shops, apprenticeship schemes, demarcation agreements, promotion ladders, job security and so on. So, while acting to try to weaken the effects of market forces through contracts and regulations, they also use their market power and strongly uphold their rights to 'free collective bargaining'.

Against this background, ideas about fairness in relation to pay are complex and confusing. Part of unions' defence of their trade is the attempt to exclude or neutralize competition from non-union labour that threatens to undercut their wage rates. Another part is the idea of the union 'rate for the

job' – that their skills and diligence deserve a reward which is a fair reflection
of their contribution to the value of the final product. The latter notion is
imprecise, and has in it some undertones of the labour theory of value (that
labour content alone provides a comparative valuation of goods) and some
undertones of neoclassical economic theory of wage rates (that they are
determined by the output of the last worker to be employed). All of these
notions have in common a basis in membership of an exclusive organization,
whose skills should be recognized and rewarded at a special rate of pay
which distinguishes this group from others. In this view, a fair national pay
structure would be the result of all the separate agreements made by
employers and trade unions.

There are obvious problems about a definition of fairness which relies on
institutional processes of this competitive kind. Although each wage rate is
the result of negotiation, it is settled in competition with other groups. There
is no mechanism for reducing the differentials that will inexorably widen
between the pay of members of strong unions and those of weak ones; each
union can prosper only by pursuing the interests of its members against all
others. Hence fairness also demands a political role of trade unions, in which
they act together on behalf of the whole working class; but this role is always
in some tension with the former one. So, for instance, the idea of solidarity
with another union in dispute with an employer raises problematic issues,
and effective support can seldom be relied upon. Alternatively, unions may
act together, through their confederation, to pursue a national pay policy
which forgoes competitive advantage. This has happened in the postwar
period in most Western European countries, under social democratic
governments, during a period when the state was able to bring representa-
tives of national capital and organized labour together to plan output,
investment and incomes. It is still the case in Austria, and especially in
Sweden, where unions have used such corporatist arrangements to reduce
differentials and strengthen the position of low-paid workers. But in other
countries these arrangements were difficult to maintain, and have broken
down or been abandoned.

In less successful advanced industrialized economies such as Britain there
is a more serious problem for this version of fairness over pay. Where the
number of better-paid, secure jobs is falling, and trade unions are losing
members, there is a rise not only in unemployment, but also in short-term,
part-time and casual employment, and in self-employment. If the trade
union movement cannot represent more than half of the potential workforce,
and if its definitions of fairness rely on excluding the rest from any share of
labour market power, then a dual standard becomes institutionalized. In
these circumstances, it is not surprising if the impoverished, disorganized,
casualized workforce adopts standards of fairness which include practices
(such as doing 'cash jobs', avoiding taxes, working while claiming and so on)
that are precisely the ones most feared and resented by the trade unions.

Part of this problem is a long-term one concerning women's pay, which has historically been well below men's in Britain, while women's membership of trade unions has also been far lower. It is difficult to explain these differentials in terms of the standards of fairness used in the labour movement; women have always been seen as a different kind of worker, often employed under different conditions, doing different jobs.[16] In his study in Kent, Pahl found that most male manual work was defined as skilled, and paid accordingly, even though it required an average period of two weeks' training, whereas most female jobs were defined as unskilled, even though the average training period was six months.[17]

In the Eastern European countries, the structure of incomes is strongly linked with the idea of a fair reward for labour, and is supposed to be based on a 'scientific' theory of production, derived from Marx's analysis. In practice, manual workers, and especially those in heavy industries, get relatively higher wages, particularly in relation to many professions (such as judges and teachers, who are mainly women, and work part-time). This can be seen either as an example of political desert (the proletariat is the socialist vanguard) or as providing the incentives to a group who do dirty and arduous jobs. But the general levels of wages in Eastern Europe are low, higher proportions of national income are devoted to capital formation (in state industries) than are absorbed in profits in capitalist countries,[18] and trade unions have no competitive economic role.

The Eastern European structure of pay has the advantage of being a unified one, because the great majority of households get their income from employment, and because the state is committed to providing paid work for all those available to do it. Its differentiations in terms of desert are therefore marginal to a pay structure which is supposed to be adequate for basic needs, and fair as between all citizens. The weakness of the system is its lack of voluntarism, and its reliance on a secondary (unofficial) labour market for people to pursue their individual income goals.

The radical issue raised by both Western and Eastern systems is whether it is possible, within the same structure of earnings from labour, to provide households with the income they need for living and with a return for the effort and skill they expend in employment. The ideas of a 'fair day's pay' and a 'fair rate for the job' suggest that people's wages are sufficient simultaneously to meet their needs and to reward them for their labour. Hence people are supposed to deserve the pay they get, and to deserve the differential advantage (or disadvantage) it reflects in relation to others' pay. It seems unlikely that employment under modern conditions can bear this weight of moral expectation. It is too much to expect our pay packets or salary cheques to be able to provide both for our common needs for security and our individual needs for recognition of merit and skill.

In small-scale informal transactions, rewards for effort or merit are usually treated quite separately from the routine everyday benefits of co-operation, and are often attached to special individual or group projects. It is therefore surprising that ideas of desert, however shadowy, should play such a large part in the sharing of resources through the formal economy. In the final part of this book, I shall discuss possible ways of separating income needs from rewards to effort, and their implications in terms of fairness and desert.

Needs and Abilities

So far I have argued that neither rights nor deserts play the primary role in small-scale negotiations about comparative welfare. Yet fairness is, I would argue, the most important value in any set of relationships of any duration. People will put up with considerable constraints or even privations in a social role, or as part of a group, provided that they are convinced that the burdens and benefits of membership of that social system or group are fairly shared out; conversely, they will leave it or rebel rather quickly once they are convinced that they are not being treated fairly – that others are benefiting at their expense.

What, then, is the basis of this notion of fairness in small-scale relationships? I would argue that it is that members contribute according to their abilities and benefit according to their needs. In the family, most of the activities of the able-bodied adults centre around providing for the common needs of the group, and for the special needs of those who are dependent in one way or another – children, disabled members, elderly members and so on. Any time, energy and space that is left over is divided up so as to allow their needs to be met in such a way as not to disrupt the group, and especially those with dependency needs.[19]

I might be accused of painting far too rosy and altruistic a picture of family life here. After all, statistics on child neglect and abuse, on granny-bashing and on the hospitalization of handicapped people all suggest a very different picture, while a divorce rate of one in three current marriages indicates a high rate of breakdown in marital co-operation. But I would argue that none of this invalidates my perspective. What is now regarded as child abuse, in the form of severe beatings, was once almost universal practice, when it was considered not merely not damaging to children but actually beneficial to them in the long run as a form of discipline.[20] Now that this view is discredited, society intervenes when it does occur, because it is considered unfair on children, as well as detrimental to their development. Similarly, rates of divorce and separation were lower when expectations of marriage were much more modest. Now that many partners expect a satisfying sexual relationship, mutual support, compatibility of interests, equality of opportunity and so on, it is not surprising that more marriages break up. Different perceptions of needs give rise to new calculations of what is fair and what is unacceptable.

Two less spectacular examples may help to make my point. The postwar generation of middle-class mothers was quite heavily influenced by a simplified version of John Bowlby's view of the needs of young children for continuous care.[21] Many believed that children under school age would suffer if they experienced prolonged separation from their mother; they carried this into their campaign for better access to children in hospitals, and also into their decisions about when and if to take up paid employment.[22] I am not suggesting that all middle-class mothers who interrupted their working lives by several years during their children's infancy were doing so purely out of altruistic motives; what is clear is that, in the light of further research which has modified Bowlby's views,[23] and the campaigns of the women's movement on access to employment, many women now believe that their young children would benefit from their having a job, and they act accordingly. The result is a shift in the balance of paid and unpaid work done by women with young children (though they are still the group least likely to have a job), in line with a new understanding of children's needs.

Second, research has indicated that men whose wives have paid employment do more in the way of domestic work than those who do not; the difference is fairly marginal, but it exists.[24] Along with the general shift towards slightly increased participation in domestic tasks by husbands,[25] this does indicate a change dictated by perceptions of fairness in terms of abilities and needs. As men's employment has become less physically arduous, and married women have increasingly joined the labour force, the idea that men have done their 'fair share' at work, and can put their feet up by the fire or slope off to the pub after their evening meal, has become discredited.

None of this should be taken as an argument that present relations between partners or between parents and children have achieved fairness by any objective standards – there is massive evidence to the contrary. What it does suggest is that some change does occur as a result of changing perceptions of individual needs and abilities, and that people do appeal to fairness in trying to readjust their roles and relationships. The women's movement can certainly claim some limited success in alerting the consciousness of many women and some men to structural unfairness in domestic roles and employment opportunities, and the beginnings of a movement away from the crasser manifestations of patriarchy. At the same time, both disabled people and those who care for them have become more outspoken about their individual needs, and how these can be balanced in the domestic setting.

When we compare this with wider society, it seems at first sight that there are parallels. The social services exist to try to redistribute welfare on the basis of need, and are financed out of a mixture of income-related contributions and progressive taxation – that is, according to ability to pay. On the face of it, therefore, the social services function as a kind of mechanism for bringing abilities and needs into some sort of equilibrium, by redistributing welfare through collective provision for various needs.

Yet there are very important differences also. First, in the domestic economy, the usual way in which abilities and needs are adjusted is through the direct contribution of paid or unpaid labour. Able-bodied adult members either earn or do unpaid work according to their abilities – ideally, all do both. Children, disabled members and the elderly are not passive recipients of income, goods and services: they have active roles, they interact with the working adults, they co-operate in tasks, they may even provide part of the income (for instance, through part-time work). In the social services, roles are far more distinct. Most workers contribute part of their income towards paying for the social services, but only a smallish proportion are actually employed in providing them. It is therefore in most workers' interests to minimize their contributions towards social services, though those employed in them have an interest in maximizing their share of the national product. As for the recipients of services, most of them are prescribed purely passive roles, and are excluded from economic life, and usually from any part in the services themselves; for example, claimants of social security are forbidden to earn, except to a minimal extent, and patients are encouraged to be inert recipients of health care. The long-term unemployed are an obvious example of a group denied participation in society, most of whom would much prefer an economic role to the state's method of 'meeting their needs' through benefits. What is more, the needs met through the social services are (with few exceptions) those perceived and defined by politicians, professionals and bureaucrats, with little or no consultation with the recipients, either as groups or as individuals. Services tend to be 'delivered' to individuals, rather than shared within an active, participatory local community.[26]

Second, the mechanism by which the relative shares are decided is quite different. The political process is not one of negotiation between groups of workers and groups of welfare beneficiaries: the latter do not come into it at all, and it is only in continental countries with a strong corporatist tradition (like Sweden and Austria) that government, employers and unions sit down together to plan the share of national product that will go to the social services. In Britain, the decision is the result of a wrangle between the Treasury and the 'spending ministries' in the Cabinet; social services are treated as one kind of 'public expenditure' which competes with others such as defence, the environment and employment services for a pre-set proportion of the national cake. The idea of negotiation plays little or no part in this process under governments which appeal to liberal principles; under past social democratic governments, elections pledges and 'social contracts' have often given way to the 'reality' of 'what we can afford'.[27]

Third, it is far from clear that the criteria used for deciding allocations to social services are a balance between needs and abilities according to *fairness*: in practice, these are not the kind of criteria that are used. Because the business of government is, like business itself, dominated by large-scale decisions about limited resources, it is primarily a redistribution that takes place according to economic criteria relating to efficiency, growth and so on. This seems to apply as much to socialist (East European) as to capitalist economies. The needs of recipients of social services are indeed considered, and there are certain political limits (probably much stricter in Britain than in the United States or the USSR) on the extent to which provision can be pruned back.[28] However, it is the state that decides, on the basis of the functioning of the whole economy, which needs are to be recognized and met by its services.

The question of how much this decision depends on criteria of fairness will be discussed more fully in the section on equality in the next chapter. My main conclusion at this point is that evaluative decisions are increasingly excluded, as far as possible, from the discussion of *overall* levels of provision. For instance, the discussion of the roles and responsibilities of individuals and the state in the British Green Paper on the Reform of Social Security was completed by the middle of page 2. Reference to fairness as a concept was confined to discussion of the relative incomes of very poor people – never to comparisons between rich and poor.[29] As in many other official documents, the attempt was made to establish that levels of benefits were 'adequate for needs', without any reference to the social roles of recipients, or to value assumptions behind provision. The whole document could be taken as strong evidence against Richard Titmuss's view that the social services represented a moral sphere of redistribution in society, to be contrasted with the amoral workings of a market economy.[30]

Within liberal theory, there are many who argue that the distribution achieved by the market is already fair (given the fairness of existing property holdings), and hence that any attempt to redistribute through social services is necessarily unfair.[31] One modification of this view is that, in spite of the intrinsic fairness of market distributions, some other value – compassion, charity or benevolence – requires that the state should relieve avoidable suffering, at least to the point of physical survival. I have already dealt with this argument in the previous chapter; there seems little reason to conclude, if one accepts the principles of liberalism, that we *should* feel compassion, and hence that the state *should* act in this way. If it acted purely to preserve public health and decency, it would probably adopt the measures of the Victorian Poor Law, not the modern social services.

In ordinary life, I have argued, we act predominantly from motives of fairness, based on perceptions of ability and need. We also rebel intuitively against the argument that it is *fair* to let people suffer, or even die unaided, and that only some other principle requires us to do something to assist them. Private insurance company ambulances in the United States may drive away from uninsured victims of road accidents, but ordinary people presumably do not, unless they have absorbed all the tenets of American liberalism. I shall return to this stubborn intuitive connection between fairness and need in the section on equality.

Conclusions

Fairness is claimed as the primary value in formal systems for sharing communal welfare, just as it seems to be the primary value of informal systems of sharing personal welfare. All major formal social systems consist of a structure of rights and obligations (individual or group) guaranteed by the central authority of the state; a system of marginal rewards and punishments according to some kind of desert (political or economic); and a system for redistributing welfare according to needs.

However, as we have seen in this chapter, the kind of fairness claimed for the formal processes of sharing does not coincide closely with the understanding of fairness that guides our informal distribution of welfare. Indeed, informal systems often seem to be designed to deal with the unfairness which is a structural feature of formal processes, because the latter were ill-equipped to make use of the give-and-take transactions which are crucial for everyday negotiations of fairness.

But I have also argued that corporate social organizations through enterprises and trade unions, provide some of the features of association (membership, sharing) that are absent from market distributions. It is very important, therefore, that this form of organizational protection seems to be available to fewer people in advanced capitalist societies as a result of recent socioeconomic change. If the boundaries of welfare are shifting so that a smaller proportion of citizens gets the benefits of corporate membership of large organizations, then fairness may demand an equivalent shift in the boundaries between the market and informal sources of welfare, so that more citizens are able to maximize their benefits from the latter sources.

One crucial test of any society-wide system for communal welfare must therefore be how it meshes into informal systems, allowing them to function effectively to achieve fair shares. It should enable flexibility of transfer between formal and informal spheres and compensation in one for difficulties in the other. For these features of welfare distribution, the values discussed in the next chapter are especially important.

Notes

1 See for instance, Garrett Hardin and John Baden, *Managing the Commons*, W. H. Freeman, 1977. Locke, in his *Second Treatise of Government*, argued that common land justifiably became private property for two reasons: first, because cultivation (labour) gave it a far higher yield, and this improvement could be achieved only by enclosure (sections 33–7); second, because the invention of money allowed people fairly to possess more land than they could use the product of, and to exchange their surplus produce for money, which could be hoarded up without injuring anyone (section 50).

2 See for instance John Plamenatz, *Consent, Freedom and Political Obligation* (1938), Oxford University Press, 1968. Plamenatz argued that some form of consent by the governed was an important element of political obligation in democratic systems. 'Under representative democracy those members of the government who make the laws, as well as those who undertake its administrative and judicial functions, can be said to represent the governed, in so far as their rights to make laws depends on consent' (p. 19). But, 'under the very best possible conditions, so far as consent is concerned, it may be true that the rights of the governors depend on the consent of a majority of the governed, but never upon the consent of all persons who can rightly be said to be obliged to obey the law. It follows from this that consent cannot be taken to be the only basis of political obligation' (pp. 23–4). He concluded that a government of this kind was 'more likely to safeguard freedom than is any other sort. For, since laws must be made and since, by their very nature, they must place restrictions upon the freedom of those persons who can be compelled to obey them, it is clear that the best way of diminishing the number of these restrictions is to ensure that they give effect to the wishes of as many of the governed as possible' (pp. 152–3). This view may be contrasted with social contract theories of political obligation, such as Locke's, which held that societies were formed as a result of an actual agreement between a body of people at a certain point of time, by which they agreed to give certain powers to their rulers, so long as their natural rights were respected. But in trying to explain why this contract should be binding on subsequent generations, Locke was forced to use such vague notions as 'tacit consent', as when he argued that by merely living in the territory of a government a man tacitly consented to all its laws, or even that a stranger travelling through a country gave 'his tacit consent, and is as far forth obliged to obedience to the laws of that government' (Locke, *Second Treatise*, section 119).

3 Locke's claim that unequal private property – resulting in the exclusion of a whole class from land tenure – was justified in terms of higher productivity from which all benefited, has already been mentioned (n. 1). Later liberal theorists, such as Adam Smith and John Stuart Mill, were less concerned to argue that the origins of unequal property lay in principles that were fair and agreed by all. Indeed, Smith suggested that they lay in force and violence, and was almost as outspoken as Marx (if less historical and specific) about the connection between unequal holdings and coercive state authority. It was the introduction of 'an inequality of fortune' that 'gave rise to regular government. Till there be no property there can be no government, the very end of which is to secure wealth and defend the rich from the poor' (*Lectures on Justice, Police, Revenue and Arms*, part 1, div. 2, section 2 – see also *The Wealth of Nations*, book V, ch. i, part 6, sections 2–12). Yet Smith's model attempted to show that, from this thoroughly *unfair* basis for society, a fair – even ideal – distribution of welfare could ensue, through the operation of the 'invisible hand' (see chapter 3). Mill too admitted that property was acquired in the first place by 'conquest and violence; and notwithstanding what industry has been doing for many centuries to modify the work of force, the system still retains many and large traces of its origins' (*Principles of Political Economy*, book II, ch. i, section 3); he hoped that in time a classless society, based on co-operation, could emerge from capitalist inequality, so long as population growth could be restrained.

A modern theory which links private property with state authority is Robert Nozick's, in which a monopoly over the use of force to protect individuals from force, fraud and theft arises spontaneously, by morally permissible means, without anyone's right being violated, and without any claims being made to a special right that others do not possess. It occurs through the self-interested and rational actions of individuals, without anyone planning it (*Anarchy, State and Utopia*, Basil Blackwell, 1974, pp. 114–18). But Nozick does not explain how people are supposed to have acquired their original property holdings; in his account they appear already equipped with jobs, salaries, baseball bats, cars and real estate. It would be more difficult to show that the processes of the market and the powers of a radically *laissez-faire* government were equally morally justified if the original distribution of property were not assumed to have been in the precise form of an affluent private housing estate in suburban America.

4 See for instance H. B. Acton, *The Morals of Markets*, Longman, 1971.

5 R. E. Pahl, *Divisions of Labour*, Basil Blackwell, 1984, p. 225.

6 Until quite recently, dockers in Salford used to assemble in a 'pen' from which they were selected for day work by foremen. The scene, reminiscent of an animal auction, but with the dockers themselves bidding to be selected, was one of the last British examples of a labour 'market' in which workers were treated as a mass from which favoured individuals were selected. This was still happening in the early 1960s.

7 See for instance S. Mintz, 'Pratik: Haitian Personal Economic Relations', *Proceedings of the American Ethnographic Association*, spring 1961, pp. 54–63; W. G. Davis, *Social Relations in a Philippine Market: Self Interest and Subjectivity*, University of California Press, 1973 (the practice there is called 'suki'); and L. Trager, 'Customers and Creditors: variations in economic personalism in Nigeria', *Ethnology*, vol. 20, 1981, pp. 133–46 ('onibara').

8 Keith Hart, 'Commoditization and the Standard of Living', in G. Hawthorn (ed.), *The Standard of Living*, Cambridge University Press, 1986.

9 Keith Hart, 'Informal Income Opportunities and Urban Employment in Ghana', *Journal of Modern African Studies*, vol. 11, no. 3, 1973, pp. 61–89.

10 Hart, 'Commoditization and the Standard of Living'.

11 These ways are usefully summarized by Geoff Hodgson in *Capitalism, Value and Exploitation: A Radical Theory*, Martin Robertson, 1982. But he goes on to criticise Marx's labour theory of value. Exploitation consists partly of pre-contractual inequality, as Marx pointed out, but also of the worker's loss of disposable time, risk of injury, lack of control over working conditions and rules of industrial discipline, and his indispensability for the modern production process. But it does not consist of the notion that value is measurable only in terms of abstract labour, as Marx suggested.

12 See for instance, F. Feher, A. Heller and G. Markus, *Dictatorship over Needs*, Basil Blackwell, 1985, pp. 99–100. They argue that this illegal 'secondary economy' is essential for the functioning of centrally planned societies, because it alone brings demand and supply into some sort of equilibrium.

13 Robert Pinker, *The Idea of Welfare*, Heinemann, 1979, argues that 'There would seem to be three major criteria by which material welfare goods and services are allocated in social life. In the economic market the criterion is one of utility, or price; in the social market the criterion is one of need. There is however a third

criterion – that of political desert – which also operates in all societies . . . .
Political criteria may take the form of ideological, religious or ethnic
discrimination' (p. 224).

14 F. A. Hayek, *The Constitution of Liberty*, Routledge & Kegan Paul, 1960, is quite
clear that the market measures social utility, not desert, and that the principle of
desert always requires an authoritative decision to be rewarded. By contrast, the
market rewards what is of value to others automatically but not on merit (p. 96).
David Miller, in *Social Justice*, Clarendon Press, 1976, discusses the idea that
work efforts should be rewarded for their social usefulness in terms of desert. He
argues that in a modern organized society, consisting of a system of interlocking
organizations, individuals' salaries depend on their positions within organizations, and desert is seen in terms of the contribution of these towards an efficient
and prosperous community (pp. 300–8). Organizations are graded according to
their contribution to the general product, and each position is remunerated
according to grade; 'organised society makes service to the community the
dominant motive in work; the justification for rewarding the incumbent of one
position more highly than the incumbent of another is that he makes a greater
contribution to social wellbeing' (p. 309).

15 See for instance J. H. Goldthorpe, 'The End of Convergence: Corporatist and
Dualist Tendencies in Modern Western Societies', in B. Roberts, R. Finnegan
and D. Gallie (eds), *New Approaches to Economic Life: Economic Restructuring,
Unemployment and the Social Division of Labour*, Manchester University Press,
1985, especially pp. 138 and 149.

16 Veronica Beechey and Teresa Perkins, 'Conceptualising Part-Time Work', in
Roberts et al., *New Approaches to Economic Life*, especially p. 255.

17 Pahl, *Divisions of Labour*, p. 174.

18 D. M. Nuti, 'The Contradictions of Socialist Economies: A Marxist Interpretation', in R. Miliband and J. Saville (eds), *The Socialist Register, 1979*, Merlin,
1979, pp. 260 ff.

19 G. S. Becker, 'A Theory of the Allocation of Time', *Economic Journal*, vol. 75, no.
299, pp. 493–517.

20 See for instance M. Hewitt and I. Pinchbeck, *Children in English Society*, vol. 1,
Routledge and Kegan Paul, 1969.

21 J. Bowlby, *Child Care and the Growth of Love*, Penguin, 1963; this summarized his
earlier work, such as 'Some Pathological Process Set in Train by Early
Mother–Child Separation', *Journal of Mental Science*, vol. 99, pp. 265–72.

22 For instance, the films of James Robertson, which inspired the National
Association for the Welfare of Children in Hospital.

23 For example, Michael Rutter, *Maternal Deprivation Reassessed*, Penguin, 1972.

24 Jean Martin and Ceridwen Roberts, *Women and Employment: A Life-time
Perspective*, Department of Employment/Office of Population Censuses and
Surveys, 1984, table 8.9, p. 102.

25 Negotiations between partners may be seen as setting up a kind of equilibrium,
not on the model of supply and demand in classical economics, but more on the
alternative model provided by Keith Roberts in his book *A Design for a Market
Economy* (as yet unpublished). He argues that, instead of the traditional graphical
analysis, we should substitute a picture of 'a ball oscillating with some degree of
friction in a parabolic well: the diminishing oscillations illustrate the way in which

successive offers by buyer and seller eventually lead to a market price'. But in a system with different degrees of freedom in various markets, 'The original parabolic well is now replaced by a surface with many dimensions, although one can still picture the ball rolling on this surface and becoming trapped when it finds itself in a deep hole from which the loss of energy due to friction does not allow it to escape. It will indeed be a local optimum, even though in general one would expect to find many such holes and no analysis is ever likely to be able to show that the ball will automatically find the global optimum, i.e. the deepest hole which is the true optimum economic state.' He later points out the whole surface may be constantly changing, rising and falling, due to international changes in supply and demand, and hence the ball may suddenly be dislodged and roll some distance again before coming to rest. This seems quite a realistic model for similar negotiations about welfare within families.

26 At the time of writing a Private Member's Bill with all party support is being debated by the British House of Commons, requiring that disabled people should be consulted, by law, by those planning services for them, on both an individual and a group basis.

27 For examples of this see Frank Field, *Inequality in Britain: Freedom, Welfare and the State*, Fontana, 1981, on the non-implementation of the Beveridge Report; and Bill Jordan, *Automatic Poverty*, Routledge & Kegan Paul, 1981, on the Callaghan government's non-implementation of the Social Contract of 1974.

28 G. V. Rimlinger, *Welfare Policy and Industrialisation in Europe, America and Russia*, John Wiley, 1971. In the USSR between 1926 and 1955 the value of pensions fell from 36 per cent to 23 per cent of the average wage (p. 280). Unemployment benefit was effectively abolished during this period, during which the collectivization of agriculture and rapid industrialization were enforced and benefits were used to reinforce the creation of an urbanized proletariat (ch. 7).

29 DHSS, *The Reform of Social Security*, Cmnd 9517, HMSO, 1985, vol. 1.

30 Richard Titmuss, *Commitment to Welfare*, Allen & Unwin, 1968.

31 F. A. Hayek, *The Constitution of Liberty*, Routledge & Kegan Paul, 1960, and Acton, *The Morals of Markets*, are two examples among many.

5

Freedom and Equality

Freedom and equality are two values which are often treated as conflicting. Liberalism is seen as giving priority to individual freedom over equality between citizens; socialism is seen as promoting equality at the expense of freedom. But this was not always the case. Several of the founders of modern political thought regarded the values as closely associated. Locke insisted that everyone had a natural right to both freedom and equality;[1] so did Rousseau;[2] and so (in a slightly different context) did Jefferson.[3]

Locke and Rousseau reconciled these two values by putting mankind in an imaginary 'state of nature', with abundant resources – enough for all to live comfortably without rationing or competition, and hence without private property.[4] Jefferson's Virginia was also a place of abundance, where land was so available that most could acquire an adequate holding.[5] The two values appear to come into conflict as soon as people have to share out productive resources, differentiate productive roles, and get different rewards from the productive system. Marx's whole analysis started from an attack on the fundamental inequality between the classes engaged in capitalist production.

Since Marx, most discussion of the relationship between freedom and equality has concentrated on issues of property and production. But this ignores all the other spheres of social life; a proper analysis of how these two values interact should take account of these also. After all, the imaginary 'state of nature' was an undifferentiated world of work, leisure, domesticity and culture, blissfully lived out in woodland glades or rustic shelters. As roles and resources for production have been divided and subdivided, so too have their political, domestic and recreational counterparts.

One recent theory has addressed these issues – Michael Walzer's *Spheres of Justice: A Defence of Pluralism and Equality*.[6] Walzer argues that these different spheres of social life should be kept separate, each with its own system for sharing welfare according to its own values and methods. It is important, for instance, that money – the medium of exchange in the economic sphere – should not be able to buy political power or domestic happiness. The rules of fairness should aim at preventing advantages from one sphere invading others, and upsetting the pluralistic structure of welfare distribution. A monopoly of the dominant social good in one sphere is not necessarily an evil; the dominance of social goods from one sphere over other spheres is always unfair.

This leads Walzer to argue that we should seek not 'simple' but rather 'complex' equality. Socialism has tried to attack the injustices that stem from one group monopolizing the economic sphere through money by making political power the dominant social good; this has meant (in Eastern Europe) the monopoly of political power by a small group, and its dominance over all spheres, which is equally unjust. Instead, he suggests, we should make sure that each sphere is autonomous, and that social goods in each are shared according to the values and principles appropriate to it. Thus, inequality in one sphere will not imply inequality in another. 'By and large, the most accomplished politicians, entrepreneurs, scientists, soldiers and lovers will be different people; and so long as the goods they possess don't bring other goods in train, we have no reason to fear their accomplishments.'[7]

What Walzer fails to see is that, even if his separation of spheres could be accomplished, which is doubtful, there is still another problem. The way that social goods are shared out in one sphere (the roles, values and principles required) must not tie people to that sphere and exclude them from others – or if this occurs it must be with the full consent of the people concerned. For instance, the social goods distributed in the religious sphere (reverence, faith, communality, a good conscience, salvation) are in some religious groups shared only among those who renounce any share of worldly social goods (property, finery, money, modern amusements, sex). In other groups – such as the Hutterites or the Amish communities – they are shared only among those who follow strict seventeenth-century rules, and stay outside modern society. Most people nowadays would regard this only as a fair way of dealing with people who actively choose membership of such groups or communities.

Of far greater importance is the fact that people who gain considerably from their participation in the major formal spheres of advanced societies (the economic and political) are left entirely free to participate as fully and advantageously as they please in almost every other sphere. But those with important roles in the domestic sphere (women) are often barred by their responsibilities from virtually any other sphere; and many in the social welfare sphere, who qualify for benefits by virtue of need, are also severely restricted in their participation in other social activities, and especially the economic sphere.

So I shall argue in this chapter that the intermeshing between formal and informal spheres of welfare is itself as important as the values and principles which govern any particular sphere. While Walzer is quite right to focus on the need to see the sharing of welfare, and patterns of equality and inequality, in terms of different spheres with different principles and processes, he is wrong to neglect people's choice in how they move from one sphere to another, either from hour to hour or over their whole lifetime. And this is largely an issue of freedom as we shall see.

Freedom

Freedom can be seen as of paramount importance for individual welfare, since without certain kinds of freedom the individual is unable to pursue his or her welfare at all. But it occupies a rather different role from that of fairness in comparative welfare and in discussions about redistribution. Freedom is one of the elements in individual welfare that we might wish to redistribute, but it is not itself a criterion for comparative welfare, whereas fairness is a criterion of comparative welfare, but is not something that can be redistributed. We can make the distribution of welfare fairer between two people by making one of them freer and the other less free; we cannot make the distribution freer by making one of them fairer and the other less fair.

Individual Freedom

In any notion of individual welfare which presumes that the individual is the best judge of his or her own welfare, freedom is an essential element. The individual must be free to choose his or her projects, and to pursue them in his or her own way. Without this kind of freedom, the subjective notion of welfare makes no sense.

Recently, individual freedom has been held to have two elements, negative and positive freedom.[8] Negative freedom is freedom from interference, whether by authority (in the forms of rules, regulations or arbitrary interventions and punishments) or by public opinion (intrusive prohibitions based on custom and morality).[9] If people are the best judges of their own welfare, then they must be allowed to choose, pursue and develop their own projects, subject only to the limitation that they should not, in doing this, limit the projects of others. There is plenty of scope for dispute about how this rule can fairly be applied in practice, since projects can include such things as the vast accumulation of private resources (limiting others' scope for accumulation, or sometimes even their scope for survival), dangerous activities (such as jumping off cliffs or collecting ferocious animals, which limit others' safe access to the environment) and activities which cause pollution or other forms of public nuisance.[10] Since Locke, there has been dispute between libertarians who believe that restrictions on individual freedoms should be kept to a minimum (though others adversely affected should be able to claim compensation) and authoritarians who have argued that the state should place strict limits on personal freedom.

The biggest single issue in this debate concerns the accumulation of private property. For libertarians, this must be permissible if a subjective definition of welfare is to be sustained. The principle of compensation should allow those who lose traditional rights to have their losses offset. But does this imply that all who lose their way of life – for example, hunter–gatherers or even peasants – should be compensated by once-for-all payments, or by state pensions in perpetuity? Authoritarians argue that only by restricting private property to resources for personal use can the state prevent some individuals from infringing on the liberties of others.

Positive freedom implies that each individual should be able to develop him or herself to their fullest potential. It implies that people should have the opportunity, the resources and the information to frame the personal projects which will most 'stretch' and fulfil them – that they should not be constrained by poverty, ignorance or obligations to others. This raises important issues about the distribution of opportunities, resources and roles; it certainly has redistributive implications. Because positive freedom implies that no one should be denied the conditions for self-fulfilment, it has often been seen as conflicting with negative freedom, which implies that individuals should be left to their own devices, and that the effects of natural advantages, luck, the market and so on should be allowed to stand, without interference from the state.[11]

In everyday life, individual freedom is clearly very important as a fundamental precondition of welfare. For anyone to claim that they lacked freedom – that they could not choose or pursue personal projects – would be in effect for them to argue that their welfare was being sacrificed to whatever or whoever was denying them this freedom. Yet, as we shall see in the next section, this is paradoxical, since all roles and relationships entail a sacrifice of freedom.

Freedom, Roles and Relationships

If all personal projects require freedom of choice and freedom of pursuit, all personal commitments involve some sacrifice of individual freedom. Any relationship, or any role in a group or organization, requires the individual to commit him or herself to certain obligations in return for certain benefits. Even the most *ad hoc* and casual friendship means giving up time, listening and being prepared to put oneself out to some extent on another's behalf. Serious relationships and central roles in organizations involve considerable sacrifices of personal time, energy and resources – in other words, giving up much of what one might otherwise devote to individual projects. The gain from commitments, of course, is shared in group projects, which may be more satisfying and fulfilling; there may therefore be a gain in positive freedom through co-operation, interaction and self-development. But there is always a loss in negative freedom, since every role and relationship exposes the individual to demands, duties, criticisms and constraints which, if imposed rather than chosen, would be experienced as interference with freedom.

Why then do people enter into commitments, especially if freedom is an essential precondition of the subjective view of welfare? The answer is obviously that the benefits in terms of personal welfare from roles and relationships is reckoned to be greater than the losses in welfare sustained through their constraints. People are prepared to trade freedom for support, companionship, love, common interests, a shared cause, the chance to help and so on. But if at a later date they find that the sacrifices they are making within their commitments are greater than the benefits derived therefrom, they will either try to renegotiate the terms of their roles and relationships, or simply withdraw from them.

I am suggesting not that freedom becomes unimportant within commitments, but that participants *perceive* commitments as compatible with personal freedom under certain conditions. These are (usually) that the commitments are chosen, and that the sacrifices of freedom made by all parties are fairly distributed in terms of the welfare derived from roles and relationships. This does not necessarily mean that the sacrifices have to be exactly equal, since some people may be willing to sacrifice more for the sake of more benefits. In every sports club there is someone who marks out the pitch, does the teas and serves behind the bar, often with minimal help from other members; yet such people seldom seem to leave in a huff. The rest usually assume that this individual derives some special personal benefit from being the heart and soul, as well as the workhorse, of the club; they usually treat him or her with respect and consideration, but not with the craven indulgence that their sacrifices would seem to demand.

The notion of an equilibrium between sacrifices and benefits in relationships implies that, in comparisons about welfare, people are able to include a calculation of their opportunities to pursue individual projects, as well as to share in joint projects with others. Obviously, some people do not attach great importance to individual projects, preferring joint ventures and shared commitments. In this case, they will find satisfactions in roles and relationships which allow little personal freedom, and may involve considerable obligations to others, which appear from the outside to be poorly rewarded.

We can perhaps best understand the relationships between freedom and welfare in everyday life by considering the roles of wife and mother. In the first half of this century (and perhaps until the mid-1960s) it was generally assumed, and probably widely believed, that married women were 'naturally' equipped to attend to domestic and care-giving tasks, and that the roles of wife and mother were intrinsically satisfying. Women were commonly supposed to *choose* to be housewives *as a project*; they were assumed to want to keep house and bring up children, just as men were to choose to be 'breadwinners'. If a role could be perceived as being in itself a project – and countless women's magazines portrayed young women romantically yearning for marriage to firm-lipped, action-man, pipe-smoking types who were scarcely likely to play much part in cooking, cleaning or child care – their marital relationships could not be counted as involving sacrifices of freedom. The woman who was able to marry the man of her choice was seen as having (more or less by definition) embraced a role which gave her more benefits than she lost, no matter how onerous her domestic life. By contrast, the woman who never married, and stayed at home to look after a disabled mother, was seen as having sacrificed all her possible projects, and having surrendered the freedom that was fundamental to her welfare.

The women's movement allowed a completely different light to be cast on these transactions. It drew attention to the grotesque disparity of opportunities and obligations between men and women in the conventional middle-class marriage. Men's obligations as providers of incomes gave them many fringe benefits, especially in terms of access to other spheres, where they could derive status, stimulation, company, escape and independence; women's role in the home condemned them to one sphere, in which their 'reward' was drudgery, boredom, isolation, dependence and often also poverty. Many women felt guilty about their resentment of their roles, and told themselves that they should willingly sacrifice their freedom for the welfare of husband and children. But the whole domestic system was in fact a travesty of fairness, since men sacrificed little of their freedom and few individual projects for the benefits of getting an unpaid housekeeper and care-giver, while women sacrificed all of theirs (including their potential careers) for the sake of dubious financial support.

Thus, the issue of freedom came to be reasserted as one of crucial importance in marital relationships. When the role of wife was seen as a project in itself, freedom for married women was apparently not an issue; once the domestic role became seen largely in terms of its sacrifices of individual projects in their spheres and its unpaid obligations, freedom was very much at stake. Hence negotiations between partners about comparative welfare in marital relationships can no longer assume that women 'choose' domesticity as a 'career', and must instead count lost opportunities in any balance of welfare advantages which aims at fairness between the partners.

Freedom in Wider Society

I have argued that freedom, unlike fairness, is not an end in itself in small-scale relationships. While personal welfare is impossible to conceive of without the freedom to choose projects and commitments, welfare in roles and relationships involves sacrifices of freedom for the sake of other benefits. Hence in any small social system (family, group, association) it is fairness that is the primary criterion for distributing welfare; freedom is one of the individual attributes that is negotiated (or traded), along with needs and abilities. The aim (consciously or unconsciously) is to reach a fair distribution of welfare, having regard to individual and shared projects, to sacrifices and benefits, needs and abilities – not to give any specific amounts of freedom to any individual, and certainly not to maximize the freedom of all. Even organizations that are focused primarily on freedom (like the women's movement) usually argue not for freedom for its own sake, but for a fair distribution of freedom.

By contrast, discussions of freedom in wider society are often conducted as if freedom is an end in itself. Liberals are especially inclined to argue that freedom is the primary value in social organization, and that both political and economic freedom (which are seen as very closely linked) are crucial for a healthy society.[12] There may be some sound reasons for this line of argument. In the first place, as we have seen, people do not choose to join societies in the way they choose to form relationships or join associations: they are born into them. They have very little influence on the rules and regulations that govern political and economic life, and which therefore profoundly influence all their other relationships. So it is perhaps desirable that individual freedom should be protected as much as possible, where escape is far more limited than in personal relationships. Second, the potential for political and economic coercion is enormous. Modern liberal capitalist societies are in many ways reactions against early tyrannies and dictatorships and more recent totalitarian systems; individual freedom has had to be won and defended against arbitrary despotism and the authoritarian tendencies of state power. Equally, market economic relations have been hard-won, through the gradual abolition of slavery, serfdom, feudal hierarchies and duties, protectionism and so on; economic coercion through both traditional status-based systems and modern totalitarian ones have been the dominant tendency to economic life. Hence liberals can claim that individual freedoms (in terms of civil and political rights against coercion and interference) are the bulwarks of our whole social order.

On the other hand, liberalism has always been much stronger on negative than on positive freedom. It has always been concerned to define what Mill described as a circle around the individual, into which neither authority nor public opinion should step to constrain or interfere.[13] Individual rights protect people from arbitrary power and malicious prejudice; they also allow great inequalities of property accumulation, and hence of resources for personal projects. If we return to our original distinction between freedom as a right to pursue projects, freedom as an opportunity to pursue them and freedom as having the means to do so, then clearly liberalism defends the first but is far more limited in its ability to provide the second and third. The problem about drawing a circle around the individual, with his or her largely arbitrary natural endowment of attributes and talents and largely historical inheritance of property, is that, in leaving such individuals free to develop theirs as best they may, it offers little opportunity to the less well endowed and poorer, who often lack the physical resources as well as the talents to pursue their projects.

Liberalism is concerned to claim that all have equal freedom in its characteristic society (as regards civil and political rights, freedom of contract and so on), but its claims are weakest in relation to people who are forced to depend on the state for income support. This is hardly surprising, since pure liberalism cannot really justify public spending to support them anyway. But even in its modified, social democratic forms, the benefits payable to claimants (even under social insurance) are conditional upon exclusion from the labour market and from full-time education – the two most characteristic public arenas for the pursuit of personal projects, for improving accomplishments and accumulating resources.[14] This radical differential in freedom between claimants and others is especially striking, since no one is allowed to *choose* to be unemployed or sick in a liberal society, so that loss of freedom accompanies misfortune, adding insult to injury.

Socialists would add to this the fundamental differential in freedom between capitalists and workers, since the latter are physically tied to their tasks for the duration of the working day, whereas the former can manage, supervise, sell their products or even play golf; they are also free to pursue other projects, including other businesses, while the work is being done. Ownership of productive resources gives them power over workers, above all to hire and fire them at will.

Socialism therefore emphasizes positive freedom, and especially that achieved through group rights, at the expense of negative freedom based on individual rights. It stresses that workers should be free, through their employment, to develop themselves and their skills, and that society as a whole should develop the resources to meet all its needs. On the side of negative freedom, traditionally oppressed groups should be free from exploitation; this can come about only if individual accumulations of property, and especially of productive resources, are strictly limited.

The sense in which individuals can be said to be free under traditional, authoritarian socialism is however obscure. The limitation on individual rights spreads out from property to much of personal life, so that ultimately individuals' talents and attributes are not their own to develop, but those of the group, or society (ultimately of the state). While stopping short of the direction of labour, the state strictly constrains personal projects in the Eastern European countries, so that certain forms of intellectual, cultural and artistic endeavours are proscribed as decadent or frivolous, and dissidence is punishable by exile or even forced labour. If we accept a personal, subjective view of welfare, this lack of individual freedom is a very serious shortcoming in Eastern European socialism, at least as serious as the very unequal distribution of freedoms in such societies as the United States.[15]

Socialism in its traditional form is more like everyday relationships in refusing to treat freedom as an end in itself, but instead insisting that fairness demands sacrifices of freedom. However, it is unlike everyday relationships in that these sacrifices are not chosen but imposed, and it is far from clear that those who get the greatest benefits from a socialist order are those that make the greatest sacrifices of freedom. Indeed, everyone makes considerable sacrifices, but perhaps most of all the intellectuals, artists and innovators, who often are either marginalized or even punished, and are seldom rewarded by the political leadership. Hence they form the most discontented group in Eastern European countries, though even workers in countries like Poland, with strong traditions of individual freedom (mainly religious in origin), strongly protest against their lack of choice in issues of association, objectives and personal commitments.

Hence the problem of equalizing freedom in society is one of the most unresolved under both types of social order. Under liberal regimes – even those which have developed welfare states – growing numbers of people dependent on state income maintenance clearly represent an exception and a reproach to the idea of equal freedom for all, while at the domestic level women are increasingly rejecting their traditional roles, but find difficulty in achieving equal status, and hence equal freedom, in wider society. Under authoritarian socialism, freedom is rather equally lacking for all, since all have prescribed and imposed regulated roles, state-guaranteed provision for needs and severe constraints on individual projects; the enterprising are especially sufferers under this regime.

Equality

I have argued that in ordinary life there is a strong link between equality and fairness. If fairness is the golden rule of small-scale relationships and the division of roles in voluntary associations, then equality is in some sense the criterion for fairness; and equality in turn implies that each person's membership gives him or her a balance of benefits and sacrifices of individual projects that works out about equally.

This should not be taken to imply that equality requires that everyone should be treated the same. On the contrary, I have argued that fairness involves a balance between needs and abilities, with occasional exceptions for extraordinary desert, and a defence of the individual rights agreed under the original terms of membership. This means that everyone is treated differently, but the eventual outcome in terms of benefits and sacrifices is about the same, taking full account of individual needs and abilities (especially the needs of dependent and handicapped members of the group).

The way in which this is achieved in small groups is quite complex and sophisticated, though seldom conscious and calculated. In families, for instance, fairness is quite closely monitored, with the understanding that everyone should be treated equally within this overall rubric. To give a very simple example, in my own large and rather impoverished family of origin, there was a somewhat obsessive observation of fairness at mealtimes. First of all, it was considered important by some members that they drink out of a particular mug; my youngest sister insisted on the pinky mug, and this was generally recognized as a need rather than a whim – only in conditions of sustained beastliness to her was she denied it. Second, there was a ritual of 'fair shares' over quantities of food. This generally took the form of exactly equal first helpings for all, followed by negotiations over whatever remained. If the meal was a very popular one, the same precise equality applied to second helpings; if not, the porcine propensities of myself and my brother were indulged, though between him and me there was an important attention to equality in excess. Finally, there were rituals around parts of certain dishes – the skin on rice pudding, the icing on cake and the top part of jars of honey and marmite (mysteriously referred to as 'the wax') – which were highly favoured by some but actually disliked by others; these in turn had to be divided up equally between those partial to them. Just occasionally, issues of desert (merit rather than pudding) entered into the partition, but generally speaking need was the predominant criterion, along with preference. I regret to say that probably the only concession to my mother's meritorious claims as the cook was a tacit agreement not to quibble and squabble about our shares when she was having a bad day.

I argued in the second chapter that informal, personal systems of co-operation such as families had the advantage of combining the routine, predictable exchange of services according to regular patterns (giving security) with flexible, adjustable responses that could be rapidly adapted to changes in individuals' circumstances (mood, health, luck, stress), and which thus allowed *ad hoc* changes to occur very quickly, sometimes without explicit re-negotiation. This means that the benefits of co-operation include a number of fairly intangible short-term gains from mutual adjustments, so that roles which are apparently rather fixed and unchanging (like father, mother and child) can actually be quickly and subtly altered to take account of other demands on the emotional and physical energies of members, temporary misfortunes and so on. Hence, although fundamental reviews of the benefits and burdens of membership are rare and difficult, frequent shifts in how roles are performed and who takes responsibility for what can achieve a great deal of flexibility, and there is always the possibility of a fundamental re-negotiation of roles in a serious crisis.

In wider society, and in formal systems of co-operation, there is less scope for rapid adjustments and re-negotiations, so more weight falls on the basic terms of membership of associations, and on the general principles according to which welfare is shared. Since relationships are more likely to be contractual, and roles fixed, it is these that determine how rights and responsibilities are divided, and resources distributed.

It is an obvious requirement of fairness in any system of co-operation that all members should participate on terms which are in some sense equal; but it is an equally obvious feature of humanity that people's abilities and needs are manifestly different, so to divide up roles and resources in ways that gave exactly the same to each would be absurd. Hence, any serious theory of fairness has to show how the terms of membership (of a group or a society) provide a basic equality of rights and duties, while at the same time allowing inequalities (for example of income or authority) which correspond with some relevant need or contribution of the individuals or groups concerned.

One very important issue is whether there can be a single principle or set of principles according to which both these questions (basic equality and permissible inequality) can be decided, so that we can tell by applying them whether a complex system of relationships is fair or unfair. Some modern authors, particularly Rawls and his followers, have argued that there are two linked principles that can do both these things: the principle of 'equal liberty' and the 'difference principle' (that inequalities are fair so long as they benefit everyone, and especially the least advantaged members of society).[16]

The main difficulty about this approach is that, although the two principles are linked, they are not applied to quite the same issues. Equal liberty is a principle that applies chiefly to the basic terms of membership, the way in which roles are allocated, the authority structure, rights and duties; the difference principle applies mainly to the distribution of resources, to who gets what. Although Rawls considers both capitalist and socialist systems, and argues that both could be made fair in his terms,[17] he is basically a liberal democrat at heart. Hence he applies the principle of equal liberty to institutions which determine political and civil rights, and to issues of equality of opportunity (ensuring that advantageous, prestigious or powerful roles are allocated only by reference to *relevant* abilities and attributes). He treats class relations, productive relations and distributive shares as being settled through the difference principle within any given system – that issues of fair inequality can be settled by determining whether or not they benefit the least advantaged group. So, for instance, whether or not a capitalist is allowed to grow richer depends on the effects this will have on an unskilled worker's income.[18]

The problem here is that the very existence of roles such as capitalist and worker are part of what is in dispute (for socialists at least) when issues of equal liberty are considered. Socialists would argue that capitalists and workers do not enjoy equal freedoms, and do not participate in productive co-operation on terms that are fair according to Rawls's first principle. Similarly, feminists would argue that traditional marital relationships do not embody equal freedom for both partners. In both these examples, those who confront the roles of the system with a radical challenge in terms of equal liberty would not allow that adjustments (in wages for workers,[19] or in 'housewives' allowances' for married women) would in principle be capable of correcting an unfair inequality in these relationships. Rawls's theory would allow a capitalist or patriarchal system of relations to be 'reformed', in the sense of readjusted, and it would also allow a socialist or feminist one to be similarly adapted; but it would not provide the criteria by which we could decide whether to move from one whole system of relations to another.[20]

One reason for this is that the basic equality in membership that concerns Rawls makes no allowance for the meeting of needs – he sees this purely as a matter of distribution,[21] and hence to be determined by reference to the difference principle. This is because he (in common with most other writers) sees needs as being met primarily by systems for productive co-operation (whether employment or family). Hence he sees the roles that people take in these systems as being prior to the meeting of their needs – welfare must be produced before it can be shared out.

But individuals have certain basic needs that arise irrespective of their roles in production or the domestic system, needs which might therefore form part of the substance of equality that makes up the terms of membership of society as a whole. We all need food, shelter, warmth, light and clothes for physical survival. We also need instruction and information to understand the world. We are all vulnerable to illness and injury and during infancy, and so need special attention when we are very young, sick or wounded; and we are all mortal, and can expect to be frail as we approach death. These are common, shared needs, which are part of the human condition.

Hence it might be part of what it means to be a member of a society (a citizen) not only that one has certain political and civil rights to equal freedom (equality before the law, freedom of association, freedom of speech and belief, and same voting rights as others), but also that these basic needs are guaranteed to be met in some way or other. So the terms of membership would include equal provision for basic (common) needs, though not for individual wants and preferences. This is what socialism attempts to do, and it seems intuitively to be an important part of what most of us mean by fairness. For instance, in families we would not expect to find that the security and protection enjoyed by some children (regular meals, a bed to sleep in) was withheld from one or more others. Some of the most shocking cases of abuse by parents of children or even handicapped adults concern their being systematically refused food, or made to sleep in dog kennels, chicken houses or outside sheds, while the rest of the family was warm and comfortable in bed.[22] This kind of unfairness over basic needs seems to be the denial of what family life is supposed to guarantee – an equal share, at least of the essentials.

The difficulty that Eastern European socialism illustrates is that these citizenship guarantees over needs cannot be reconciled with equal freedom if the *whole* system of productive co-operation is then geared to meeting such needs. This is because a system which tries to guarantee all needs is constructed only in exchange for compulsory co-operation, and there is little or no official scope for individual welfare projects, or individual civil or political rights.

But if we can distinguish between common basic needs and those that are specific to individual projects and commitments, it may then be possible to provide guarantees only for those essential needs which should be equally met for all, irrespective of their roles in productive co-operation, and to leave those which are matters for individual choice to be provided through various forms of voluntary association – including employment and the household. Hence, equality would be ensured by one form of provision in a single sphere, which then would allow individuals to participate in other spheres, distributing other social goods according to other principles. This would permit a reconciliation of freedom and equality which included some elements of the liberal view of welfare along with others from the socialist view, as follows.

1 As in the socialist view of welfare, it recognizes that each individual's welfare depends on the satisfaction of basic needs which should be met through a system of social co-operation and solidarity overseen by the state. This includes not only law and order and defence, but also education, health care and enough income to meet basic needs. This is part of the state's responsibility for protecting individuals from harm and exploitation. By giving all citizens unconditional security over basic needs, it allows their participation as equals in other spheres, where this principle of equal distribution of benefits does not necessarily apply, such as the commercial sphere.

2 As in the liberal view of welfare, it recognizes that above this basic level of needs each individual should be free to pursue his or her own projects and commitments, and to acquire the resources he or she needs to achieve these.

3 Individuals would be able to participate in many different forms of social co-operation, distributing a variety of social goods according to different principles, on the basis of voluntary association. Because each individual has a state guarantee of provision for basic needs, he or she does not depend on any one form of co-operation to meet essential requirements. Hence participation can be truly voluntary, and the fundamental terms of social co-operation can be negotiated from a basis of equal freedom – including those of employment and household roles.

4 It would be acknowledged that some individuals (for instance those with handicaps) need more resources to bring their living standards up to the same level as those without special needs.

Of Rawls's two principles, the first (equal freedom) seems much more convincing than the second (the difference principle). The idea that inequalities that give rise to welfare gains for all are justified has attractions for liberals – it formed the basis of Locke's 'productivity principle', and his justification of unequal holdings of exclusive private property. But it is not really the way that fairness is treated, especially in small-scale, informal systems of co-operation.

Obviously, the goal of co-operation is to maximize the total amount of welfare to be shared out. But the principles of fairness according to which sharing takes place concern rights, deserts and needs, as was shown in the last chapter. They are derived either from the terms of membership, or from the relative efforts, contributions or needs of members. Any or all of these can justify unequal shares in the final partition of welfare goods. But this is a different issue from maximization of production.

For instance, in the example of Rita and Beryl Johnson given in chapter 2, it was the mother who went into full-time employment and the daughter who stayed at home to run the house and look after her brother, because Beryl had higher earning power than Rita at that stage of their lives. This justified a differentiation of their *roles* in terms of maximizing the welfare of the household; but it did not justify an unequal distribution of the shares of welfare between them. Beryl did not claim that she should have more pocket money, or more leisure time, because she was the one in employment. Similarly, if one of a couple was working at home and another outside it, the home-based worker might be allocated a room in which to work and the employed person might not get a room to him or herself – but this would be a decision from efficiency, which would be part of the original terms of co-operation, and would not influence the basis on which their joint income was shared out.

The advantage of an approach to fairness which aims to give equality as the starting point of co-operation, rather than using redistribution as the means of equalizing the outcome, is that it leaves people far freer to organize their own co-operative associations, and to adjust the benefits according to their subjective views of their personal welfare. Clearly, this will mean that the shares they get are *not* equal, by any external, objective standards. They will be differentiated, and they may appear unfair to an outsider. But if people start as equals, particularly if their basic needs are guaranteed, then they always have the security to withdraw from any co-operative association (including employment), without losing the means of autonomy and subsistence. I argued in chapter 2 that people *seek* fairness, which is part of every co-operative association, and that fairness is the underlying value of society. If this is so, social institutions which guarantee equal autonomy should as much as possible allow people to co-operate on their own terms, and to seek fairness in their own way. Since, as I showed in chapter 2, the subjective view of welfare necessarily entails both that each individual seeks his or her welfare according to chosen projects and that each co-operates in a manner that involves standards of fairness, this seems a much more satisfactory approach than using services to redistribute welfare according to pseudo-objective criteria.

Conclusions

Freedom and equality are both important elements in fairness. To be fair, the terms of membership of any association, including a society, must give equal freedom and equal responsibility. But the best way to achieve this may not be to apply the same principles to all the spheres of social co-operation and to require equalization of welfare in each, or a demonstration that all benefit from particular inequalities. Instead, it may lie in defining the basic needs of individuals, and using the political sphere to provide for these needs. This in turn may allow the other spheres to share their characteristic social goods fairly. For instance, if women do not depend on men for food and shelter, they become free to enter into marital partnerships on terms which allow the benefits and burdens of co-operation to be more fairly shared. If workers do not depend on wages for subsistence, they can enter employment contracts from a position of relative security. The requirement of fairness in all these forms of co-operation is therefore to allow individual projects to be meshed with communal ones. In the informal sphere this can be achieved by detailed negotiation; in the commercial'sphere it can be done through market exchange.

At this point we seem to have reached a justification for something like a welfare state – a sphere of public agencies, concerned with guaranteeing basic needs for individual citizens. But we have also suggested certain features of the provision to be made by these public agencies which do not correspond with the principles used in present social services. It is these principles that will be the subject of the next chapter.

Notes

1 John Locke, *Two Treatises of Government* (1698), Cambridge University Press, 1967, *Second Treatise*, sections 6, 25, 54, 57.
2 Jean-Jacques Rousseau, 'A Discourse on the Origin and Foundation of Inequality among Men' (1755), in *The Social Contract and Discourses*, J. M. Dent, 1952, preface and part I.
3 Thomas Jefferson, 'Fundamentals of Rightful Government', in Edward Dumbauld (ed.), *The Political Writings of Thomas Jefferson*, Liberal Arts Press, 1955.
4 Locke's state of nature was social but pre-political; Rousseau's was pre-social – people were isolated individuals, self-sufficient and harmless to others.
5 Thomas Jefferson, 'Notes on Virginia' (1784), in Andrew Lipscombe (ed.), *The Writings of Thomas Jefferson*, Jefferson Memorial Association, 1903, vol. 2, especially pp. 229–30.
6 Michael Walzer, *Spheres of Justice: A Defence of Pluralism and Equality*, Martin Robertson, 1983.
7 Ibid., p. 20.

8 Isaiah Berlin, 'Two Concepts of Liberty', in *Four Essays on Liberty*, Oxford University Press, 1969.

9 J. S. Mill, 'Essay on Liberty' (1859), in *Utilitarianism, Liberty, Representative Government*, J. M. Dent, 1912.

10 Locke argued that the invention of money exonerated enclosers of land from the duty (in natural law) to leave 'as much and as good' for other commoners (*Second Treatise*, sections 33–7 and 50), and that higher productivity through enclosure justified the creation of an uncompensated class of landless labourers (*First Treatise*, section 43). Robert Nozick deals with the principle of compensation at some length. As a libertarian he is concerned to minimize interference with property accumulation and risk-taking but acknowledges that (as first proposed by Fourier) individuals might deserve compensation for losing certain liberties (which previously enabled them to subsist, such as hunting and gathering rights) as a result of the process of civilization (*Anarchy, State and Utopia*, Basil Blackwell, 1974, p. 178, footnote). He also acknowledges that history gives no generally applicable account of the justifiable extent of compensation, or of social protection.

11 See for instance Robert E. Goodin, 'Freedom and the Welfare State: Theoretical Foundations', *Journal of Social Policy*, vol. II, no. 2, 1982, pp. 149–76.

12 For instance, John Stuart Mill, 'An Essay on Liberty', especially ch. 1, and F. A. Hayek, *The Constitution of Liberty*, Routledge & Kegan Paul, 1960. Hayek sees the rule of law, and equality before the law, as fundamental for freedom, and contrasts the virtues of a free society with the vices of a controlled, authoritarian one.

13 Mill, 'Essay on Liberty'.

14 See Bill Jordan, *The State: Authority and Autonomy*, Basil Blackwell, 1985, pp. 258–64.

15 Rudolf Bahro, *The Alternative in Eastern Europe*, New Left Books, 1978, and F. Feher, A. Heller and G. Markus, *Dictatorship over Needs*, Basil Blackwell, 1985.

16 John Rawls, *A Theory of Justice*, Clarendon Press, 1972. His two principles are supposed to be derived from what free and rational people concerned to further their own interests 'would accept in an initial position of equality as defining the fundamental terms of their association' (p. 11). His potential citizens are imagined as choosing these principles behind a 'veil of ignorance', knowing nothing of their class position, social status or hereditary endowment of health or intelligence in the futute society (pp. 14–15).

17 Ibid., pp. 270–4.

18 Ibid., pp. 78–80.

19 Marx regarded wage rises as being no compensation for the exploitation inherent in capitalist production; it 'only means in fact, that the length and weight of the golden chain the wage-labourer has already forged for himself allow it to be loosened somewhat' (*Capital*, (1867), Penguin, 1976, vol. 1, ch. 25, p. 769).

20 Rawls sees the process by which his potential citizens choose their principles as being in several stages. The first stage is absolutely general, and made without knowledge of anything except some rival theories of justice. The second is based on knowledge of 'general facts about society, such as its size and level of economic advance, its institutional structure and natural environment, and so on' (p. 200); in other words, the potential citizens then apply the two general

principles to social institutions, rules, roles and responsibilities already established, since Rawls says that each society has its own 'traditions, institutions and social forces . . . and its particular historical circumstances', and that 'the theory of justice does not include these matters' (p. 274). So they do not have to choose, for instance, between capitalist or socialist institutions – surely a fundamental issue for the potential citizens of any society.

The limitations of Rawls's theory might be illustrated by reference to a group of potential citizens applying the principles of justice to mid-seventeenth-century England. They would certainly have been able to choose between the rival claims of king and parliament over individual freedom and political authority; but they would not have been able to choose between the rival arguments of those advocating a radical redistribution of land for subsistence farming and those advocating the extension of large-scale property holdings, wage labour and commercial markets, even though the former were apparently arguing for greater equality and the latter for greater inequality (though with a promise that even unskilled labourers would benefit through higher wages). This is because the two systems did not even have 'primary social goods' in common, to measure comparative value – in the first system the 'primary social goods' were land and tools (for subsistence production), and in the second money (for capital and wages).

21 Rawls, *Theory of Justice*, ch. 43, pp. 274–84.

22 See for instance the inquiry into the death of Stephen Menhenniot, a mentally handicapped young man who was treated like an animal on his father's farm. Depriving children of meals and virtually starving them to death was a common feature of the two greatest child care scandals of postwar Britain, the cases of Denis O'Neill and Maria Colwell. See Tom O'Neill, *A Place Called Hope*, Basil Blackwell, 1981.

Part Two

Socioeconomic Change and Welfare

6

A Welfare State?

At the end of the last chapter, a glimpse of a possible reconciliation between individual and communal welfare seemed to be emerging. Perhaps the values of fairness, freedom and equality, all of which play an important part in small-scale distribution of welfare, could after all enter into wider society through the notion of equal provision for the basic needs of all. This idea seems intuitively promising, and of course it also points towards the kind of welfare state that has been developed in Western Europe and Australasia, to a lesser extent in the United States and Japan, and to some extent in Eastern Europe, since the Second World War.

The notion of a welfare state raises the fundamental question of why we have a state at all, and what its purpose is. After all, much of my argument so far has suggested that in families, small groups and voluntary associations welfare is distributed according to the principles of fairness and equality, with some regard being paid to freedom also. I have throughout implied that there is a good deal of consensus in most communities about how these principles can be applied to small-scale roles and relationships, and that mechanisms can be set up to settle conflicts through the rules and the agreed rights of the membership – ultimately, if conflicts cannot be settled, then individuals can leave and join other groups. If all this is true, why do we need the state?

The state defines the territory and membership of a society, regulates its internal affairs, conducts relations with other states (by peaceful and warlike means), and provides it with identity and cohesion.[1] It presides over a number of different spheres of communal life and orders the relations between groups, associations and institutions. It oversees their regulation of their members, and regulates their relations with each other. The state is important because it is the system for watching over all the other systems of activity in a community, both formal and informal. In ruling over its territory, the state also defends its inhabitants against others' attempts to rule over all or part of it.

So the state regulates both the boundaries and the rules of the many spheres in which welfare is shared in societies. It is responsible for overseeing the fairness of the rules that apply in each sphere, and for defining people's rights (freedoms) to move between spheres. Political authority has a sphere of its own, whose shape and scope varies between societies; the way it orders the rest of society depends in turn on who holds political power, and what processes limit it.

Theorists about the state can be divided into two (rather heterogeneous) groups. On the one hand, there are writers who argue that the state needs to be strong because of the potentially fragmentary, conflictual and destructive tendencies in wider society. This group includes individualists like Hobbes, who saw people as inherently vainglorious, competitive, envious and quarrelsome, and commercial society as exaggerating these natural traits. He also saw rivalry and resentment between groups (especially those based on religious enthusiasm) as particularly dangerous. The 'natural' state of society was therefore one of war, with its notoriously risky consequences for the individual. Hence what was needed was a strong state to overawe its subjects, and master their turbulent passions.[2] The same group includes many German writers, among them Hegel and the militaristic school of the late nineteenth century (Clausewitz, Gumplowicz, Hintze et al.), who regarded the strong state as embodying values and virtues of morality, leadership, cohesion, consensus, unity and purpose which would be wholly lacking in a society left to sordid intergroup wrangles.[3] Their glorification of the state allowed them to value state-building (through war as well as through institutional frameworks) as a good in itself; Bismarck might be taken as an example of their philosophy in action.[4] Finally, Marx was influenced by Hegel; and in his notion of the class basis of state power he laid the foundations for the Leninist approach, which insists that a strong state is needed to promote the interests of the proletariat, to control an ever-scheming residual bourgeoisie and to suppress external subversion and counter-revolution.[5] It is also the expression of the political leadership's framework for managing the planned economy and meeting social needs.

The second group is concerned to limit the power of the state and define the rights of the individual. This has been the approach of liberalism since Locke, but it is really much more an attempt to justify a *certain kind* of strong state than it seems. Writers of this persuasion are always as interested in economic liberty as they are in political freedom, and they emphasize the state's role in protecting property, punishing deviance, upholding contracts and holding the economic ring to allow markets to function smoothly. Among this group, Adam Smith stands out as especially benevolent, since he alone took an optimistic view of human nature (paradoxically, based on a rather cynical trust in people's instincts for self-preservation and profits, and the workings of the invisible hand).[6] Locke himself, Defoe, Bentham, John Stuart Mill and the rest of the British school all gave strong emphasis to the importance of law and order, strict and deterrent principles of poor law administration and controlling the breeding propensities of the lower orders.[7] Although they were concerned to exclude the state as far as possible from economic life, and from the social world of the middle classes, they saw it as a very necessary force to control the turbulence, improvidence and fecklessness of the working class, and to protect their own freedom. This group's most characteristic modern spokesman is Hayek, who argues that the threat of coercion is the only way of preventing coercion, that hence a monopoly of it is given to the state, and that the state's abstract and general rules protect the known private spheres of individuals against interference by others; hence, 'even the coercive acts of government become data on which the individual can base his own plans'.[8]

Both schools of thought have influenced the actual development of the state – the first mainly on the continent, and especially in terms of international relations, and the second mainly in Britain and the United States (subsequently also Japan). As far as economic systems are concerned, neither view has achieved predominance. The first, which favours protectionism, planning and state intervention, has at times been very successful (rapid economic growth was achieved through totalitarian methods in Hitler's Germany and Stalin's Russia; Britain used central planning successfully during two world wars; and the more permissive planning and corporatist methods of postwar European countries were also highly effective); but at other times the liberal approach has been equally advantageous (as in nineteenth-century Britain and twentieth-century United States).

We might conclude that state power has certainly been successful in international relations (witness the comparative dominance of nation-states like Britain, France, Holland and post-Bismarck Germany over the old imperial structures of Europe between the fifteenth century and the end of the First World War). The system of nation-states has also produced comparative territorial stability, in spite of frequent outbreaks of armed warfare.[9] Perhaps the most obviously successful function of the state has been to anchor economic relations to particular territories, and hence provide institutional protection for (a variety of) productive and property forms.[10] It is difficult to give an all-purpose historical judgement on the state; it is even harder to imagine a world without states, even though this often seems desirable, especially when tension between the superpowers threatens nuclear catastrophe.

The Theory of the Welfare State

From what I have said so far about the state, it is obvious that, in return for the authority it is given by (or takes from) its subjects, it should offer them all some kind of protection from harm, and some benefits in terms of order, predictability and security. The primary duty of the state has always been to defend the inhabitants of its territory from attack by the inhabitants of others, and particularly from organized invasion by other states.[11] The second duty is to protect them from harm at each other's hands – and to ensure that the rules they make for each other, and that it makes for them, are observed, and offenders are punished. There is room for disagreement about whether the state should be mainly a punitive arbitrator which prosecutes lawbreakers or a benevolent mediator in disputes between its citizens, but it clearly has some responsibilities in terms of law and order. Finally, the state has a duty to regulate itself, its own institutions and its processes, to protect citizens against arbitrary authority, and to give them opportunities to influence its policies and decisions.

One of the most important issues of the twentieth century, which has resurfaced recently with a vengeance, is whether the state also has a responsibility to protect all its citizens from harm by *guaranteeing* that their basic needs will be met in all circumstances, through the provision of social services. It seems obvious that the state must have some such obligation, since it is supposed to be a protective organization for all in its territory, and is supposed to save them from preventable harm. But whether it should do this in a generalized and systematic way is open to dispute. On the whole, the strong state tradition of Hobbes and the German school favoured a paternal state that was concerned with the welfare of the poor, while the British and American liberal tradition took a much more restrictive view, and tended to regard those who applied for state income support as deviants who were as much in need of training or punishment as of assistance.[12] It was not until after the Second World War that there was a general move towards universal social services.

As we shall see in this chapter, this move combined ideas about common basic needs with a model of the economy and of social life. The notion that the state had a duty to meet universal basic needs up to a minimum through non-stigmatized social services was not introduced out of a clear blue sky, or in an intellectual vacuum. It rested on certain assumptions about economic and social systems, and on how they distributed welfare in society. My purpose will be to clarify these assumptions.

I shall argue that the principles under which social services were created in postwar Britain were characteristic of the liberal view of the state, whereas those used in the Western European countries were influenced more by the German tradition. The differences and similarities between the two will be examined.

Beveridge and the British Welfare State

The Second World War was an important watershed in social policy, because it is only since its end that the state in capitalist countries has given universal guarantees on basic needs to all citizens.[13] But it would be quite wrong to suppose that this represented a completely new way of thinking about citizenship or the role of the state. Rather, it was an extension of certain tendencies in both liberal and corporatist (continental, strong state) societies which had existed before the war. Both kinds of systems felt the need to create a new relationship between the state and the citizen, and both believed – once the aftermath of the war had been survived – that their economies and social structures could sustain the expansion of social rights.

In Britain the thinking behind the creation of the welfare state was given exceptionally clear and forthright expression by Sir William (later Lord) Beveridge. In his famous Report, *Social Insurance and Allied Services*, and his other writings, he enunciated the principles that he considered proper for the social services, and the assumptions on which he recommended their adoption. Inevitably, his scheme was not accepted in its pure form, and no politician or administrator has ever justified the modifications made then or since with anything like the same clarity. So Beveridge is the best source for the thinking behind the British social services, and is still particularly interesting, because all his instincts were those of a liberal in the British tradition.

In Beveridge's thinking, two main strands were woven together: that of universal social rights to a national minimum, and that of the continued importance of individual effort and family support. These strands were drawn together at the start of his Report when he wrote that

> social security must be achieved by co-operation between the state and the individual. The State should offer security for service and contribution. The State in organising security should not stifle incentive, opportunity, responsibility; in establishing a national minimum, it should leave room and encouragement for voluntary action by each individual to provide more than the minimum for himself and his family. (para. 9)

These two apparently contradictory principles, which had always been held by liberals to be incompatible, he reconciled through a third – that of universal insurance. 'It is, first and foremost, a plan of insurance – of giving in return for contributions benefits up to subsistence level, as of right and without means test, so that individuals may build freely upon it' (para. 10). The title to security was therefore gained through work, and each individual was guaranteed flat-rate benefit – supposed to be enough to meet his or her basic needs – from the pooling of risks, out of total contributions.

Beveridge saw this insurance cover as a fall-back for certain contingencies ('interruptions or termination of earnings'). The main source of income for basic needs would be the earning-power of men, as heads of households; they in turn would provide for their wives and children. The labour market and the family were thus the primary means of distribution and redistribution. What people had in common was their roles as workers and family members; the factory and the family were the systems of co-operation that met their common requirements. Other basic needs, for health care and education especially, would be met by social services provided by the state in kind.

Writing in 1942, Beveridge was able to look forward to a postwar society in which the state could actually strengthen the market economy through Keynesian measures, and hence he could make certain assumptions about income from employment. He concluded from interwar surveys on poverty that the vast majority of people whose income did not meet their basic needs were living in a household where the head was retired, unemployed or sick; and that, of the rest, the major cause was families with more than one child. (This last conclusion misinterpreted the evidence, such as it was, which suggested that low wages were the major cause, and that many families with only one child were living in poverty.)[14]

Beveridge regarded it as both possible and essential for the state to maintain full employment (in the sense of allowing all *men* seeking a job to find one) as part of its responsibility for guaranteeing the incomes of all citizens. In another report, published in 1944, he acknowledged his debt to Keynes, whose *General Theory of Employment, Interest and Money* had been published in 1936. He argued that, by changes in interest rates, taxation and public spending, the state could manipulate the overall level of demand, and should maintain it at such a level that the number of job vacancies was always slightly higher than the number of men looking for work. 'It must be the function of the State in future to ensure adequate outlay and by consequence to protect its citizens against mass unemployment, as definitely as it is now the function of the State to defend the citizens against attack from abroad and against robbery and violence at home.'[15] In *Social Insurance and Allied Services*, he spelt out his assumption on economic policy in the following terms:

> most important, income security which is all that can be given by social insurance is so inadequate a provision for human happiness that to put it forward by itself as a sole or principal measure of reconstruction hardly seems worth doing. It should be accompanied by an announced determination to use the process of the State to whatever extent may prove necessary to ensure for all, not indeed absolute continuity of work, but a reasonable chance of productive employment. (para. 440)

Beveridge also saw a national health service as essential for an effective income maintenance scheme, to ensure that the full costs of health care were covered. 'Restoration of a sick person to health is a duty of the State and the sick person, prior to any other consideration' (para. 426). He thought it should be free, and available irrespective of national insurance contributions. However, not all conditions which made people unable to work had their income needs covered by insurance benefits. Beveridge saw disability exclusively in terms of industrial injury, and made no provision for people handicapped from birth. Presumably this was partly because there were fewer handicapped and disabled people who survived childhood at this time, and partly because they were seen as being properly cared for in hospitals, and hence as the province of the health service.

Beveridge's assumptions about family roles and responsibilities were fairly explicit, and were conventional for the period. Most people lived in families, with a male 'breadwinner'; married women did work which was 'vital but unpaid' in the home, as part of a 'team' with their husbands – all domestic tasks were therefore her duties (para. 107). Only a small minority of married women sought employment, and their wages should be seen as providing for needs other than the basic ones of households (para. 108). Women's basic needs could be met at less cost than men's (paras 218–23) and children's costs were less than adults' (paras 227–8), though this was age-related. The larger the household, the less was the average cost of basic needs per head (paras 229, 418). Divorce and separation were rare; when they did occur, one party could be clearly identified as 'to blame' (para. 34).

Beveridge's insurance scheme brought married women in as 'a special insurance class of occupied persons' whose unpaid work complemented their husbands' employments. He therefore wanted the husband's contribution to be made 'on behalf of himself and his wife, as for a team, each of whose partner is equally essential, and it gives benefit as for the team' (para. 107). It was supposed to cover married women not only against widowhood and maternity needs, but also against separation and divorce, so long as this was not 'through their own fault or consent' and they lost maintenance from the husband as a result (para. 347).[16] Beveridge thought that an unmarried woman, living with a man as his wife, should get maternity benefit and dependant's addition for unemployment and sickness benefit, but not widow's benefit (para. 348).

Because he thought that men's wages would be adequate for the basic needs of husband, wife and one child, he argued that family allowance (child benefit) should be paid for second and subsequent children, at the rate which he calculated to be the average costs of subsistence for children aged 0–15. This came out at 58 per cent of the single adult rate – almost certainly an underestimate of the actual costs.[17]

Housing costs posed Beveridge his most difficult problem, because these varied so much between households and between areas of the country. He acknowledged that there was a strong case for varying benefits according to actual housing costs, but ended (mainly because of his adherence to the principle of universal flat-rate benefits) by recommending a notional housing element, equivalent to 'average rents', in all the adult benefit rates. This greatly weakened his claim that the rates of national insurance benefits were to be sufficient for 'all normal' subsistence needs (i.e., basic needs).

What Beveridge hoped he had achieved was a universal guarantee of a minimum income, enough for 'subsistence in all normal cases' (para. 307), on terms that were dignified for all who claimed. This was supposed to be achieved through the insurance principle; people would feel entitled by virtue of their contributions, and because they were not getting 'something for nothing'. They would also find the scheme more acceptable because of his assumptions about employment and marriage. In fact, few married women were contributors in their own right, and although Beveridge was adamant that they were not treated as dependants, but were included in their husbands' contributions, the distinction was semantic; they could not claim as individuals unless they were employed and paid full contributions. Other people, such as the handicapped, long-term unemployed and school-leavers without jobs, were also 'invisible' in Beveridge's scheme – their needs were not recognized as being on a par with full adult citizens.

Furthermore, the terms of benefit were very much the same as they had been before the war. To get unemployment benefit, the claimant had to show that he or she was looking for full-time work, was available for such employment, was not doing a part-time job (even unpaid) on any day for which the claim was made, and so on. All this was fair if, as Beveridge assumed, full-time work at decent wages was available for anyone who wanted it – but his assumption about wages was never valid, and his assumption about the volume of employment has become increasingly less realistic from the 1960s onwards.

Beveridge's scheme was a bold attempt to reconcile social rights to a guaranteed minimum income with liberal principles of freedom and the subjective view of welfare. It directly addressed a number of longstanding British liberal fears and prejudices, and challenged them with a radical new approach. It gave a right to an income which met basic needs, but it defined these in terms of households, and assumed that the combination of a state-reinforced labour market and family allowances would be sufficient to give the employment and the wages required. It acknowledged that, without compulsory insurance and family allowances, the labour market could not meet basic needs, and that the state had to base its policies on sharing responsibilities with the family, rather than on a fear of fecklessness and population growth. It recognized the need for free health services, universal secondary education and improved public housing at reasonable rents.

Unfortunately, Beveridge's scheme was undermined from the start of the process of implementation. His separation and divorce benefits were scrapped in the White Paper of 1944, thus destroying the notion of 'partnership' in married women's coverage, and reducing them to the status of dependants.[18] Unemployment benefit was to be time-limited to a year and not open-ended, as Beveridge wanted.[19] Above all, the whole subsistence basis of his costings (which meant that national insurance benefits should have been enough for basic needs, and was the substance of the scheme's claim to fairness and dignity) was abandoned. The government allowed only

31 per cent for inflation since 1938, when by 1946 the actual level was 54 per cent;[20] it used old and discredited cost-of-living indices; its notional rents were quite unrealistic (taking advantage of Beveridge's acknowledgement of defeat on this point); and family allowances were cut from his recommended 7s. to 5s. per week, well below the actual cost of bringing up a child.

The result was that from the start there was a large and growing need for claimants of national insurance benefits to claim means-tested national assistance also. By 1955, two-thirds of claimants of the latter were national insurance beneficiaries, and half were pensioners. There was a built-in inadequacy in the social insurance scheme, acknowledged in the 1944 White Paper – it was a 'reasonable insurance against want', but relied on the savings or sacrifices of claimants to make up the gap between rates of benefit and basic needs, or required them to go for means-tested benefits to meet it. This was quite unacceptable in Beveridge's own terms, since he had argued that national assistance should be perceived as less desirable, since 'otherwise 'the insured persons get nothing for their contributions' (para. 369). In practice, the rise in numbers of claimants of national assistance (later, supplementary benefits) has created a constant policy dilemma in the British system. Attempts to cream off some claimants by the introduction of earnings-related benefits[21] between 1961 and 1975 have been dismantled (for people of working age) by the Conservative government since then, and in any case have been much more than offset by the enormous increase in claims from people not covered by insurance benefits, such as the long-term unemployed, school-leavers and single parents.

But this development has not been sufficient to relieve poverty, and particularly that resulting from low wages. Since people in full-time employment are excluded from supplementary benefit, the problem of low-income families (re-identified in the mid-1960s) demanded a different solution.[22] Successive governments have opted to give means-tested benefits related to family size (family income supplement) and housing costs (rent and rate rebates, now housing benefit), thus spreading income-related schemes further, adding to complexity, and creating the poverty trap. The dilemmas created by these measures will be discussed in chapter 7.

The third main policy development since the creation of the national insurance system has been non-contributory non-means-tested benefits for disabled people and those who care for them. Here governments have had to tiptoe not only around the insurance principle, but also along the tightrope set by Beveridge's assumptions about the family. The rules governing these benefits faithfully reflect traditional assumptions about the role of married women as unpaid care-givers. For instance, the conditions for receiving *attendance allowance* (1971) were framed in such a way as to demonstrate that the care and attention given to a disabled person must be far greater than that given (on an unpaid basis) by mothers, wives or daughters to an able-bodied adult or child. The disabled person must need either frequent attention throughout the day in connection with his 'bodily functions',[23] or continual supervision throughout the day in order to avoid substantial danger to himself or others. Children are eligible only if they are over 2 years of age (because all children under that age would need that kind of attention, and most get it free from mothers), and those under 16 must show that they require supervision 'substantially in excess of that normally required by a child of the same age or sex'.

Similarly, *invalid care allowance* (1976) was until very recently payable only to men and single women who gave up *paid* work to look after someone who was in receipt of attendance allowance. The care had to be regular and substantial – every day of the week for a total of at least 35 hours. The claimant could not be in paid work or under 19 in full-time education, or over pensionable age.[24] Married women and cohabitees were excluded, unless (in the case of married women) they had ceased to live with their husbands and also received less than £20.45 (1985) per week in maintenance from them. In other words, married women and female cohabitees were expected to look after any chronically sick or disabled relative (child, spouse or parent) on an unpaid basis, without state support. These rules were successfully challenged in the European Court by Jackie Drake, a married woman caring for her mother, in June 1986, and have now been substantially revised in line with that decision.

West Germany, the Social Market Economy and the Social Insurance Scheme

The origins of the German social security system make an interesting contrast with that of Britain. The theoretical basis was in many ways similar, but the emphasis was quite different, partly because of Germany's very different intellectual and political traditions, and partly because of the immediate postwar situation.

In the late nineteenth century, the German nation-state was built around military strength and the notion of socially aware hereditary rulers. The middle class was politically weak, individualism in the British liberal tradition commanded little support, and even in economic terms the ideas of free trade and *laissez-faire* were little respected. The state regulated both economic and social life; it was active in industrial expansion, protectionist and paternalistic. Bismarck's social policy was aimed at weakening socialist opposition and incorporating the working class into the state's order; he never pretended to be either a democrat or a reformer.[25] His policies were based on state aggrandizement, contempt for liberalism and fear of socialism.[26]

Because of the economic disasters of Germany's period of liberal democracy after the First World War, the defeat of Hitler left a political vacuum in Western Germany, and an urgent need for new philosophies and policies. Leading industrialists had been compromised with the Nazi ragime, and free enterprise was not a strong element in the German tradition. On the other hand, there were dramatic social problems – millions of refugees, homelessness, unemployment and environmental chaos. The intellectual response of the Christian Democratic political and intellectual leaders was to devise a new theory – the Social Market Economy – which emphasized, first, individual initiative and second, state-guaranteed security. It was roughly the same mixture as in Beveridge, but the order was significantly reversed: for the Germans it was liberalism that needed strengthening, and hence individual freedom that was stressed as primary, while social protectionism (which had always been much stronger in Germany, before and after Bismarck) was made the secondary element.

The man generally given greatest credit for West Germany's economic miracle was a major theorist of the Social Market Economy. Before conceding that 'social security is certainly a good thing and desirable to a high degree', Ludwig Erhard wrote, in *Prosperity through Competition* (1958):

A free economic order can only continue so long as the social life of the community contains a maximum of freedom, of private intitiative and of foresight. If, on the other hand, social policy aims at granting a man complete security from the hour of birth, and protecting him absolutely from the hazards of life, then it cannot be expected that people will develop that full measure of energy, effort, enterprise and other human virtues which are vital to the life and future of the nation and which, moreover, are the prerequisites of a social market economy based on individual initiative. The close link between economic and social policy must be stressed; in fact, the more successful economic policy can be made the fewer measures of social policy will be necessary.[27]

The last sentence emphasized the strong theme in German thinking on integrating social and economic policy, and on making growth in social services expenditure dependent on growth in the whole economy. While the initial theoretical basis of the German system was neo-liberal, its consolidation became linked with the philosophy of social planning, and the corporate management of the economy. Just as the Christian Democrats established the Social Market Economy on individual initiative, so the Social Democratic Party (SPD) consolidated it through its concept of the Social Plan.

The intellectual basis of the Social Plan was provided by Gerhard Mackenroth, who argued that both economic and social policy required planning to harmonize resources with needs through priorities, and that it was far more desirable to finance social services out of growth than from consumption or investment.[28] The SPD's Sozialplan of 1957 aimed to establish 'an overall economic and social view, a basic plan, and a systematic, continuous expansion of the foundations of our entire economy'.[29] Reversing the emphasis of their Conservative rivals, they insisted:

> society has to assume the *basic changes* of life in health, work, capacity, and human dignity. Only then does the individual have the *possibility* of responsibly shaping on his own a life for himself and his family . . . our time is in accord with *an intermingling of social measures and personal initiative*. . . . A comprehensive social reform cannot be limited to help in times of need. It calls forth the resources of the community and of the individual to *prevent need from arising*. It creates *the precondition for the citizen's right to self-responsible existence.*[30]

The West German insurance schemes had been better developed than the British before the war, but were divided between a number of different systems covering different risks and different groups of workers. They were also administered through decentralized organizations. The postwar reforms did not unify or centralize the schemes on the British model. The largest – for pensions and industrial injury – was widened in 1957 to cover almost all workers (including farmers and other self-employed workers), and was put on an earnings-related basis, so that post-retirement income was based on lifetime salary rather than aimed at meeting subsistence needs, and industrial injury benefit was related to notional lost earnings.

Unemployment insurance was gradually extended between 1953 and 1957, until the coverage was approximately the same as for sickness insurance, and the duration of benefit was a year. Rates of benefits were also steadily raised. A number of measures (including grants and low-interest loans) were introduced to help workers with the costs of changing jobs, to help construction workers during bad weather, to subsidize jobs for the long-term unemployed and so on, giving a strong emphasis on rehabilitation of the unemployed back into the labour market. The number claiming unemployment assistance (means-tested, and at much lower rates) fell to 17,000 by 1962.

Family allowances for the employed and self-employed were introduced in 1954 for the third and each subsequent child, and were extended to the second (on a means-tested basis) in 1961. Allowances increased considerably from the second to the fifth and subsequent children, so large families were considerably subsidized, since there was also a system of progressive tax exemptions for children. However in this scheme, as in others, the West German income maintenance system was even more tied to employment than the British.

The distinguishing features of the German income maintenance were therefore its strong insurance basis (with different risks covered by different schemes), its local administration (with strong employer and union representation), its link with work and earnings (even provision for 'dependants' of workers is more limited than in Britain,[31] and benefit rates reflect differentials established in the labour market), and its provision for training and rehabilitation. Women suffer a double disadvantage, because their earnings are habitually lower, and because their employment record is usually interrupted by childbearing and child care, which is especially relevant for pensions and invalidity benefits.[32] Part-time workers who do less than 20 hours per week (most of whom are women) are not covered by unemployment insurance. The means-tested assistance scheme (Sozialhilfe) has scale rates which are much lower than their British supplementary benefit equivalents, and is locally administered, with far greater discretionary elements. Hence there is poverty in West Germany still, especially among groups not covered by insurance, in particular the handicapped, the old and single-parent families.

However, there is relatively much less poverty among those in full-time employment.[33] Unlike Britain, most continental countries have well-developed minimum wages legislation as a remedy against poverty among the working population, but West Germany has relied on economic growth, high wages and nationally binding pay agreements. Also, German trade unions (like those in Sweden) have negotiated to *reduce* differentials at the lower end of the wages structure, so the unskilled are less disadvantaged than in some other European countries.[34]

Liberal and Corporatist Approaches

We have seen that there were certain marked similarities between the philosophies and the methods of the British and West German income maintenance schemes, which influenced the rest of their social services provision. Both linked benefits with the labour market through insurance, both assumed full employment and adequate earnings for men, and both treated married women as coming into schemes through their husbands' contributions. They therefore contained common inbuilt assumptions about the market economy and the 'domestic economy' of households, and how these were linked together through employment, earnings, insurance and unpaid care-giving.

However, there were also important differences about the way the two approaches were managed at the level of national economic and social policy. In the British approach (which is largely also adopted in Australasia, where social security schemes are quite well developed, and in the United States, where they are less comprehensive and where there are also no family allowances, no national health service and little public sector housing), economic policy and social policy are treated separately.[35] Social services compete with other forms of government expenditure (such as defence and law and order) for resources, within an economic structure which is adjusted through year-to-year budgets, and managed mainly through the Treasury. In most of the West European countries, by contrast, the tradition is for both economic and social policy to be planned by the state, employers and employees, within corporate structures which set longer-term targets and make agreements about resource allocation. This corporatist approach, involving what are referred to as the 'social partners' and aimed at achieving consensus about a growing social services sector, was very successful so long as sustained economic expansion was achieved in Western Europe. With the slower growth that has prevailed since the mid-1970s, both 'indicative planning' of economic targets and consensus about social expenditure have waned or perished, though these methods are still fairly successfully followed in smaller countries with a high degree of social cohesion, homogeneity and political continuity, such as Sweden and Austria.

In the British approach, the welfare state is seen largely as a separate sphere, outside the economy, distributing resources according to different principles (moral rather than utilitarian, in some theorists' views).[36] In the continental approach, the term 'welfare state' is taken to include the management of the whole economy, including the social services and the postwar settlement by which trade unions were included in the corporate institutions for planning and agreeing the allocation of resources. In this approach, therefore, growth of spending on social services is part of what is bargained about by the leading interest groups, through the state's structures, and what is planned at top level, both in the medium and the long term. Consensus over goals is not assumed but is actively sought by the state, and the 'social partners' are required to co-operate in fixing the shares to go to all sectors of society, not just their own. So economy and social welfare are not seen as separate spheres, as in the British approach, but as interdependent; growth in neither sphere can be sustained without the co-operation of the major interests in the 'national enterprise'. It is particularly part of the West German tradition that unions bargaining over wages pay close attention to prospects for profits, growth and inflation as well as for their members, and also to social goals. Hence, although industrial conflict is not uncommon, and has increased in recent years, it is contained within a tradition of moderate and 'responsible' wage demands.

This approach was perhaps furthest developed in the Scandinavian countries, and especially in Sweden, where the Social Democratic Party and the trade unions were in a specially favourable position. The forms of 'social citizenship' developed in Sweden were not exclusively based on social insurance principle. In particular, with very high levels of trade union membership (about 80 per cent of the workforce), and with women part-time workers as part of the organized labour movement, they negotiated to *reduce* differentials in earnings and final incomes through central bargaining machinery. Even in the face of growing conservative opposition and new problems of reconciling full employment with economic growth, Swedish governments bargained with unions to trade wage restraint for a share of profits and increased industrial democracy, as well as collective ownership of shares in the country's predominantly private sector.[37] Thus in Sweden the principle of social citizenship which is used to reduce income and status differentials between welfare state beneficiaries and market participants has been a stronger feature of corporatist national economic management than in West Germany or even Austria, mainly because of the political solidarity and power of the labour movement.

In the British approach, the state's responsibility for meeting basic needs is confined to the systems and processes of its public agencies. This is true to the liberal tradition of segregating the state and the economy, and trusting to market forces rather than state intervention. It also encourages the notion that recipients of social services are especially needy people, different from the active and able-bodied members of society – an idea which does not accord easily with that of a universal minimum. The continental approach stems from a view of the state as having wider responsibilities for maintaining social cohesion, for setting goals and standards and for establishing processes whereby all can share (through corporate associations) in the planning and management of society. In theory, this means that all have responsibility for identifying basic needs and organizing services to meet them; in practice, it may mean that certain powerful leaders do so on behalf of the rest. But it does appear to have involved the trade unions in particular in greater concern for social services, and in greater willingness to sacrifice sectional interests for the sake of the worst-off groups.

In Britain there have been two rather feeble attempts to imitate the European approach – by the Wilson Labour government in 1965–7 (the National Plan), and by the Wilson–Callaghan Labour government in 1975–9 (the Social Contract). In the first case it has been pointed out that the plan involved a slowing down of the growth in expenditure on social services that had occurred under the previous (Conservative) administration;[38] in the second it involved cuts in public expenditure generally and in social services particularly.[39]

Developed Western European countries spend a higher proportion of their national incomes on social services generally than do Britain, Australia, the United States and Japan.[40] This is particularly the case in income maintenance. In 1980 Britain actually spent the lowest proportion of its GDP on social welfare of any country then in the European Community – even Ireland spent proportionately more.[41] Yet everywhere consensus about social welfare spending was crumbling, and attacks on institutions, methods and concepts were increasing – even in countries like Sweden, with the strongest welfare state traditions and the highest proportions of spending.

Conclusions

The period between 1945 and 1975 has been represented as an era of 'social democratic compromise' in Britain and Europe, and to some extent also in the other developed liberal capitalist countries. I have suggested that there were two quite different versions of this compromise, even though they had important things in common. In concluding this chapter, I shall emphasize their shared assumptions, all of which have become highly questionable since the mid-1970s.

1 *Full employment* could be achieved by the state's skills in economic management. Although liberal countries used orthodox methods of fiscal and monetary adjustment whereas continental ones used planning, both believed that their versions of Keynesianism could achieve a situation where able-bodied men could get full-time jobs at adequate wages. This was an essential element in their view of how basic needs could be met, primarily through the labour market, and secondarily through social insurance.

2 *Household members* would share the incomes earned by the breadwinner between them, so that the domestic economy would manage both income and their own informal labour in such a way as to bring individual social needs into equilibrium with resources. This was possible because most households were assumed to contain either two able-bodied adults, or at least one insured person.

3 *Growth* could be seen as sustaining rising standards of living throughout society, and providing the basis for expansion of state spending on social services. Even demographic shifts (such as the increase in the proportion of frail elderly members of the population) could be managed through growth, without sacrifices by traditionally privileged groups.

4 *Consensus* was secure – in Britain through the morally persuasive canons of the welfare state, in Western Europe through participation in corporate structures. The social services were therefore immune from fundamental attacks by people who rejected the principles on which they were founded. Except at the margins, social policy was not a matter for political conflict.

I hope I do not need to point out that none of these assumptions applies in the 1980s. However, I shall present in the next two chapters an analysis of the major economic and social changes which have undermined these assumptions and made them outmoded, before continuing with a more detailed account of the current dilemmas of policy in the major social services.

Notes

1 See Bill Jordan, *The State: Authority and Autonomy*, Basil Blackwell, 1985, ch. 1.
2 Thomas Hobbes, *Leviathan* (1651), Basil Blackwell, 1966, chs X–XIII.
3 For the continental school of thought on the state see Kenneth Dyson, *The State Tradition in Western Europe: A Study of an Idea and Institution*, Martin Robertson, 1980. See also Jordan, *The State*, ch. 6.
4 So also might Machiavelli – though Bismarck was far more successful in practice. For his theory of statesmanship, see *Reflections and Reminiscences of Otto Prince von Bismarck*, ed. A. J. Butler, Smith Elder, 1898, vol. II.
5 V. I. Lenin, 'The Proletarian Revolution and the Renegade Kautsky', in *Collected Works*, Lawrence and Wishart, 1964, vol. 25, pp. 472 ff.
6 Smith was particularly optimistic that the spread of commercial relations, and the replacement of a feudal status-based society by a capitalist labour market, would reduce crime by reducing the number of idle retainers: 'it is not so much the police that prevents the commission of crimes as having as few persons as possible to live upon others. Nothing tends so much to corrupt mankind as dependence, while independence still increases the honesty of people. The establishment of commerce . . . is the best police for preventing crimes. The common people have better wages in this way than in any other, and in consequence of this a general probity of manners takes place through the whole country' (Lectures on Justice, Police, Revenue and Arms, in H. W. Schneider (ed.) *Adam Smith's Moral and Political Philosophy*, Harper, 1948, II.i.i). This may be contrasted with the views of Jeremy Bentham, who advocated 'preventive police' based on the surveillance of individuals, their guidance into harmless amusements, the licensing of activities and trades, street lighting, regulation of firearms and other potentially dangerous implements, public information about crime, etc. (L. J. Hume, *Bentham and Bureaucracy*, Cambridge University Press, 1981, p. 95).
7 See for instance John Locke's memorandum to his fellow commissioners in the Board of Trade, 1697, which blamed increased unemployment and claims on 'vice and idleness', 'debauchery', and 'begging drones'. Hard labour, military service and the house of correction should be punishments for unlicensed begging; anyone found with a counterfeit licence should have his ears cut off for a first offence, and transported for a second. Claimants' children over 3 years of age should be set to work, and earn their keep (*Board of Trade Papers*, Journal B, pp. 242–326; quoted in H. R. Fox Bourne, *The Life of John Locke*, King, 1876, vol. II, pp. 377–87). Daniel Defoe expressed himself in equally forthright and punitive terms in his pamphlet, *Giving Alms no Charity, and Employing the Poor a Grievance to the Nation* (1704), S. R. Publications, 1975. John Stuart Mill believed that the Victorian Poor Law was a big improvement on the old system; its intentionally deterrent principles and institution treatment were necessary. He also justified compulsory emigration (deportation) of paupers to the colonies (*Principles of Political Economy*, (1848), in *Collected Works*, vos 2 and 3, 1965, X.ix.7), and despotic rule over peoples 'in a state of savage independence' who should be taught before all else to obey (*Some Considerations concerning Representative Government*, in *Utilitarianism, Liberty, Representative Government* (1861), Dent, 1912, ch. 2).

8 F. A. Hayek, *The Constitution of Liberty*, Routledge & Kegan Paul, 1960, pp. 20–1.

9 Michael Mann has calculated that, 'Throughout the whole history of the West from 500 BC to the present day, the average state has engaged in at least one open, organised war with another state in about 50 per cent of years.' Interestingly, since the seventeenth century Prussia/Germany has been involved in the fewest war-years of the major Western powers. M. Mann, 'Capitalism and Militarism', in M. Shaw (ed.), *War, State and Society*, Macmillan, 1984, p. 32.

10 Jordan, *The State; Authority and Autonomy*, ch. 9.

11 However, as Michael Mann's account of wars and states points out, the notion of defending territory and property implies that the community is a territorial one, with some notion of property rights, and a system of rules to uphold them. Hence, an internal order upheld by the state is probably logically and historically prior to interstate relations, whether peaceful or warlike. Before communities had territories or property, quarrels were mainly ritualized threatening gestures, and in the face of any real threat people simply ran away. M. Mann, 'Captialism and Militarism', p. 30.

12 For comparisons between the two traditions see for instance P. Flora and A. Heidenheimer (eds), *The Development of Welfare States in Europe and America*, Transaction Books, 1981, and Joan Higgins, *States of Welfare: Comparative Analysis of Social Policy*, Basil Blackwell and Martin Robertson, 1981. For comparisons between paternalism and the new Poor Law of 1834, see Bill Jordan, *Poor Parents: Social Policy and the Cycle of Deprivation*, Routledge & Kegan Paul, 1974, and *Freedom and the Welfare State*, Routledge & Kegan Paul, 1976.

13 'Now, when the war is abolishing landmarks of every kind, is the opportunity for using experience in a clear field. A revolutionary moment in the world's history is a time for revolutions, not for patching'. Sir William Beveridge, *Social Insurance and Allied Services*, Cmd 6404, HMSO, 1942, para. 7.

14 Frank Field, *Inequality in Britain: Freedom, Welfare and the State*, Fontana, 1982, points out that the interwar surveys carried out in Sheffield, Manchester and Plymouth gave no basis for relating poverty to family size, and that a survey in Bristol indicated that 40 per cent of poverty occurred in households with three or fewer persons, only a minority of which included elderly people. Similarly, in 1936 Seebohm Rowntree found that 42.3 per cent of poverty was due to the inadequate wage of the chief wage-earner, and only 28.6 per cent due to unemployment; family size was secondary to low wages as a cause of poverty (p. 83).

15 Sir William Beveridge, *Full Employment in a Free Society*, Allen & Unwin, 1944, p. 29.

16 Beveridge also thought that women should be paid a 'marriage grant' as a single payment, to mark the fact that 'on marriage every woman begins a new life in relation to social insurance . . . To mark this transition it is proposed that she should receive a marriage grant which, besides giving money when there is likely to be a felt need for it, has the administrative convenience of encouraging early notification of marriage to the Security Office' (para. 110). The next paragraph begins, 'During marriage most women will not be gainfully employed' (para. 111).

17 Budgetary studies in Europe and the United States, both before and since the

Second World War, indicated that the costs of bringing up a 14 or 15-year-old are at least equal to those of an adult, and later US estimates indicate that the range extends from 33 per cent at under one year to 93 per cent for a 12–15-year-old, and over 112 per cent for a 16–19-year-old (Field, *Inequality in Britain*, p. 43). See also David Piachaud, *The Cost of a Child*, Child Poverty Action Group, 1979.

18 *Social Insurance*, Cmd 6550, HMSO, 1944, p. 29.

19 Ibid., p. 17.

20 Field, *Inequality in Britain*, p. 89.

21 The main motive for the introduction of earnings-related benefits was undoubtedly that it allowed earnings-related *contributions*. There was alarm in the late 1950s that the National Insurance Fund was in the red, and that it could get more so. The Act of 1959 therefore was concerned mainly with deriving more contributions from better-paid workers, rather than with the needs of pensioners. The Labour government extended the principle in the National Insurance Act 1966 to sickness, unemployment, industrial injuries and widows' allowances (Vic George, *Social Security: Beveridge and After*, Routledge & Kegan Paul, 1968, p. 38). In 1975 the State Earnings-Related Pension Scheme (SERPS) provided a much more comprehensive one than the Act of 1959 had done, including occupational schemes to secure an earnings-related addition based on the best 20 years of employment, as a supplement to the basic state pension.

22 Peter Townsend and Brian Abel-Smith, *The Poor and the Poorest*, Bell, 1965.

23 According to Lord Denning, 'bodily functions' consist of 'breathing, hearing, seeing, eating, drinking, walking, sitting, sleeping, getting in or out of bed, dressing, undressing, eliminating waste products, and the like, all of which an ordinary person who is not suffering from a disability does for himself. But they do not include cooking, shopping, or any of the other things which a wife or daughter does as part of her domestic duties or generally which one of the household does for the rest of the family' (R. v. N.I. Commissioner *ex parte* Secretary of State for Social Services (1981), 1 WLR 1017 (CA)).

24 Pensioners can continue to claim if they were doing so before they reached pensionable age.

25 Bismarck's domestic *realpolitik* consisted in playing off interest groups against each other to the advantage of the state, and he used the working class against the liberal bourgeoisie on several occasions. For instance, his reason for allowing universal manhood suffrage was that he believed that 'In a country with monarchical traditions and loyal sentiments the general suffrage, by eliminating the influences of the liberal bourgeois classes, will also lead to monarchical elections' (speech to Reichstag, 1866; quoted in G. A. Craig, *Germany 1866–1945*, Clarendon Press, 1978, p. 45).

26 'Bismarck was to establish himself in history as a great conservative statesman, but he was conservative in an unusual way. Though he greatly admired traditional beliefs and institutions, he had no faith in their strength.' A. J. P. Taylor, *Bismarck: The Man and the Statesman*, Hamilton, 1955, p. 63. He feared revolution and probably overestimated the strength and determination of his socialist opponents.

27 Ludwig Erhard, *Prosperity through Competition*, Thames & Hudson, 1958, pp. 185–6. Later in the same passage he also referred to the welfare state as 'a modern delusion'.

28 Gerhard Mackenroth, 'Die Reform der Sozialpolitik durch einen deutschen Sozialplan', *Schriften des Vereins fur Sozialpolitik*, new series, vol. IV, 1952, pp. 39–76; quoted in G. V. Rimlinger, *Welfare Policy and Industrialisation in Europe, America and Russia*, John Wiley, 1971, pp. 155–6.

29 Sozialdemokratischen Partei Deutschlands, *Sozialplan fur Deutschland*, Dietz Verlag, 1957, p. 12; quoted in Rimlinger, *Welfare Policy*, p. 158.

30 Ibid., p. 9.

31 Karl Furmaniak, 'West Germany: Poverty, Unemployment and Social Insurance', in Robert Walker, Roger Lawson and Peter Townsend (eds), *Responses to Poverty: Lessons from Europe*, Heinemann, 1984, p. 146.

32 Ibid., p. 157.

33 Ibid., p. 136.

34 Ibid., p. 142.

35 The differences between the liberal 'differentiated welfare state' and the corporatist 'integrated welfare state' are very usefully summarized in Ramesh Mishra, *The Welfare State in Crisis: Social Thought and Social Change*, Wheatsheaf, 1984, ch. 4, esp. table 4.1, pp. 102–3.

36 See for instance Richard Titmuss, *Commitment to Welfare*, Allen & Unwin, 1968.

37 G. Esping-Andersen and W. Korpi, 'Social Policy as Class Politics in Post-War Capitalism: Scandinavia, Austria and Germany', in J. H. Goldthorpe (ed.), *Order and Conflict in Contemporary Capitalism*, Oxford University Press, 1984. They describe the policies adopted by the Social Democratic government in 1984 as a new phase in social citizenship. 'The strategy is therefore to introduce a new set of citizen rights to collective capital ('economic citizenship') as a means of resolving the existing contradictions between social citizenship with full employment and economic growth' (p. 196).

38 Brian Abel-Smith, *Labour's Social Plans*, Fabian Tract 39, 1966, p. 5.

39 See speeches by Dennis Healey (Chancellor of Exchequer) and James Callaghan (Prime Minister), 25 February 1976 and 27 April 1976. Both emphasized the need to transfer manpower and resources out of the public sector and into manufacturing industry. Mr Callaghan said, 'It is important that productive jobs should be created and that we should rely on investments in which a successful return can be expected. That is the way to achieve more employment rather than by transferring more and more jobs to the public sector.'

40 Frank C. Castles, *The Working Class and Welfare: Reflections on the Political Development of the Welfare State in Australia and New Zealand, 1890–1980*, Allen & Unwin, 1986.

41 Robert Walker, 'Resources, Welfare Expenditure and Poverty in European Countries', in Walker, Lawson and Townsend, *Responses to Poverty*, table 2.12, p. 47.

7

Employment

Employment is the mechanism through which most of the welfare generated by the formal economy in advanced capitalist countries is shared out. In Britain, for instance, two-thirds of all personal income is made up of wages and salaries, about a tenth is from self-employment, and another eighth is from social security benefits (most of which are related to contributions through employment); there is also a smaller proportion made up from occupational pensions.

This seems to fulfil the promise on which modern economic development was founded. In agrarian societies the proportion of people who worked for wages was low; most people worked with family or communal resources for themselves or each other. People had claims on each other's time, energy or produce, by virtue of their place in a system of status or kinship; they shared the rest among their own. Markets in land and labour gradually increased the commercial economy and reduced the subsistence one. It was the higher productivity of capitalist agriculture and industry, and the assurance that it would provide a fair share of greater national income *for all*, that gave this form of economic development its moral force.[1] Higher wages were what compensated those who lost the resources for subsistence in this process.

But it was differences in productivity, both between the capitalist and the subsistence sectors and within the former, that gave the whole system its dynamism, and these differences have grown over time. Labour was drawn into the more productive branches, first, of agriculture and then of industry; but it has since been pushed out again by still more productive methods, which have saved labour costs. In agriculture this started to happen in the mid-nineteenth century; in industry it is happening all over Western Europe at present.

The subsistence and informal economies have constantly adapted to these changes in labour utilization in the formal economy. In the early stages of economic development, people still retained some fall-back resources for subsistence production or some links with subsistence farming kin. Next, they diversified their waged work, with men pursuing a number of occupations simultaneously or seasonally and women contributing through part-time or out-work. Then gradually, married women withdrew from the labour market and expanded the amount of unpaid work they did in the home, while men had full-time jobs in a single occupation.[2] Recently, a pattern more like the earlier one has been re-emerging, as men's jobs have become scarcer and less secure, and more married women have been drawn back into paid work.

We cannot understand these changes simply in terms of a division between paid and unpaid work. In many ways the spheres of self-employment, personal service employment, home-based out-work and domestic work are closely related. People who are marginal to the labour market may take refuge in any of these during a period when the high-productivity sector is shedding workers. In Britain between 1871 and 1891 the numbers of people employed in manufacturing increased by only 18 per cent; those employed in distributive trades and miscellaneous services (including private domestic service) increased by 31 per cent.[3] Between 1920 and 1938, manufacturing employment declined by 3 per cent and distributive and miscellaneous service employment grew by 33 per cent.[4] But in the more prosperous years between these two periods, manufacturing employment grew by 31 per cent, whereas distributive and personal service jobs increased by only 6 per cent.

All modern societies consist of people whose jobs are linked with high-productivity processes and those who do low-productivity work, either as wage-earners, on a self-employed basis or as part of unpaid roles. The balance between the tasks done through each of the latter kinds of work is constantly changing, and responds to quite small alterations in formal systems. For instance, a married woman might well spend less time looking after her own children and take a part-time job looking after someone else's, in response to a minor change in the rates of child benefit and income taxation.

In one sense, the promise of economic development has indeed been kept; we do all benefit from high productivity in one sector of the economy. A motor car is much cheaper, in terms of an unskilled labourer's wages, than a horse and carriage was in the eighteenth century; and a housewife can do her cleaning much more quickly and efficiently with a vacuum cleaner than she would with a scrubbing brush. But the processes that link people into a share of increased prosperity are far more complex and precarious than Adam Smith and his followers suggested. They have also become more complex and precarious than Sir William Beveridge anticipated or planned.

We saw in the last chapter how, in the postwar period, the managed economy was linked with the household through the social services, and especially social security. Social rights were established through employment, via contributory payments, by the male head of household on behalf of his wife and dependants. Child benefits gave assistance with the extra costs of larger families. Wages were assumed to give adequate income for household needs; economic management was assumed to be able to provide full employment, for men at least. In a sense, social security benefits are a form of compensation for those forced out of the formal economy (temporarily or permanently) to allow them to survive in the informal sector.

All of these assumptions are now highly questionable in Western European societies. Employment in the high-productivity sector seems to be shrinking more continuously than ever before. Employment in the low-productivity sector has increased, but has also become more fragmented, more casual, less secure and reliable. Where households have a male head with a job in the high-productivity sector, they often have other members with additional component earnings, contributing to a comfortable household income. Even households with several members employed in the low-productivity sector are benefiting from the latest developments in economic change. But one-earner households are less obvious beneficiaries, and there is a growing sector of no-earner households whose share of society's income from paid work now often depends on social assistance – payments under principles derived from the Poor Law, which were supposed to have disappeared with the advent of the welfare state.

If male employment no longer automatically provides a fair share of the welfare that is distributed through the money economy (in wages and social security benefits), then the postwar link between jobs and household incomes in terms of social rights comes under question. Socialists tend to argue that it implies that rights to employment must be guaranteed, even if this lowers productivity and efficiency, and reduces the benefits of the international division of labour. Market-minded pragmatists insist that all that is needed is a new system of means-tested income maintenance, which gives social assistance to the poorest households, whether their members are in employment or not, but which imposes work obligations through various sanctions (such as the US 'workfare' scheme).[5] A third alternative, which will be discussed in chapter 9, is that all citizens should have their basic income needs met *before* they enter either the labour market or the household.

Restructuring of Employment and Earnings

It is by now a cliché that (since the mid-1960s) international capital has been restructuring world industrial production through the medium of multinational corporations. The relocation of much heavy industry and the manufacture of simple commodities in Latin America and the Caribbean, in southern Europe and the Middle East and in the newly industrializing countries of South-East Asia has involved new patterns of labour utilization. Labour-intensive production has been pushed out towards the periphery, and capital-intensive methods have been concentrated in the older industrialized core countries. As a result, numbers in industrial employment have grown sharply in the newly industrializing countries, and have shrunk in the advanced industrialized ones. For instance, between 1974 and 1983, paid employment in manufacturing increased by 76 per cent in South Korea, 42 per cent in Hong Kong, 41 per cent in Singapore, 39 per cent in Yugoslavia and 32 per cent in Turkey; it declined by 15 per cent in Denmark, 16 per cent in West Germany and 28 per cent in both Britain and Belgium.[6] The jobs lost were mainly those of men; between 1970 and 1983 there was a decline of 4.2 million in male employment (6 per cent) and a rise of 4.1 million in female employment (12 per cent) in the nine original countries of the European Community.[7] In addition to fewer industrial jobs, there have also been shorter industrial working hours, both in terms of weekly hours offered to manual workers and in terms of hours worked in a year, throughout the European Community.[8]

Although unemployment rates in the West are extremely variable, the main factor in rising rates has unquestionably been the decline in industrial employment, with older industrialized countries like Britain (14 per cent), the Netherlands (18 per cent) and Belgium (20 per cent) near the top of the league, along with others like Spain and Ireland (20 per cent), where rapid growth in industrial jobs was suddenly checked in the mid-1970s.[9] On the other hand, some smaller countries like Sweden, Norway, Switzerland and Austria have achieved much lower unemployment rates (2–6 per cent) despite shrinking industrial workforces, mainly by means of sustaining and adapting the political mechanisms for managing economic and social change that were established in the postwar period.

It is interesting to compare new Western European patterns of labour utilization with those of the United States and Japan. In the United States the marked decline in the workforces of the old heavy industries of the northern and eastern states has been compensated by new jobs in lighter high-tech manufacturing in the southern and western states. Even so, employment in manufacturing declined slightly in the period 1970–83, and overall employment was sustained only by the enormous growth of jobs in services, mainly in new small firms.[10] In Japan, the rapid automation of production in large-scale industry (with widespread introduction of robots and 'flexible manufacturing systems') has been achieved by displacing many older skilled workers into small peripheral firms and sub-contractors, leaving a smaller core of younger technicians in larger enterprises. Workers on the industrial periphery have much lower and more variable wages than those in the core of large firms.[11]

Both Japan and the United States in their different ways offer a recent refutation of the theory that industrial societies lead to ever-increasing proportions of employment in large-scale, bureaucratically organized enterprises.[12] Instead, these enterprises are diminishing their workforces, and hiving off production under subcontract to smaller concerns. In Western Europe also there is strong evidence of increases in part-time work, short-term contracts, self-employment and other forms of labour utilization which break up large organized structures, both of enterprises and of trade unions.[13] Whereas in the postwar period the idea of cheap labour supplies and a 'dual labour market' was associated mainly with the availability of refugees and migrant workers from eastern and southern Europe,[14] now, increasingly, flexibility is achieved by the use of subcontracting and a variety of new forms of employment contract, especially in services.[15]

The overall balance between agricultural, industrial and service employment is now remarkably similar in all the advanced industrialized countries of the West. Older industrial countries such as Britain and Belgium are now much more like the United States and Japan. Whereas in Belgium in 1930 47.5 per cent of all workers were employed in industry, 17.5 per cent in agriculture and 35 per cent in services, the ratio is now 30.5 per cent in industry, 4.7 per cent in agriculture and 66.6 per cent in services. In the United States it is 27.6 per cent in industry, 3.5 per cent in agriculture and 69 per cent in services; in Japan, 34.8 per cent in industry, 9.3 per cent in agriculture and 56 per cent in services.[16]

Yet these similarities disguise enormous variations, especially within the service sector. For instance, in the United States both growth and restructuring of employment have occurred in this sector, entailing new industries and new organization of the labour process, and especially the growth of new small firms based on information technology. In Japan, by contrast, the service sector is backward, and microelectronic innovations which have revolutionized manufacturing have been introduced only slowly. It is the services sector that is likely to provide the key to much of the future of employment and earnings.

Employment in Services

If the industrial sector provides a picture of declining numbers of better-paid jobs for men, the services sector provides one of rising numbers of part-time and mainly low-paid jobs for women. In the nine countries of the European Community, employment in services increased by 11.5 million between 1970 and 1983 (24 per cent).[17] In all the West European countries women's participation rates have grown, and only in Japan (among the advanced industrialized countries of the capitalist world) have they remained static. Part-time work now makes up 17.3 per cent of employment in services in the European Community countries, but in some countries the proportion is much higher – 32.5 per cent in Denmark, 27.1 per cent in Britain and 27.5 per cent in the Netherlands. (This proportion has doubled since 1975.)[18]

However, the significance of these changes requires analysis in terms of structural alterations within service employment. In their book *The New Service Economy*, Gershuny and Miles have argued that it cannot be explained in terms of increased demand for, or consumption of, marketed services. Neither services consumed by industry nor those consumed by individuals have grown significantly – indeed, the latter have declined as a proportion of GNP in many European countries.[19] They develop a model, based on their research, in which productivity growth in services lags behind that in industry, but pay tends to rise in line with pay in the industrial sector. This means that over time the price of goods falls in relation to the price of services. Demand for services is price-elastic, and hence tends to decline. The rise in the relative price of services more than cancels out the income elasticity of demand for services.[20] This explains why marketed services are less consumed at each income level over time in their study; but of course, demand *has* grown for non-marketed services (mainly state social services) where the price effect is disguised by subsidies or the absence of charges to consumers. Here, tax revolts and fiscal crises represent the equivalent of falling demand for services in the market sector.

The effects of these processes on employment are very mixed. In Western Europe services to business (insurance, banking, finance, etc.) have grown rapidly as employers (doubled since the 1940s) but they still form only 10–15 per cent of total employment; hotels, catering and retailing have grown slowly; transport has stayed roughly constant; but employment in community services (health, education and other collective services) has grown rapidly – by 23 per cent in France, 17.5 per cent in West Germany and 10 per cent in Britain since the mid-1970s.[21] In all the major European Community countries except West Germany and Italy, employment in community services exceeded manufacturing employment by 1983; in Denmark it was more than double. As an average proportion of all employment in Western Europe, community services were around 25 per cent.[22]

Gershuny and Miles argue that what has been happening in marketed services is a shift towards 'self-servicing'. As goods have become relatively cheaper and services relatively more expensive, consumers have bought new equipment to combine with their own unpaid labour as a replacement for direct services.[23] Cars, televisions and washing machines have replaced a good deal of public transport, theatres, cinemas and laundry services. They argue that with the advent of information technology this trend will spread to non-marketed services. As the relative costs of social services rise, and consume a larger and larger proportion of national resources, new combinations of goods and unpaid labour will gradually replace directly provided services. The Open University is a model for this trend; expensive investment by both the university and the student in equipment and course material, coupled with the state provision of infrastructure, result in what is finally a much cheaper product, because of the mass membership of courses and the fact that students can study in their own homes while following a full-time or part-time job. Health and personal social services could perhaps use similar methods to allow patients/clients to monitor their own wellbeing and communicate with experts through microelectronic information systems. Gershuny and Miles suggest that this might result in much fewer direct service-giving jobs, and a much larger input of unpaid labour in community services such as education and the care of elderly and handicapped people.[24]

The Gershuny–Miles analysis emphasizes 'self-servicing' at the expense of other very important changes in employment patterns. The figures for employment in social services in particular are distorted by a lack of recognition of the importance of part-time work. For instance, the British national health service is now the largest single employer in Europe, yet over half of health service ancillaries and over a third of nurses are part-time workers.[25] With the growth of employment in social services, the proportion of women in the whole British workforce who work part-time has grown from 40 per cent in 1971 to over 45 per cent in 1983;[26] in spite of the large increase of women workers overall, there are proportionately fewer *full-time* women workers than there were in the early 1960s. To some extent this offsets the price effect described by Gershuny and Miles, since most of these workers are low-paid. Furthermore, in Britain half of all part-time women workers earn too little to pay income tax and 40 per cent earn too little to pay national insurance contributions, which facilitates the payment of low wages.[27] The privatization of several services has been based on the use of this method of saving labour costs, allowing a further fragmentation and casualization of employment in this sector.

All this has important implications for earnings and for household incomes. If the main increase in employment which offsets the loss of better-paid industrial jobs for men is a growth of low-paid part-time jobs in public services for women, then certain households are experiencing considerable loss of earnings. All the evidence suggests that a polarization of households is occurring, with the increase in female service employment mainly benefiting households which already have at least one male earner. In Britain, 61 per cent of households with a male 'head' in work have a wife in some kind of paid employment, but only 30 per cent of those with a male 'head' unemployed have a wife with a job.[28] This polarization over earnings, and hence incomes, is reflected in opportunities for the 'self-servicing'. Pahl's study of the Isle of Sheppey found that, because equipment needed for home improvement, car maintenance and the like is expensive, multi-income families were in much the best position to use self-servicing methods to improve their living standards – they did so mainly by 'moving up' the owner-occupied housing market through home improvement. Self-servicing of this kind was virtually absent in households dependent on state benefits.[29]

Furthermore, the Gershuny–Miles scenario for the future takes no account of effects on the domestic division of labour. On the face of it, they would appear to suggest that women, who have been the main beneficiaries of the increase in service employment, will be required to give up their jobs and return to the domestic sphere, to combine their unpaid labour with new and more sophisticated electronic devices, which will allow them to stocktake, shop, maintain security, provide education for their children and care for their elderly relatives, monitor their own health and keep fit, without ever leaving their homes. This is not every woman's dream of Utopia. It is perhaps through the role of women that we can best consider the implications of all these changes in labour utilization, and their consequences for earnings and social roles.

Women's Work

In many ways, the restructuring of the labour market has affected women more than men. In the 1930s only about one in seven married women in Britain had paid employment, and historically the trend seemed to be that more and more would withdraw to domestic life; now, 60 per cent have paid jobs.[30] In Scandinavian countries the rate is higher still.

Where Britain and the United States contrast with the Scandinavian countries is over the earnings of these women workers. In Sweden, for instance, where part-time work is more prevalent than anywhere else in Western Europe, women's pay is far more equal with men's than in Britain, and part-time workers' is more equal with full-time workers'. This may be because 80 per cent of the workforce, including women, are members of trade unions in Sweden,[31] whereas only just over 50 per cent are trade unionists in Britain, and only a third of part-time workers are trade union members.[32] In Britain the married woman's tax allowance and the national insurance contribution threshold encourage employers to use low-paid part-time women workers, whose costs have an effective discount of over 40 per cent for this reason. Yet women part-time workers are much more likely to be very satisfied with their jobs than male full-time workers, and much less likely to be very dissatisfied.[33] Furthermore, Pahl found that in the Isle of Sheppey women workers needed an average of six months to be trained for their jobs, though these were low-paid and classified as unskilled, whereas men needed only a fortnight's training for theirs, though these were higher-paid and were classified as skilled.[34]

A large part of the increase in service employment for women consists of increases in domiciliary and day care for elderly and disabled people, most of which was previously not done at all, or was done on an unpaid basis by family members. In so far as most of those unpaid tasks were done by married women, and most of the new paid jobs go to married women, what has happened has been a restructuring of women's work, with more done as a paid service and less on an unpaid basis (the opposite of a move towards self-servicing). Similarly fast-food chains, a major new source of employment in the United States and Britain, have provided a lot of low-paid part-time work for married women, and have reduced the amount of food preparation and cooking done on an unpaid basis. All this has more than compensated for the decline in employment opportunities in laundries, on buses and in cinemas.

The balance between paid and unpaid work for women is set by many factors, including relativities of incomes and the tax-benefit system. When the rich are very rich and the poor very poor, the former tend to have many servants and attendants and do little for themselves; as incomes equalize and labour costs rise, even the wealthy start to do their own cooking and gardening.[35] But suppose that there was then a cut in the upper reaches of income tax, and a simultaneous cut in the rates of benefit for people outside work and in low-paid employment. The likely result would be that the rich would take on more cleaners, gardeners, cooks, caddies, gillies, houseplant watchers, nannies and the like; and that the poor would take up these jobs, not out of a sense of vocation to serve the rich in these capacities, but to make good the shortfall in their incomes. In fact, it is perfectly possible in theory that the amount of extra work done by these new employees could exactly equal the amount of self-servicing no longer done by the rich, and that the amount of pay they received for doing it would exactly equal the amount of benefit they lost as a result of the cut. In this case, the total amount of goods and services produced and consumed in the economy would be exactly the same, though the new situation would show up as a large increase in employment and in national income in the economic statistics. As there are many more nannies, cleaners and cooks than gillies or caddies, and as women do more unpaid work than men, their roles would be much more affected. Women are also much more likely to adjust their work and hours to family responsibilities, and to make short-term adjustments by way of casual part-time jobs in response to changes in household circumstances.

Recently, market-minded governments have become more concerned with employment in the services sector, because it is so much cheaper to create 'low-tech' jobs than high-tech industrial ones. They have also become interested in the employment effects of tax cuts (often combined with disguised or open benefit cuts) as a method of job expansion, in preference to other policies, such as investment in infrastructural improvements. It is clear that this makes the relationship between paid and unpaid work, and between the economy and the household, of crucial importance, and raises the social services to a key position in economic management, both as income redistributors and as employers.

Occupational Welfare

It might be assumed that low-paid, insecure jobs were among the least satisfying – that the welfare that accompanies employment is correlated with the income derived from it. To some extent this is apparently true; the British *General Household Survey* has found that over 50 per cent of male managers expressed themselves as 'very satisfied' with their jobs as a whole, compared with 46 per cent of male foremen and non-manual supervisors, while only 37 per cent of skilled and 35 per cent of unskilled male manual workers said they were very satisfied. Conversely, only 2 per cent of male managers were very dissatisfied, compared with 8 per cent of unskilled workers.[36]

However, the proportion of women in each occupational group who were very satisfied with their jobs was considerably higher at each socioeconomic group than men – over 60 per cent for full-time female managers of large establishments and 48 per cent for unskilled manual workers – with fewer very dissatisfied. The largest differences of all were between full-time and part-time workers. The average of all part-time workers who were very satisfied was 52 per cent, compared with 42 per cent of full-time workers (and 40 per cent of full-time male workers). Part-time male workers were just as likely to be very satisfied with their jobs as part-time women workers.[37]

Another important factor in job satisfaction was age. Young people aged between 20 and 24 were least likely to be very satisfied, especially male full-time workers (only 34 per cent). Job satisfaction then inceased with age, with over 75 per cent of those over retirement age with full-time jobs expressing themselves very satisfied with them. Married people were more likely to be very satisfied with their jobs than single people, and widows were much more satisfied than separated and divorced people (62 per cent very satisfied, compared with 44 and 42 per cent).[38] In other words, age, part-time working and marital status were at least as important in determining likely job satisfaction as the nature and pay of the job itself.

We also know that among women in Britain in full-time employment 40 per cent say that they need the money for basic essentials and 13 per cent for extras, whereas among part-time women workers 28 per cent say that it is to earn money for basic essentials, and 28 per cent for extras.[39] The most common features mentioned by women workers for choosing a job were liking doing it, friendly people to work with and security, with pay some way behind, and good prospects much lower still; part-time workers mentioned convenient hours as much as the first two factors.[40]

It is well known that married women respond much more strongly to tax and benefit incentives and disincentives than married men in decisions about taking paid employment, and about hours of work.[41] It seems that, given adequate employment opportunities and access to jobs, they are able to adjust their working hours and conditions to the framework of constraints, and to derive satisfaction from paid jobs which may not fully use their productive or creative potential. By contrast, young people – who are also known to be responsive to tax and benefit factors – are more choosy about their jobs and working conditions.

This raises important questions about the nature and purposes of job creation and training programmes for young people, and particularly about the idea of making these compulsory (under threat of losing benefits). Although all the evidence suggests that young people, like those in other age groups, find unemployment frustrating, and hence want jobs, there is also much evidence that they do not derive welfare from just any occupation. It cannot therefore be assumed that creating meaningless work or ill-disguised occupational therapy – especially under conditions of compulsion – gives young people a sense of sharing in the welfare distributed through employment. On the contrary, it may confirm their feelings of exclusion and alienation.

Conclusions

The labour market in the advanced capitalist countries is now characterized by much more variable patterns of types of contract, hours of work and earnings than in the 1960s. More jobs are short-term or part-time, more work is done away from main production sites, large firms are contracting, the number of small enterprises is growing, more people are self-employed; in addition to all this, there are high rates of unemployment in most of Western Europe, especially among men. What we are seeing is a return to a situation more like that before the Industrial Revolution. It was only with the widespread adoption of factory methods of production that most workers began to do full-time jobs in a single occupation; before that most men had several occupations and worked seasonally, or in bursts, or in two jobs at once, while most women also had part-time employment. It has only been in this century that the pattern of a 'breadwinner' and an unpaid housewife became the dominant norm, and that the industrial labour market came to fit this domestic pattern.

Ideas about fair shares in the distribution of earnings are derived from the history of industrialization, and the expectation of future economic development in a similar direction. Industrial society has been seen as a structured, stratified arrangement of organized occupational groups, competing in a unified labour market, and rewarded according to negotiated rates of pay for their skills.[42] If this expectation is confounded by identifiable tendencies towards dualism and segmentation, then traditional ideas about 'fair pay' and income distribution come into question along with the very notion of a labour 'market'.[43]

So employment, though it still shares out about as large a proportion of national income now as it did in the 1960s, does so in very different ways, and the old linkage between jobs and households through earnings and social security has become very rusty, even broken in places. Households themselves have also been changing – in composition, roles and patterns of behaviour. This will be the subject of the next chapter.

Notes

1 'A King of a large and fruitful territory there [uncolonized America] feeds, lodges, and is clad worse than a day labourer in England' (John Locke, *Two Treatises of Government* (1698), Cambridge University Press, 1967, *Second Treatise*, section 43). Similarly, 'When providence divided the earth among a few lordly masters, it neither forgot nor abandoned those who seem to have been left out in the partition. These last too enjoy their share of all that it produces. . . . In ease of body and peace of mind, all the different ranks of life are nearly upon a level, and the beggar, who suns himself by the side of the highway, possesses that security which kings are fighting for.' Adam Smith, 'Theory of Moral Sentiments', in H.W. Schneider (ed.), *Adam Smith's Moral and Political Philosophy*, Harper, 1948, part IV, ch. i.

2 For example, in Belgium the number of women working in manufacturing in 1846 was almost the same as the number of men (310,000 compared with 329,000). It remained roughly constant for the next hundred years, and in 1961 stood at 285,000, while the number of men in manufacturing had risen to 961,000. In Italy, the number of women in manufacturing fell from 1,358,000 in 1871 to 1,245,000 in 1921, and in mining, construction and manufacturing the figure was 1,553,000 in 1961; the number of men in manufacturing rose from 1,446 in 1881 to 4,657,000 in 1931 and 6,333,000 in 1961. In the United Kingdom, women made up 35 per cent of the manufacturing workforce in 1851, but only 29 per cent in 1961. B. R. Mitchell, *European Historical Statistics, 1750–1970*, Macmillan, 1975, table C1, pp. 153–63. Marx described those on the margins of the labour market as the 'industrial reserve army' (*Capital*, (1867), Penguin, 1976, vol. 1, ch. 25), a very apt phrase for women, who were quickly drawn into the workforce during the two world wars.

3 C. H. Feinstein, *Statistical Tables of National Income, Expenditure and Output of the UK, 1855–1965*, Cambridge University Press, 1976, table 60, p. 131.

4 Ibid., table 59, p. 129.

5 See for instance Patrick Minford, D. Davies, M. Peel and A. Sprague, *Unemployment: Cause and Cure*, Martin Robertson, 1983.

6 International Labour Office, *Yearbook of Labour Statistics, 1984*, ILO, 1984, table 5A, pp. 354–7. Manufacturing output increased by an annual average of 0.9 per cent in the 20 countries of Western Europe between 1975 and 1981, compared with 7.5 per cent in the countries of East and South-East Asia (excluding North Korea and Japan) during the same period. United Nations, *Statistical Yearbook, 1982*, UN, 1985, table 4, pp. 9–12. Similarly, the growth of industrial output in the Caribbean, Central and South American countries was more than twice as rapid between 1975 and 1982 as that of the North American countries. Ibid., table 9, pp. 20–4. Of course, the industrial output of the newly industrializing countries is still tiny compared with that of the United States and Western

Europe, but the impact of this shift on *employment* has been enormous, especially since it has been estimated that in the newly industrializing countries about four times as many employees are used as in industrialized ones for the same process.

7 Eurostat, *Employment and Unemployment, 1985*, Statistical Office of the European Communities, 1985, table II.4, p. 122. In the nine countries the number of jobs for women (38.8 million) now exceeds the number of jobs in industry (36.2 million), while the declining number for men will soon be less than the total number in services (60.7 million).

8 Ibid., tables VI.1 and VI.7, pp. 241 and 254. In France the average weekly hours offered to manual workers in industry declined from 46 in 1970 to 39 in 1983, in Italy from 42.5 to 37.5, and in Belgium from 42.5 to 35.

9 ILO, *Yearbook of Labour Statistics, 1984*, table 9A, pp. 455–9. Unemployment is now concentrated among older and younger workers, with those under 25 years of age forming nearly 50 per cent of registered unemployed in Italy, 45 per cent in France and 40 per cent in Britain. Ibid., table 9B, pp. 465–9.

10 In the United States, population growth was accompanied by an overall increase of employment of 25 per cent between 1970 and 1983. Eurostat, *Employment and Unemployment, 1985*, International Comparisons, pp. 106–7. A national survey found that enterprises with under 100 employees generated 3.4 million of the 4.85 million new jobs created in 1979–80 – 70 per cent. David L. Birch and Susan MacCracken, 'The Small Business Share of Job Creation: Lessons Learned from the Use of a Longitudinal File', *MIT Program on Neighbourhood and Regional Change*, Massachusetts Institute of Technology, 1982.

11 Among manufacturing firms with over 1,000 employees, 96 per cent had introduced microelectronics into products, processes or both by 1982. *A Survey of Technological Innovation in Japanese Firms*, Japanese Ministry of Labour, 1982; quoted in Shirley Williams, *A Job to Live: the Impact of Tomorrow's Technology on Work and Society*, Penguin, 1985, p. 56. For the structure of Japanese firms see J. Atkinson, 'The Flexible Firm takes Shape', *Guardian*, 18 April 1984, and for the impact of this on women and older workers see K. Yonemoto, *Robotisation in Japanese Industries: Socioeconomic Impacts by Industrial Robots*, Japanese Industrial Rights Association, 1983, and Williams, *A Job to Live*, p. 64. The dual structure of a high-productivity, high-wage sector and a peripheral, casualized or subcontract sector with much lower productivity and wages has existed in a marked form in Japan since the nineteenth century or even earlier – see M. Morishima, 'The Transformation of Japanese Society from Centralized Feudalism to Dualism', paper given to ESRC Symposium on Socioeconomic Change in the West, Cambridge, April 1986.

12 For an account of these theories and a critique of them see J. H. Goldthorpe, 'The End of Convergence: Corporatist and Dualist Tendencies in Western Societies', in B. Roberts, R. Finnegan and D. Gallie (eds), *New Approaches to Economic Life: Economic Restructuring, Unemployment and the Social Division of Labour*, Manchester University Press, 1985.

13 S. Berger and M. J. Piore, *Dualism and Discontinuity in Industrial Societies*, Cambridge University Press, 1980, and F. Wilkinson (ed.), *The Dynamics of Labour Market Segmentation*, Academic Press, 1981.

14 C. P. Kindleberger, *Europe's Postwar Growth: The Role of Labour Supply*, Harvard University Press, 1967.

15 Guy Standing, 'Meshing Labour Flexibility with Security: An Answer to British

Unemployment?' *International Labour Review*, vol. 125, 1986, pp. 87–107.

16 Eurostat, *Employment and Unemployment, 1985*, table II.6, p. 124, and pp. 106–7.

17 Ibid., table II.5, p. 123.

18 Ibid., tables VI.3 and VI.4, pp. 250–1. Sweden has an even higher rate of (mainly female) part-time employment.

19 J. Gershuny and I. D. Miles, *The New Service Economy: The Transformation of Employment in Industrial Societies*, Pinter, 1983, pp. 32–3.

20 Ibid., pp. 40–1. Comparing services as a proportion of consumption in 1959 and 1977, 'at each level of real income, households spend less in services in the later period than they did in the earlier' (p. 50), though of course higher-income households tend to spend more in services than lower-income (Engels's Law).

21 Eurostat, *Employment and Unemployment, 1985*, table III.1, p. 130.

22 Ibid.

23 Gershuny and Miles, *The New Service Economy*, p. 84.

24 Ibid., p. 89.

25 H. Land, 'Time to Care', paper delivered to Critical Social Policy Conference, 22 April 1985.

26 Office of Population Censuses and Surveys, *General Household Survey, 1983*, HMSO, 1985, table 7.8, p. 108.

27 J. Martin and C. Roberts, *Women and Employment: A Lifetime Perspective*, Department of Employment and Office of Population Censuses and Surveys, 1984, p. 43.

28 *General Household Survey, 1983*, table 7.17, p. 115.

29 R. E. Pahl, *Divisions of Labour*, Basil Blackwell, 1984, pp. 327–34.

30 Martin and Roberts, *Women and Employment*, table 2.4, p. 12.

31 P. Gourevitch, A. Martin, G. Ross, C. Allen, S. Bourstein and A. Markevits, *Unions and Economic Crisis: Britain, West Germany and Sweden*, Allen & Unwin, 1984.

32 *General Household Survey, 1983*, table 7E, p. 100.

33 Office of Population Censuses and Surveys, *General Household Survey, 1980*, HMSO, 1982, p. 85 and tables 5.12 and 5.13, p. 102.

34 Pahl, *Divisions of Labour*.

35 In Britain in 1861, 11.5 per cent of the workforce were still in private domestic service – the third largest single category of employment after manufacturing and agriculture. C. H. Feinstein, *Statistical Tables of National Income, Expenditure and Output of the UK, 1855–1965*, Cambridge University Press, 1982.

36 *General Household Survey, 1980*, table 5.16, p. 104.

37 Ibid., tables 5.12–5.14, pp. 103–3.

38 Ibid.

39 Martin and Roberts, *Women and Employment*, table 6.12, p. 70.

40 Ibid., table 6.15, p. 72.

41 See for instance the results of the SIME–DIME income maintenance experiments in the United States, quoted in Neil Gilbert, *Capitalism and the Welfare State: Dilemmas of Social Benevolence*, Yale University Press, 1983, pp. 36–8 and 98.

42 C. Kerr, J. T. Dunlop, F. H. Harbison and C. A. Myers, *Individualism and Industrial Man*, Harvard University Press, 1960.

43 A. Stewart, R. M. Blackburn and K. Prandy, 'Gender and Earnings: The Failure of Market Explanations', in Roberts et al., *New Approaches to Economic Life*.

8

Households

The household is the basic unit of co-operation in society. I argued in the first part of the book that households, like other small informal groups, were organized mainly round a notion of fairness, with contributions according to abilities and benefits according to needs, and that they tried to equalize the welfare of their members.

In this, households have the advantage of being sufficiently small and intimate to maximize the flexibility of personal negotiations about welfare shares. But their disadvantage is the differentiation in the members' roles. When households were subsistence production units, this was not marked; men, women and children worked together on the same tasks. With economic development, the roles of father and mother became more differentiated. I have argued that the structure of the nuclear family of the postwar era assumed that a married woman embraced the roles of wife, mother and domestic worker as a project, and that, once this assumption was challenged, women could be seen to be less free than men, and hence their household role seen to be unfair. In the last chapter I analysed married women's re-entry into the sphere of paid employment, along with the other changes in patterns of labour utilization and earnings in the advanced capitalist countries. In this chapter I shall consider how the structure of households and the ways they share welfare have changed in response to altered perceptions and the new economic environment, and the implications of these changes.

As the social unit that mediates between the individual and wider society, the household has to balance not only the competitive and co-operative aspirations of its members, but also the demands of the other social spheres for both competition and co-operation. In the economic sphere, capitalist society is structured so that people's shares from participation (through employment) go mainly into the household. From one perspective, the family – as the major institution for consuming personal income, accumulating and transferring personal wealth and privilege from generation to generation – is the mainspring of individualistic competition, and the social grouping which most inhibits co-operation among larger groups or classes. It is a cliché nowadays, for sportsmen (especially), when asked to justify their apparent ingratitude, disloyalty or greed in moving to a more lucrative contract with a foreign club, or to live in a tax haven, to say 'I'm doing it for my family.'

From another perspective, the household is the main forum in which sharing and giving can take place, where people can set aside their atomistic existence as market producers and consumers and show real concern for the needs of others. From this point of view, the problem posed by the household as a unit of social organization is not its values but its small size and exclusiveness. Because unequal resources from the economic sphere enter households, and because give and take is confined within the domestic sphere, the caring and sharing that takes place within these units does little to ensure fairness in wider distribution, or to meet certain social needs.

I have argued that the domestic sphere is closely related to other informal spheres of social organization – friendship networks, voluntary groups, neighbourhoods and communities – and that these systems are adapted in response to the impersonal processes of the formal systems. My argument so far would suggest that these informal systems tend to 'humanize' the outcomes of the formal ones, to redistribute welfare in the direction of fairness, equality and personal needs. However, in so far as all these informal networks tend to be organized on class lines, or at least to select people of similar socioeconomic status, they can all be expected to some extent to reinforce fundamental inequalities in the original distribution of resources through formal processes. All the research suggests that people tend to choose marriage partners, friends and acquaintances from similar backgrounds to their own, to join clubs which are relatively socially homogeneous, and to live in neighbourhoods where they meet others like themselves more often than people from different income groups. The housing, leisure and holiday markets are structured in such a way that richer people can pay for exclusiveness in the informal parts of their lives, even if they have to rub shoulders with the poor in the streets, in the shops or even at their workplace.

So there are three sets of questions that I want to address in this chapter. In the first place, I want to look at how households themselves are changing, in composition, structure, roles and processes. Second, I want to analyse how these changes relate to those in formal systems, and how they affect the overall distribution of welfare in society. Third, I want to consider their effects on individual projects, and on fairness as between men and women.

Household Composition

The most striking change in the pattern of household composition since the Second World War is the decline in the proportion of households consisting of two adults and dependent children. Whereas in 1951 these represented 40 per cent of all households in Britain, by 1983 they were only 30 per cent.[1]

Meanwhile, the proportion of households consisting of one person only had increased from 10.7 per cent in 1951 to 23 per cent in 1983. Similar patterns can now be found in all the major European countries, with even higher proportions of single-person households in West Germany and France, and lower proportions of couples with children in these countries also.[2] Single parents with dependent children form 4 per cent of British households, a proportion exceeded only in West Germany of the major European countries. All these changes mean that in Britain and elsewhere in Western Europe less than half of the individuals in the total population live in households consisting of couples and dependent children.[3]

The fastest growing age category in Western European populations is the elderly. In Britain the number of people aged 75 and over increased from 1.8 million in 1951 to 3.1 million in 1981.[4] People aged 65 and over formed 15.2 per cent of the British population in 1981; in the ten countries of the European Community they formed 14.2 per cent of the population.[5] It is especially among elderly people that the highest ratios of single-person households are to be found – in France, 51.5 per cent of people over 65 live alone, in Belgium 53.6 per cent, in Italy 49.5 per cent.[6] In Britain the proportions of elderly people living alone are rather lower, but are increasing rapidly: among those over 75, the proportion grew from 40 per cent in 1973 to 47 per cent in 1983.[7]

However, there are also growing proportions of people in other age groups who live alone; in Britain in 1983 only 2 per cent of people under 25 did so, but the proportion of single-person households aged 25–44 doubled between 1973 and 1983 to 4 per cent, and the proportion aged 45–64 increased from 8 to 9 per cent.[8] Single-person households raise particular problems for housing and income maintenance services, since their housing and fuel costs are disproportionately large. Elderly single-person households also consume disproportionate amounts of health and personal social services resources.

Other European countries have much higher proportions of single-person households among younger age groups than Britain. In West Germany and France, for instance (both of which had a higher overall proportion of single-person households than Britain) the proportions of these in 1971 where the householder was under 45 were 26.4 and 24.6 respectively, compared with Britain's 12.6 per cent.[9] In West Germany the proportion of single-person households aged under 25 was 7.4 per cent and in France 7.7 per cent, compared with Britain's 1.5 per cent in 1977.[10]

Not only are a growing number of elderly people being cared for by family members (usually in the households of daughters), but the care-givers themselves are an ageing population. In Britain in 1983, 5 per cent of all men over 80 and 12 per cent of all women over 80 were living with their children.[11] But the pool of potential family carers is shrinking. In Britain it has been estimated that an average couple in their eighties might have 40 surviving female relatives, whereas a couple reaching that age after the year 2000 will have only 11.[12]

The picture that is emerging, therefore, is one of a continued fall in the average size of households, but also one of an enormous variety of household compositon. As the British Office of Population Censuses and Surveys remarks, what is outstanding is the 'diversity of family groups present in contemporary households'.[13] Similarly, the Eurostat Statistical Office, though drawing attention to the continued existence of extended families in the more agricultural societies of Ireland and Italy, remarks on the dominance of the 'mono-nuclear and smaller families':

> The smallest families and the families with largest proportions of working members are to be found in France, Germany and the United Kingdom. Such families are therefore in receipt of several salaries. Particularly noteworthy is the high proportion of working wives in these countries, even though they often work part-time. . . . single-member households – although relatively uncommon – are encountered more frequently, extended families are quite rare and quite a large proportion of nuclear families consist of couples with no children.[14]

Yet what is disturbing is the evidence that, in spite of this strong trend towards a dominant structure of households that are well adapted to the new structure of labour markets (multi-earner, fewer dependants), there is still a substantial minority of households (even those that should apparently fit well with this pattern) which have very low earnings, or no earnings at all. This is most marked in Britain, where almost half (47.2 per cent) of all the individuals living in the bottom 20 per cent of income units are couples with children, and exactly half of these households had a male 'head' in work, while in the other half the male head was unemployed – suggesting that unemployment, low wages and single-earner households all contribute to the relative increase in poverty in this type of household. In 1971 only 39.7 per cent of individuals in the bottom 20 per cent of income units were couples and children.[15]

But despite this growth in poverty among British families with children, this was not the only group which increased its proportion of members in the bottom 20 per cent of income units. Single people of working age increased from 9.7 to 15.7 per cent, and one-parent families from 8.8 to 9.9 per cent, between 1971 and 1982; even couples without children increased from 7.0 to 8.0 per cent. Only pensioners declined considerably in their population – from 34.9 to 19.2 per cent.[16]

Household Roles and Tasks

How does the internal organization of households (roles, activities, management of resources) relate to that of wider society, and especially to the economic sphere? What do households *do*, and how do they decide how to do it? To try to answer these questions, we have to rely on a rather different sort of research and analysis from the ones that provide information from the formal spheres of social organization. I shall draw particularly on an important and extensive recent study by Ray Pahl, *Divisions of Labour*.

Pahl looks at the household organization of work (both paid and unpaid) in terms of strategies for 'getting by'.[17] The partnership between men and women to get a livelihood is not necessarily consciously constructed or agreed – it may be implicit or customary. A household work strategy, according to Pahl, is one which makes 'the best use of resources for getting by under given social and economic conditions'.[18] This necessarily consists of a mixture of paid work outside the household, unpaid work within it, and unpaid work both for and by the members of other households. The object of the whole exercise is to get the necessary resources, and to get the work done.

Historical research shows that in Britain there was no sudden transition between an era of exclusively subsistence production and one of waged labour; from the early mediaeval period most people had some resources for production for their own use and also did paid work, often on a day or seasonal basis.[19] It was not until the seventeenth century that landless labourers became an identifiable, impoverished class in Britain, and the wives of superior tradesmen were given the roles of unpaid domestic adornments, who took no part in production.[20] In the eighteenth century most men still had several occupations, and most married women also did paid work.[21] So it was not until after the industrial revolution, and especially in this century, that most households came to depend on the earnings of a 'breadwinner' in a single occupation, and the full-time domestic services of his wife. Furthermore, it was only then that most men expected to be employed all the year round, and not to have to rely on part-time or casual work and savings from previous seasonal work to make good gaps in earnings. Social security benefits for interruptions of earnings completed this circle of increased specialization of labour outside the household, and its tendency to specialize work roles within it also. Men came to provide the resources for getting by, and women the labour for transforming these resources into services to meet the needs of family members.

Pahl argues that household strategies have been adapted to the labour market changes described in the last chapter, and to other shifts within the formal spheres. Not only have women returned to a far more active economic role, mainly through part-time paid employment; there has also been an upsurge in self-servicing activities, especially centred on home improvements.[22] Do-it-yourself building and maintenance has become the fastest growing sector of the building industry. As owner-occupation has become the dominant tenure in the housing market, and as inflation has made houses the dominant form of personal wealth, increased activity has come to involve both husbands and wives.[23] As opportunities for increased earnings through male employment diminish, self-servicing becomes a relatively more productive form of work and use of household resources.[24] Pahl argues that home ownership has come to be of greater political significance, in terms of consciousness, than the occupation of the 'breadwinner', and that home-owners make up the majority of the 'middle mass' in British society. 'Of all the forms of work, the one that has the most political significance for the middle mass is self-provisioning.'[25]

But Pahl makes it clear that the increase in self-servicing by households is conditional on income from employment. People need good incomes to be able to afford the equipment to carry out home improvements, just as they need good and secure incomes to be able to buy houses to improve. Multi-earner households meet these income needs best, and also provide the most flexible and efficient labour supplies for self-servicing activities; it is in such households that most self-servicing occurs. Furthermore, 'while there may be signs of some shift towards greater sharing of tasks in households where both members are in employment, when the male is unemployed there is no sign of such a shift.'[26] Pahl describes a polarization between households which are most active, both in the external labour market of paid work and in self-servicing, and households on benefits, often living in local authority houses, where there is no paid employment and little self-servicing activity.

What Pahl seems to be describing from his massive survey evidence is a return to something like the situation before the modern era. Instead of depending primarily on the full-time earnings of a male breadwinner, households that are more successful appear to depend on a combination of several incomes, some of them from part-time work or 'spare-time' jobs, and on the use of income from these sources to provide equipment for equally productive unpaid work in the form of home improvement, car maintenance and so on. But, unlike eighteenth-century Britain, today's society does not give equal access to these opportunities, because they do not depend on common rights, widespread resources or plentiful seasonal jobs. Instead, they depend partly on having exclusive property rights (owner-occupied housing), partly on having expensive private equipment (cars, power tools) and partly on access to employment, which is very unequally distributed, since households headed by claimants of benefits are effectively barred from part-time work.

'Getting By' and 'Getting On'

Pahl's work is of great value and interest, but in some ways his conceptual framework does not do justice to his material. The household strategies he describes are clearly something more than ways of 'getting the work done' or 'getting by': some of them are aimed at improving the household's relative status, at increasing its resources, and hence its control over external events. His own evidence suggests that much self-servicing work, far from being mere maintenance, is actually a major means of improving the household's position in society. People do up their houses to sell them and move to more desirable areas, to homes with higher status and value. He describes 'the vigour with which people renovated or improved their houses' in relation to the 'rising or falling status' of individual streets or roads in the area.[27] 'People who want a better way of life for themselves and their families perceive that they can most readily achieve this through a distinctive mix of all forms of work by all members of the household.'[28]

It is clear from Pahl's own account of researches into mediaeval households that the same was true from early times. In R. M. Smith's picture of thirteenth-century Suffolk, there were three major groupings: those with so few resources that they relied mainly on paid work outside the household; those with more resources who both gave and took in substantial amounts of unpaid household work among kin and neighbours; and those rich enough to pay for all the services they received from outside the household. The middle group was much the most quarrelsome as well as the most collaborative, as households strove to improve their position in a perpetual flux. There was an active market in land, and holdings of this most essential resource were constantly changing.[29] Later studies show a similar picture of individuals and households struggling to gain autonomy and command over resources in competition as well as co-operation with others; village communities were far from stable and unchanging, and land markets provided one of the means of constant change, while informal labour provided another. Pahl's account of the Isle of Sheppey in the 1980s makes it clear that his 'middle mass' of owner-occupiers were very similar in their competitive aspirations, and he himself describes them as firmly in the tradition which Alan Macfarlane traces back to the thirteenth century – one of robust individualism, independence and commercial striving.

Pahl's distinction between 'middle mass' and 'underclass' is made substantially in terms of housing tenure, on the grounds that owner-occupation favours the life-style of domesticity and provides both scope and incentive for self-servicing which brings rewards of status and resource accumulation. By contrast, among tenants, and especially local authority tenants, poverty and lack of incentive for such unpaid work go hand in hand. However, just as in the Middle Ages, the real situation is not nearly so static.

People's situations can change quite quickly, and not all households respond in the same way to apparently similar circumstances. The growing market in council houses, self-employment and opportunities for cash jobs all allow much more fluidity than Pahl's categories would suggest.

Early indications from our own researches in Exeter[30] suggest a wide variation in reactions to apparently similar economic circumstances. In a sample of 13 households (our pilot study for a project on labour market decision-making in low-income households), we found two men of working age who were not actively seeking work – one claiming unemployment benefit, the other supplementary benefit (he would have been liable for maintenance payments to an ex-wife and children if he had been in employment). But we also found four men whose decisions about work were framed in terms of avoiding the necessity ever to claim supplementary benefit again, because of the inadequacy of the benefit rates, restrictive conditions, delays, inefficiency, insult or degradation. The three self-employed men in the sample had all taken on this form of work after redundancy or being sacked; all three related their decision to being on state benefits previously and finding it difficult to manage financially. Yet another two men saw benefits as a fall-back because employment was inevitably insecure and unpredictable; but the three who had been in full-time regular employment with the same employer for most of their adult lives took no account of benefits in framing their decisions. It was also interesting that, of the three families who were buying their own council houses, two were self-employed, and had made the decision to buy despite experience of job insecurity and (in one case) having been recently claiming means-tested family income supplement and housing benefit. Five men and one woman admitted to doing 'cash jobs' which were not declared to the income tax authorities; these included the self-employed men, who regarded it as a legitimate way of 'getting on' (by limiting their tax bills), and two were building workers, one of whom also worked occasionally for cash when claiming supplementary benefit.

Once we recognize that households may try (either over a long period, or in an intense burst) to increase their holdings of resources, their earning power, their status in relation to others or their efficiency in self-servicing, we can see that important issues of fairness are at stake here. Some ways of giving people enough resources to get by disadvantage them in their joint projects for getting on. Self-employment is very risky compared with living on benefits, yet some people are prepared to take this risk rather than endure the constraints (and perhaps also the struggle and stigma) of being claimants. Owner-occupation is risky compared with being a tenant, especially when it involves losing housing benefits and incurring higher mortgage payments. These examples raise the issue of whether it is possible to meet people's basic needs without limiting their opportunities for projects in other spheres.

Household Strategies and Individual Projects

The other important issue is whether marital partners have fair opportunities to follow their individual projects. Pahl's way of looking at household strategies in terms of getting by emphasized co-operation in making the best of energies and resources. There was little evidence in his data of the strains and tensions which lead to the high rates of divorce and separation in modern society. Do the new divisions of labour he uncovered really meet criteria of fairness and allow both partners enough freedom to pursue their personal welfare? Pahl found that households with several earners and high levels of informal (self-provisioning) work divided these unpaid tasks on less gender-based lines; those with unemployed 'heads', in which less informal work took place, were structured on traditional gender-based allocation of tasks. But this tells us nothing about the conflicts between individuals associated with either strategy. It may well be that higher work rates and more active co-operation provoke heightened tensions and conflicts. Certainly Smith found this in thirteenth-century Suffolk; the middle range of households, which co-operated most by lending and borrowing informal labour, also had the most quarrels and disputes between them.

It would hardly be surprising if this were the case. In modern advanced economies, women are beginning to get greater access to the labour market, but they are still seen mainly as secondary earners, and their levels of pay reflect this, as do their hours of work. On the other hand, they are more likely to be very satisfied with their jobs than men, and less likely to be very dissatisfied. Furthermore, in the present state of the labour market, they may well have more control over their working conditions. With these very different experiences in segmented and contrasting labour markets, co-operation in joint projects raises many role problems. How exactly can welfare be equalized, and fairness in benefits from and contributions to household welfare be achieved, when so many men do better paid full-time work in unchosen and partly disliked jobs, and so many women do badly paid part-time work in chosen and liked jobs? And how can the roles be equal when the woman depends on the man for income, still does most of the domestic and care-giving 'maintenance' work, and usually gives up a possible 'career' in full-time work to bear children? This raises a whole series of difficult issues of comparability, and gives endless scope for resentment and dispute once basic trust and goodwill are eroded. Co-operation does not start from an equal partnership between couples.

Research gives some indications of the factors which make for strain between household strategies and individual projects, and the ways couples try to resolve it. In the survey by Jean Martin and Ceridwen Roberts of *Women in Employment*, the average gross hourly earnings of husbands was £3.00, compared with wives' £1.90 (full-time) and £1.60 (part-time).[31] The combination of higher earnings, better career prospects and full-time employment for husbands meant that wives sometimes adjusted their work to their husbands' employment needs: 20 per cent said their work status was affected by the husband's employment; of these, half of the working and three-quarters of the non-working wives found their husbands' working hours inconvenient.[32] In their large sample, 99 per cent of married women did at least half of the domestic work, but of the wives in full-time employment, 44 per cent said they shared housework tasks equally with their husbands, while 23 per cent of part-time employees described domestic work as equally shared.[33] On the other hand, 13 per cent of wives who were full-time employees said they did all the housework and 41 per cent that they did most of it.[34] Most wives (77 per cent) said they thought the amount of domestic work their husbands did was 'about right', and only 20 per cent said that they did not do enough.[35]

The fact that husbands and wives both gave exactly the same overall assessment of the fairness of their division of domestic labour suggested that some conscious attempt had been made to negotiate about this. Fifty per cent of wives thought that child care tasks were equally shared, and 67 per cent of those working full-time described it as shared equally. Here, 85 per cent of wives and 79 per cent of husbands felt their division of labour was 'about right'.[36]

Martin and Roberts also found that over half of their sample of married women said that their husbands would be happy for them to take paid work only if it fitted in with family life, and that nearly two-thirds of those not working said their husbands liked them to be at home when they were.[37] Of those wives working full-time, three-quarters said they liked having some money to spend as they chose, and that they liked being able to contribute to family income; 61 per cent said that earning their own money gave them a sense of independence; and 44 per cent said they did not like being dependent on their husbands for money. By comparison, only 29 per cent of non-working wives said they missed the feeling of independence that earning their own money would give, and only 23 per cent said that they did not like being dependent on their husbands for money.[38] Other research has shown that the system of pooling family income predominates in households where husbands and wives are in employment, whereas that of the husband giving an allowance to his wife for housekeeping is confined mainly to one-earner households.[39]

But there are other important welfare problems within households. The needs of dependants are not always compatible with the abilities and the projects of able-bodied adults. Although I argued in chapter 4 that most households seem to be organized around an attempt to meet need as fairly as possible, need does not always arise in easily manageable forms, nor do members always have the resources to meet it. For the well-to-do this problem can be overcome through the market. The duty of able-bodied adults to care for their dependants is a moral responsibility, not a physical requirement; rich people are held to have discharged their obligations fully when they pay others less well-off than themselves to be nannies, nurses, governesses, companions or servants. Hence even exceptional dependency needs may not pose any difficulties for the rich – they simply buy in the services they require.

For ordinary people on average incomes, however, a severely handicapped child, or an elderly person in the household who is frail in body or mind, can place enormous demands on human and material resources. Not only do such members tie up time and energy that might otherwise go to paid and unpaid work; they also create care-taking roles which are unlikely to be equally shared between able-bodied adults. This often means that one partner becomes specialized in earning much-needed income, while the other becomes a specialist carer. In the absence of adequate child benefits, even a larger-than-average number of children can have this effect on marital roles.[40]

It would seem obvious that the state's personal social services exist precisely to offset this inequality between households, which means that the overall resources and available abilities of some are severaly reduced by dependency needs. Yet in fact, the evidence is that in Britain most such households get very little in the way of services in kind. Domiciliary care (home helps, meals on wheels, home nursing), day care and social work support all go overwhelmingly to disabled, handicapped or frail elderly people living on their own, while residential care is an alternative to family care.[41] State social services give much less direct assistance to households where a dependent member is being cared for by relatives.

If we look at the case of households which fail to meet the dependency needs of children who are not severely handicapped, a similar picture emerges. The state finds it difficult to *share* the care of children with families who are short of resources, either materially or emotionally. In general terms, social workers try to assess whether families can bring their children up or not, and they admit children to public care if the parents are deemed incapable. Requests for reception into care during difficult periods (family disruption or problem behaviour by the child) are treated with suspicion, and taken as signals of parental inadequacy rather than requests for a sharing of responsibility, or an expert service.[42] Jean Packman in a recent study found that most social workers saw care as a last resort, as a sign of family failure, and preferred routes into care involving compulsory removal of children, even when voluntary care had been requested. Where children were not admitted to care, services and support offered were limited; a third of respondents, when asked what social workers had done to help, gave answers which the researchers put in the generic category 'Bugger all'.[43]

It seems that the state's personal social services are used mainly as alternatives or substitutes to the unpaid care given by households, rather than as supplements to household abilities and resources; the same could also be said about services for the chronically ill and handicapped. In this way they mirror state income maintenance systems, which largely replace earnings from the labour market. But there has been increased demand for these services, simply by virtue of the changing composition of the population and of households. A combination of improved health services and demographic change has meant that there are more elderly people in the population, that more of them have severe or moderate disabilities, and that more are living alone or with relatives.[44] The implications of these facts for health and personal social services policy will be considered in chapters 11 and 12.

Conclusions

Theorists who have suggested that a moral order underlies the formal structure of society have usually located this order in the household. The family is seen as the sphere of altruism, caring and compassion not only in religious thought, but also in early modern political theory. Social science has continued to see household roles as crucial for sharing welfare, and modern welfare state systems assume – and try to reinforce – a structure of mutual family support.

But if the domestic system distributed welfare perfectly fairly among household members, then each member would be guaranteed his or her due once the average resources per individual of each household (in terms of income and wealth) were equalized. The unit of account in social policy would be households, since fairness within them would be assured. Members could safely be left to make this distribution among themselves.

Yet we know it is not so simple. The sharing of welfare in households is a matter for constant negotiation and adjustment. The roles demanded of members by formal systems – employee, schoolchild, tenant, pensioner and so on – in turn influence roles in the doemstic sphere. So the roles of husband and wife, parent and child, carer and dependant are shaped and reshaped in response to changes in formal systems, in a complex and changing process. Formal roles outside the household give members a very different (and unequal) basis for negotiating the terms of these membership roles within it.

Inequalities in resources and needs further complicate the picture. The rich can pay outsiders to be daily or temporary members of their households, performing certain tasks as employees. The comfortably-off have some choice over which tasks to do for themselves and which to pay for. This leaves a proportion of households who lack the income or the labour power to provide for themselves – who rely on state benefits and services to meet their basic needs over long periods of time.

These processes themselves tend to some extent to distribute welfare more fairly. As the rich pay for services, they give extra income to less prosperous households; as the state's services grow, they give employment and earnings as well as low-cost resources to the poor. Recently, these extra employees in both marketed and state services have been married women, which has enhanced their opportunities outside the domestic sphere.

But I have argued that not all recent changes tend towards greater fairness within or between households. More households depend wholly or mainly on state benefits and services. These create domestic and social roles which restrict participation in other spheres. Many women are still trapped within the household, especially single parents, those with young children, disabled or elderly dependants and wives of unemployed men. Opportunities for sharing domestic tasks are limited by the full-time basis of most male employment. Women's earnings in most capitalist countries are still artificially low. The rich have more choices over roles than the rest. All this means that members of households cannot be assumed to negotiate about how to share welfare from a starting point of equality, or to be able to reach a final distribution which is fair for all.

Furthermore, if fewer households have any member with access to the security, status, pay and prospects associated with employment in the corporate sector, then the informal resources of households are becoming more important in issues of overall fairness in society. This implies that the boundaries of welfare need to be shifted so as to allow informal household co-operation to take place with adequate resources, under conditions of adequate security. If corporate social organization is waning at the expense of growing market isolation, then individuals may need to pursue a larger proportion of their welfare projects in the informal sphere, and social welfare provision should be organized to take account of this.

Notes

1 Central Statistical Office, *Social Trends, 1970*, HMSO, 1970, table 15, p. 58; Office of Population Censuses and Surveys, *General Household Survey, 1983*, HMSO, 1985, table 3.5, p. 14.
2 Eurostat, *Economic and Social Features of Households in the Member States of the European Community*, Statistical Office of the European Communities, 1982, table II.4, p. 75.
3 *General Household Survey, 1983*, table 3.6, p. 14.
4 Central Statistical Office, *Social Trends, 1984*, HMSO, 1984, table 1.2, p. 18.
5 Eurostat, *Demographic Statistics, 1984*, Statistical Office of the European Communities, 1985, table 2, p. 146, and table IV, p. 71.
6 Eurostat, *Economic and Social Features of Households*, p. 24.
7 *General Household Survey, 1983*, table 3A, p. 11.
8 Ibid.

9　Eurostat, *Economic and Social Features of Households*, table 1.5, p. 40.

10　Ibid., table II.15, p. 88.

11　*General Household Survey, 1983*, table 3.7, p. 15.

12　J. Ermisch, *The Political Economy of Demographic Change*, Heinemann, 1983, p. 283.

13　*General Household Survey, 1983*, p. 16.

14　Eurostat, *Economic and Social Features of Households*, p. 8.

15　DHSS, *Reform of Social Security* (Fowler Report), Cmnd 9519, vol. 3, Background Papers, fig. 1.3, p. 9. In fact, of those families with a male head in work, the vast majority would be single-earner households. Roger Mitton, Peter Willmott and Phyllis Willmott, *Unemployment, Poverty and Social Policy in Europe*, Occasional Paper on Social Administration 71, Bedford Square Press, 1983, p. 27, found that, among the bottom 20 per cent of household incomes in France, Belgium and Britain, 'Households with more than one worker were rarely in poverty, even though secondary members often had low earnings.'

16　*Reform of Social Security*, vol. 3, Background Papers, fig. 1.3, p. 9.

17　R. E. Pahl, *Divisions of Labour*, Basil Blackwell, 1984, p. 20.

18　Ibid.

19　Pahl quotes a number of local studies of records from English parishes, particularly R. M. Smith, 'Kin and Neighbours in a Thirteenth-century Suffolk Community', *Journal of Family History*, vol. 4(3), 1979, pp. 219–56; M. Chaytor, 'Household and Kinship: Ryton in the Late Sixteenth and Early Seventeenth Centuries', *History Workshop Journal*, vol. 10, 1980, pp. 25–60; and R. Machin, *Probate Inventories and Manorial Excerpts of Chetnole Leigh and Yetminster*, University of Bristol, 1976. See also the studies quoted in Alan Macfarlane, *The Origins of English Individualism*, Basil Blackwell, 1978.

20　For the emergence of a class of landless labourers see Christopher Hill, 'Potage for Free-born Englishmen: Attitudes to Wage Labour in the Sixteenth and Seventeenth Centuries', in C. H. Feinstein (ed.), *Socialism, Capitalism and Economic Growth*, Cambridge University Press, 1967. For the transformation of the role of women see Margaret George, 'From "Goodwife" to "Mistress": The Transformation of the Female in Bourgeois Culture', *Science and Society*, vol. 37(2), 1973. For the ideological basis of these changes, John Locke's writings are an interesting source, especially his 'Some Considerations of the Consequences of the Lowering of Interest, and Raising the Value of Money', in *The Works of John Locke in Four Volumes*, W. Strachan et al, 1777, vol. II, especially pp. 10–46. See Bill Jordan, *The State: Authority and Autonomy*, Basil Blackwell, 1985, ch. 2. See also C. B. Macpherson, *The Political Theory of Possessive Individualism: Hobbes to Locke*, Oxford University Press, 1962. Pahl argues, following K. D. M. Snell ('Agricultural Seasonal Employment: The Standard of Living and Women's Work in the South and East, 1690–1860', *Economic History Review*, 1980, p. 413) that the use of heavier scythes from 1750 excluded women from the harvesting of wheat and rye, and initiated a gender-based division of labour in British agriculture, though women continued to have an important role in farm work, which varied between regions.

21　Pahl, *Divisions of Labour*, p. 48. He also quotes R. W. Malcolmson, *Life and Labour in England, 1700–1780*, Hutchinson, 1981, p. 57: 'the family economy was not normally centred around a single breadwinner: rather it was assumed that the family's sustenance would depend on the productive contributions of all its members, each of whom helped to sustain the whole. A wife was always a working woman.'

22 Pahl cites a good deal of evidence from building trade sources about the growth of do-it-yourself activities. In 1981 almost 60 per cent of households owned a power drill (p. 104), and 84 per cent of adults aged 25 or over painted interior woodwork, 40 per cent put up shelves, 28 per cent plastered and 13 per cent installed some form of heat installation in any year (table 4.4, p. 105, from *The Polycell Report on the DIY Market*, Pergamon, 1981).

23 Statistics show an increase in do-it-yourself home improvements done jointly by husband and wife; nearly half are now done jointly, and 60 per cent in the northern region. Pahl, *Divisions of Labour*, table 4.3, p. 103.

24 For another account of the growth of the domestic sphere as 'the sphere of autonomy', see Andre Gorz, *Farewell to the Working Class: An Essay in Post-Industrial Socialism*, Pluto, 1980.

25 Pahl, *Divisions of Labour*, p. 334.

26 Ibid., p. 327.

27 Ibid., p. 326.

28 Ibid., p. 327.

29 Ibid., pp. 21–3; quoting Smith, 'Kin and Neighbours in a Thirteenth-century Suffolk Community'.

30 Simon James, Bill Jordan and Helen Kay, 'Labour Supply Decisions in Low Income Households', Exeter University, unpublished. This was a pilot study for research to be undertaken in 1986–7. The interviewer asked members of low-income households to describe changes in paid employment during the previous three years, to mention the factors which influenced the changes, their aims in making them, and how the decisions had worked out. She also asked about overtime, promotion and training in the same terms, and about changes in housing. Income tax and social security benefits were not mentioned in the questions, and it was only at the end of the interview that respondents were asked whether they had ever been influenced by these factors, if they had not already indicated this in their answers. The aim was thus to see how people actually framed decisions about paid work, whether they knew about poverty-traps, and if so how they conceptualized the problems of high effective marginal tax rates in their decision-making.

31 Jean Martin and Ceridwen Roberts, *Women and Employment: A Lifetime Perspective*, Department of Employment and Office of Population Censuses and Surveys, 1984, p. 98. These are averages for the two-thirds of women who knew about, or were prepared to reveal, their husbands' earnings. Women not in paid employment had husbands with slightly higher earnings, on average. Only 7 per cent of wives earned the same as or more than their husbands. Heather Joshi, *Women's Participation in Paid Work: Further Analysis of the Women and Employment Survey*, Department of Employment Survey no. 45, 1984, found that marriage and children not only caused a break in women's careers, but also caused them to take part-time work for which they were overqualified. She estimated the loss of women's earnings over a lifetime through this factor at 25–50 per cent.

32 Martin and Roberts, *Women and Employment*, p. 99 and table 8.6, p. 100.

33 Ibid., table 8.7, p. 101 and p. 100.

34 Ibid., table 8.7. Of the part-time working wives, 26 per cent said they did all of the domestic work, and 51 per cent, most of it. The husbands' view tended to be that fewer wives did all of the work and more most of it; the same proportion described it as equally shared.

35 Ibid., table 8.8, p. 101. More wives who were not working thought their division of labour was 'about right' (80 per cent), and full-time working wives were marginally the least satisfied (74 per cent).

36 Ibid., pp. 101–2, and tables 8.9 and 8.10, p. 102. Here women not working were marginally less satisfied with their division of labour than women in paid work.

37 Ibid., table 8.19, p. 107.

38 Ibid., and table 8.18, p. 106.

39 Jan Pahl, 'The Allocation of Money within the Household', in M. Freeman (ed.), *State, Law and the Family*, Tavistock, 1984. Overall, around 55 per cent of British households use the pooling system (in which both partners have access to all or nearly all the household money and both are responsible for managing the common pool and for expenditure drawn from it) and 23 per cent the allowance system (in which the wife gets a set amount of money for certain expenditures, while the husband retains the rest and pays for all other items).

40 The Equal Opportunities Commission estimates that there are at least 1.25 million full-time carers in Britain, mostly caring for an elderly person; 75 per cent of these are women, the largest group being daughters (27 per cent), followed by wives (17 per cent) and mothers (13 per cent) – but 16 per cent of carers are husbands. Equal Opportunities Commission, *Caring for the Elderly and Handicapped: Community Care Policies and Women's Lives*, March 1982. In her *Shadow DHSS Circular on Carers* (February 1986), Harriet Harman of the Labour Party argued that the full-time caring role carried six times the average risk of physical and mental breakdown.

41 R. M. Moroney, *The Family and the State: Considerations for Social Policy*, Longman, 1976.

42 Jean Packman, *Who Needs Care? Social Work Decisions about Children*, Basil Blackwell, 1986.

43 Ibid., p. 185.

44 See for instance Alan Walker, *The Care Gap: How Can Local Authorities Meet the Needs of the Elderly?* Local Government Information Unit, 1965.

Part Three

Social Policy and Welfare

9

Social Policy and Basic Needs

In the first part of this book I argued that there was an informal, co-operative basis of all social relations, which underlay formal systems of allocating roles and resources. The values which inform this moral order are also applied to large-scale, impersonal systems of co-operation, and this was shown to be problematic in many ways. Whereas in small-scale informal associations it is possible to make negotiated adjustments in welfare shares, formal systems do not readily allow this.

This means that the terms on which individuals enter into large-scale co-operative associations are a very important determinant of the fairness of the outcomes of their participation in them. Unless some way can be found to ensure that individuals join wider society as (in some sense) equals, and have the opportunity to withdraw from disadvantageous transactions with some security, it is likely that they will be harmed or exploited. The alternative to providing some initial form of equality is to provide a whole range of interventions which alter the outcomes of formal systems by compensating individuals in the name of fairness.

In advanced capitalist countries, the state has become increasingly involved in provision of both kinds – in trying to give individuals the education, health and personal security they need for effective economic and social participation, and in trying to compensate them when they are unsuccessful in those spheres. If anything, the balance seems to be shifting in the direction of the latter kind of provision, particularly in the form of financial and material support for people who have been unable to gain an adequate share from employment. This in turn has led to renewed disputes about whether the social services operate fairly, and whether they incorporate standards of fairness.

In this chapter I want to focus on the case for the first kind of provision and specifically for giving resources sufficient for basic needs as part of the state's relationship with the individual citizen. Political authority provides a *general* framework of rights and responsibilities in society. The state defines the relationship between itself and its citizens (what it owes them and what they should do), and between citizens. So the overall framework in which co-operation takes place has changed and developed along with new definitions of the rights and duties of citizenship.

If households can be assumed to be capable of meeting the basic needs of all their members (for example, by subsistence production), then the state has no role in social provision – the household has a simple duty to provide for itself, and the state gives (in return for taxes and military service) law and order and defence. So long as waged employment by members can be perceived as the household 'providing for itself', the labour market changes none of this. But as soon as the state gives work, income or productive resources to individuals or households, it redefines the rights and duties of citizenship. If the recipients of state provision are potential wage-earners, their obligations are likely to include the duty to accept available paid employment, to maintain their dependants, and to follow a settled (law-abiding) way of life.[1] If they are outside the labour market, their rights and duties will be defined according to their household status. All this was most obviously the case under the original Poor Laws, and still persists in modern social assistance schemes based on household means tests. Social insurance schemes establish more complex rules of entitlement through contributions in employment, but the duties they imply are similar.

The postwar welfare state's moral foundation therefore lies in the notion that households 'normally' meet the basic needs of their members through income from the labour market and through unpaid work for each other. The state undertakes to substitute for this income or this care where they are unobtainable in this 'normal' way. That makes very large assumptions (as we saw in chapter 6) about the ability of the labour market to provide employment, the willingness of employers to provide adequate wages, the ability of married women to meet dependency needs, and their willingness to do this on an unpaid domestic basis.

There are many indications that the moral foundations of the welfare state are crumbling. Not the least of these is the appeal by market-minded political leaders (especially Ronald Reagan and Margaret Thatcher) to the moral values of the last century, or to even older religious traditions. The direction of these appeals is to a faith in the power of markets to replicate the subsistence economy – to distribute resources in such a way that households can 'provide for themselves'. It is also to strengthen belief in the notion that almost all households have within them the labour power to care for 'their' dependants. These appeals are made against a background of the manifest failure of markets to make any such distribution, and the growth of the proportion of households obviously incapable of caring for themselves. The welfare state is failing, not because it undermines the ethics upon which the labour market and the family are founded, but because those ethics no longer reflect the realities of employment and household composition in modern advanced capitalist states.

I want to argue that our moral duties to each other have not changed as a result of socioeconomic development. We still owe it to each other to give and take, to be fair, to respect each other's rights to choices, and to share welfare according to abilities and needs; we still find it easiest to do this in households and in networks of informally chosen friends and acquaintances. What has changed is the formal system in which we find our roles and get our resources, and this in turn has altered what we are sharing in the informal system, and how we go about sharing it. These changes require a redefinition by the state of our rights and duties in relation to itself and to each other – a redefinition of the terms of citizenship.

We can only share the resources we have; we can only use the abilities we possess; we are constrained by the roles available to us in the formal system. One of the major restrictions on the application of fairness and co-operation in the informal system is now the workings of the welfare state itself. The social services do not meet basic needs adequately, and in meeting those needs for which they do provide, they constrain opportunities for sharing welfare fairly, between and within households.

Social policy in a market society is always concerned primarily with the distribution of income. Under advanced capitalist development, the distribution accomplished by earnings and social security is unfair, and impedes a fairer sharing out of welfare in the domestic system. I shall argue that a new system for income maintenance, which aimed to meet each individual's basic needs *before* he or she entered the labour market or the family, would both allow a fairer redistribution within formal systems of employment and earnings, and would enable a fairer sharing of tasks within domestic roles. In this way social policy would reinforce the moral order, rather than obstructing it.

The subjective view of welfare assumes that people can form projects and commitments and bargain about shares. Ideally, roles and relationships in every sphere should start from a basis of equal *autonomy*.[2] This implies that both partners (or all participants) bring to their joint enterprises equal understanding of their own potential, equal abilities (though not necessarily the same ones), equal commitments to their own personal projects, and equal involvement in the success of their joint ventures. In reality this is seldom the case, but roles which institutionalize and reinforce inequalities of awareness, of opportunities for self-development and choice, tend to increase unfairness and widen differences between the personal welfare shares of individuals. Social policy should aim at least to equalize 'basic supplies' between individuals,[3] so that in certain broad respects the things they have in common are more important than those that divide them. In this way, social services become a source of social solidarity (co-operation between all citizens) and not social division.

If people's labour market and household roles cannot be relied upon to give them the basic supplies necessary for this fundamental equal autonomy among citizens, then the income maintenance system should aim to provide for basic income needs on an individual basis, so that citizens can meet to negotiate their formal and informal roles as free and equal citizens. Their duty is then simply to co-operate with each other, according to the principles outlined in the first part of this book. Given the security of an independent income, enough for basic needs, employers and employees, men and women, disabled and able-bodied, could negotiate the terms of formal and informal co-operation without unfair duress or constraint.[4]

I shall argue that this new approach follows logically from the moral principles of give and take, from the socioeconomic developments of advanced capitalism, and indeed from recent adaptations of income maintenance schemes to these changes. I shall show this last point by analysing recent income maintenance policy dilemmas in two European countries – Britain and the Netherlands.

Britain: Harmonizing Means Tests

In Britain the need for change in the income maintenance system has been recognized by the Conservative government, which in 1985 published proposals for the reform of the social security system. Both the analysis and the proposed reforms suffered from the inadequate terms of reference of the inquiry into income maintenance problems: it addressed only the benefit side, and ignored income taxation. This meant that, although the government's Green and White Papers were obsessed with rising costs, they never considered the question of who paid for income maintenance provision, or how. Social security was treated as a form of public expenditure, when in fact it is a system for transferring income so as to redistribute welfare both between individuals and between periods of people's lives. Because of the inadequate framework of these reports, it seems pointless to analyse or criticize them in any detail; instead, I shall simply identify the important trends for income maintenance provision, and show why the government was driven towards the recommendations which it adopted.

Overall expenditure on social security has increased by 452 per cent in real terms (at 1984–5 prices) since 1949/50, and in terms of a percentage of GDP from 4.7 to 11.1 per cent.[5] The greatest growth in the numbers of claimants has occurred among pensioners (from around 4 million to around 9 million) and unemployed people (from about 200,000 to 1 million claimants of unemployment benefit) in this 45-year period.[6] If the principles of Beveridge's social insurance scheme had been retained, we could therefore expect to find the greatest proportional growth in expenditure on retirement pensions and unemployment benefits. But this is not at all the case. In 1949/50, spending on pensions formed 41.7 per cent of all social security expenditure; between 1959/60 and 1979/80 it made up between 48 and 49 per cent; but by 1984/5 it had fallen again to 42.2 per cent. Unemployment benefit made up 6 per cent of total social security payments in 1949/50 and 4 per cent in 1984/5.[7]

The main reasons why there has been a less-than-proportional growth in pensions and unemployment benefits is that the value of national insurance benefits has been held down (and recently cut), whereas total spending on means-tested benefits has increased. In 1949/50, if we exclude family allowances and war pensions from the calculation (they made up a total of about a quarter of overall income maintenance expenditure), national insurance benefits accounted for 83.3 per cent of social security spending, and national assistance (then the only means-tested scheme) for 16.7 per cent. By 1984/5, national insurance benefits made up only 65.4 per cent of social security spending, and all means-tested benefits 34.6 per cent (of which supplementary benefits formed around 70 per cent); child benefits made up about 12 per cent of overall income maintenance spending, and non-contributory benefits (including war pensions) about 5 per cent.[8] The same trend can be seen in table 1.[9]

This shift from contributory insurance benefits to means-tested ones has been greatly accelerated under the Conservative government. Between 1979 and 1984 they saved an estimated £8.2 billion, mainly by abolishing earnings-related sickness and unemployment benefits and holding down the rates of insurance benefits generally; but spending on means-tested benefits increased dramatically. For instance, expenditure on housing benefits rose from £1,890 million in 1979/80 to £4,160 million in 1984/5 (at constant 1984/5 prices), an increase of 220 per cent;[10] the number of claimants of family income supplement increased from 78,000 to 204,000 from 1979 to 1983 (155 per cent);[11] and spending on supplementary benefits increased from £4 billion in 1978/9 to £6.4 billion in 1984/5 at constant prices (60 per cent).[12] Of the latter increase, the main component was increased unemployment; over 1.8 million unemployed people were claiming supplementary benefit in 1983 (of which around 1.2 million had been unemployed for over a year), compared with about half a million unemployed claimants of supplementary benefit in 1978.[13]

It might be expected that this major shift from insurance to means-tested benefits would have meant that the burden of financing income maintenance was moved off employers and employees and on to taxpayers; but this was not the case. In 1949/50, overall social security spending was financed in the proportions of 20.4 per cent from employer's contributions, 24.6 per cent from employees' contributions and 51.6 per cent from taxation.[14] In 1984/5 the proportions were 25.3 per cent employers' contributions, 24.3 per cent employees' and 49.2 per cent taxation. This was because the burden of the National Insurance Fund had shifted heavily on to employers' (from 32.2 to 44 per cent) and employees' contributions (38.8 to 42.2 per cent), and off taxation (23.5 to 11.5 per cent) in the same 45 years.[15] Meanwhile, of course, income taxation itself had shifted, from being borne almost exclusively by the rich (in 1949 the top 1.5 per cent of income tax units contributed over 50 per cent of income tax revenue) to falling heavily on

Table 1 Real expenditure on the social security programme by type of benefit, 1984/5 prices (£ million)

	1949/50	1959/60	1969/70	1979/80	1984/5	% increase 1949/50–1984/5 (rounded)
National insurance benefits	4,164	7,078	12,574	18,627	20,848	400
Income-related benefits	837	1,093	2,412	4,183	9,276	1,010
Non-contributory benefits	1,575	1,658	2,377	5,543	6,174	290
	6,576	9,829	17,363	28,353	36,298	450

Source: DHSS, *Reform of Social Security*, table 2.3

average and even below-average earnings – most recipients of means-tested benefits in full-time employment also paid income tax.

So the British Conservative government is caught in a trap of its own making. Its economic policies depend heavily on creating new 'no-tech' jobs in services – mainly through self-employment for men and low-paid part-time work for women. But its own philosophy of incentives requires that people should have financial inducements to do these jobs. The government is trapped between the notion that state income maintenance schemes 'should not discourage self-reliance or stand in the way of individual provision and responsibility',[16] and that 'no individual should be left in a position where through no fault of his own he is unable to sustain himself or his family.'[17] Extension of means-tested benefits, and especially those for people in work, has been intended to 'target' assistance to those in 'genuine need'; but it has also reduced incentives.

Accordingly, the Green and White Papers, while concerned to continue the pruning back of national insurance benefits (such as the State Earnings Related Pension Scheme), focused mainly on the means-tested benefits – their complexity and their paradoxical effects. Despite specifically excluding the income tax system from the review, and rejecting any idea of integration between taxation and benefits, the government's Green and White Papers both gave considerable importance to 'the possible links between *social security and tax*'.

> The Government share the view that in certain respects the present social security system is not well co-ordinated with income tax, particularly as the two systems affect low-income working families. A well-known feature of current arrangements is that in some circumstances an increase in earnings for a low-paid family head can lead to a small *loss* in net income, reflecting the combined impact of increased tax payments and reduced receipt of income-related benefits.[18]

The proposed changes aim at creating a single simplified means test which can be used for supplementary benefit (to be renamed 'income support'), family income supplement (FIS, to be renamed 'family credit') and housing benefit.[19] For all three benefits, income would be calculated on a post-tax basis, rules about capital would be the same, and the same scale rates for children would apply. The changes would double the number of people eligible for FIS (family credit), but reduce eligibility for housing benefit by (among other things) making every household responsible for at least 20 per cent of its local authority rates. In the Green Paper an illustrative graph was provided of the effects of the family credit scheme, taking account of changes in supplementary and housing benefits; however, as there were no figures on the axes, this provided only a shadowy illustration. The first diagram showed available household income first rising above the sup-plementary benefit level with increased earnings, then falling again and dipping below that level, before rising more steeply again. The second showed a smooth if very gentle rise throughout an unknown range of increased earnings.[20]

In practice, when the Social Security Bill was published in January 1986 it confirmed what many people had suspected: that this could be achieved only by cutting the disposable incomes of households on the lower earnings from full-time employment, and extending the range of incomes facing effective marginal tax rates of around 90 per cent right up to near-average earnings. In other words, the price for abolishing the strong form of the poverty trap (effective marginal tax rates of over 100 per cent for a narrow range of incomes) is to widen the weaker form of the poverty trap, so that a much larger group of poorer households face rates of effective taxation which would be totally unacceptable if applied to the rich.

This shows that the Conservative government, despite rejecting the idea of integrating the income tax and social security systems, is moving much closer to the idea of a negative income tax scheme.[21] It is subjecting the incomes of the whole of the bottom quarter of income units to a system which effectively ties them to the poverty line. The simplified post-tax means test really means that all these households, whether they are in full-time work or out of it, will have their final incomes determined by the supplementary benefit (income support) scale rates, with a sliding scale of disregarded income for people working more than a certain number of hours. This separates poor households from the rest of the population, who will face far lower tax rates, far more attractive labour market incentives and far better opportunities to control their own lives.

The national insurance scheme becomes, in effect, the social security system for the market sector, providing limited benefits (insufficient for subsistence) but without means test or stigma. Yet even this segmentation is insufficient for the government. Below the means-tested system which will become the ground floor of income maintenance, there will be a new stigmatized and discretionary scheme – the 'social fund'. This will be the repository for the present discretionary powers of the supplementary benefit officers (single payments for exceptional needs and payments for urgent needs). It will have the 'flexibility' to meet individualized needs arising from debt, destitution, 'community care' and emergencies, though in practice research has shown again and again that discretionary payments stem from the inadequacy of the scale rates and the impossibility of long-term budgeting on present benefit levels for those with no margin of error.[22]

Both Green and White Papers claimed to be concerned with fairness, but they addressed this issue only in relation to comparisons between people out of work and those on low wages, and between claimants who got discretionary assistance and those who did not. The wider issues of fairness in society, of social rights, of domestic roles, of employment opportunities and so on were not addressed at all. Having opened by saying it was important to decide on the mutual responsibilities of the individual and the state, the Green Paper dealt with this vast question in a couple of hackneyed paragraphs.

Yet there was something radical in the attempt to harmonize means tests through taking account of the combined effects of tax and social security. It was a form of radicalism forced on the Conservative government by the socioeconomic changes its policies had hastened. It seems increasingly likely that these same changes will make impossible any return to Beveridge principles of the kind advocated by the Child Poverty Action Group and the Labour Party. Instead, Britain faces a choice between this kind of generalized simplified means-test approach (which would emerge as a negative income tax scheme if taken to its logical conclusion) and the basic income proposal I shall outline at the end of the chapter.

The Netherlands: A Partial Basic Income?

The Dutch income maintenance system makes an interesting contrast with the British one. Generally, although per capita income in the Netherlands is only just above Britain's, rates of benefit are a good deal higher. The system relies much more on minimum wages to guarantee household incomes, and less on means-tested benefits. But there are important common problems, also.

The Netherlands generally spends a much higher proportion of its gross domestic product on social welfare services than Britain – 30.7 per cent in 1980 compared with 21.4 per cent.[23] Expenditure on income maintenance has grown much more rapidly in the Netherlands than in Britain – from 8.1 per cent of net national income in 1960 to 23.4 per cent in 1983.[24] Old age pensions are on average 58 per cent higher per person in the Netherlands than in Britain;[25] child benefits are 38 per cent higher,[26] and unemployment benefits are 306 per cent higher.[27] Yet unemployment itself is higher also – an average rate of 17.3 per cent of the employed labour force in 1984 – and 52 per cent of the unemployed had been out of work for over a year, despite the fact that the rate was only 7.4 per cent in 1980.[28]

The minimum wage in the Netherlands provides a guaranteed minimum income for those in work and, through a mechanism called 'coupling', a base level for social security benefits. It was established in the immediate postwar period, and rose rapidly during the period of full employment to reach 75 per cent of average gross earnings of all manual workers in manufacturing industry by 1979. This is higher than in France or Belgium, and about the same as in Denmark.[29] About 10 per cent of Dutch workers received the minimum wage in 1976, and about half of these were under 23. The minimum wage is increased every six months in line with the centrally negotiated wages index. Since 1971, when 'coupling' was introduced, all insurance benefits are also increased at this time, and these are related to previous earnings.[30] But because universal family allowances are lower than the social assistance scale rates for children, some single-earner households on the minimum wage with children in them fall below social assistance levels.[31]

Numbers claiming benefits have grown enormously in recent years. The percentage increase in claimants of old age and widow's pensions between 1960 and 1984 was 72 per cent; of sickness benefits 147 per cent; of disability benefits 361 per cent; of unemployment benefits 3036 per cent; and of national assistance 293 per cent.[32] But the structure of the Dutch population is also changing rapidly, so this vast relative increase in unemployment (as compared with pensions) is unlikely to persist. Between 1980 and 2030 the number of elderly people is predicted to double, whereas the number under 15 will fall by over 30 per cent; elderly people will rise from 11.5 per cent of the population to 22.8 per cent, and from 17.4 per cent of the working age-population to 36.6 per cent, while children under 15 will fall from 22.6 per cent of the total population to 15.2 per cent.[33] Household size, which has fallen from an average of 3.5 persons in 1960 to 2.8 in 1980 (similar to Britain), is likely to go on falling as elderly households increase and the number of children decline; but single-parent households (5.6 per cent of the total already) look like growing in number.

A recent semi-official report (by the Netherlands Scientific Council for Government Policy) presents a far more thoroughgoing analysis of the implications of all these changes for the income maintenance system than the one given by the British Green and White Papers of 1985.[34] It concludes that the whole basis of the income maintenance system needs revision because of socioeconomic change. What is needed is a scheme which allows more personal freedom and choice, but also protects people against fluctuating earnings and uncertain employment.

A system based on the notion of a breadwinner is out of date when so many married women are entering the labour market, and so much work is becoming part-time,[35] but present social security schemes also inhibit the flexibility of the labour market, and – being financed mainly out of levies on labour – raise labour costs, making labour very expensive in relation to capital. Finally, the Report raises the important issue of whether, given the increasing variety of household composition and roles, benefits should be paid on an individual basis or should continue to be related to household needs. It argues that these issues are more important than the simple one of what level of public spending should be made on income maintenance.

The new system they propose is quite complex, but carefully designed in line with their objectives. These are to give adequate guarantees of household income without reducing incentives excessively; to reduce labour costs, especially in certain industries and services; to increase employment by stimulating the demand for labour; and to be fair and neutral as between the various sizes and forms of households that now make up Dutch society.

In their scheme, the Netherlands Scientific Council suggest four main elements: a universal partial basic income, general loss of earnings insurance, national assistance, and voluntary loss of earnings insurance. The most innovative of these proposals is the partial basic income (PBI). This would replace the minimum wage as the cornerstone of the income maintenance system, and would be paid *unconditionally* to *individuals*, at a rate equivalent to the present national minimum for a married woman (that is, the difference between the rate for a couple and that for a single householder – approximately 30 per cent of the national minimum wage). A higher PBI would be paid to the elderly, widows, handicapped and permanently disabled people, to raise their guaranteed unconditional income to the present national minimum. The main aim of substituting the PBI for the minimum wage for all wage-earners would be to reduce labour costs, by reducing gross wages and salaries and widening the tax base. The extra costs of the PBI would be financed out of corporation tax, VAT, import duties, pollution taxes and so on, thus shifting taxation off labour and on to expenditure. This should increase the demand for labour and for labour-intensive commodities.

The individual basis of the PBI would represent a step in the direction of fully individualized benefits, though the Council points out that this principle, while it avoids the intrusiveness and stigma of household means tests, aggregation of requirements and treating women as dependants of men, does disadvantage single-person households. The report states:

> If the desire for individual economic independence is to be taken as the starting point for official policy, a completely individualised system of income transfers would need to be introduced on a personal basis . . . Traditional role patterns may have been eroded, but, in so far as new ones crystallize out, it cannot be assumed for policy purposes that any one or more of these will emerge as dominant. This means that a choice in favour of either the individualization principle or needs/economic means criteria in the social security system will cause tensions one way or another. As long as the diversity of household forms persists, no ready-made solution will be available. Instead, efforts will have to be made to find a solution that as far as possible steers a neutral course.[36]

This means that the PBI is held at a below-subsistence level, so that, although most working people would reach the present national minimum by a combination of PBI and earnings, a few low-wage-earners might fall below this; they would then qualify for national assistance, calculated on a household means test. Although the aim would be to keep this number as low as possible, clearly it would rise if the intended effect of lowering wages in certain sectors occurred, and this might be cumulative if the PBI remained at the same level. Similarly, for people out of work, the general loss of earnings insurance (GLI), which would provide a compulsory supplement to the PBI for unemployment, sickness and short-term disability, would be designed automatically to bring households up to the national minimum, and would include the self-employed. But the GLI would be time-limited (half the period of contributions), so during recessions unemployed people (especially those with unskilled jobs, and hence insecurity of employment) could swell the numbers on national assistance. Voluntary loss of earnings insurance would provide the earnings-related element in the insurance scheme, though unlike the present social security system the earnings-related contributions and benefits would no longer be compulsory.

The Netherlands Council's proposals are an ingenious compromise between a number of different principles, but they do not have the same air of expediency as the British government's plans. They are deliberately designed, not to divide and segment Dutch society, but to introduce some dynamism and growth into an economic system which has become rather stagnant, with undesired and unplanned social consequences. The Council is very concerned about the falling share of income from enterprises and self-employment in national disposable income (from 27 per cent in 1960 to 13 per cent in 1983, but down to 10 per cent in 1980), which seems to fall in step with the rising share of income transfers to the economically inactive (from 12 per cent in 1960 to 26 per cent in 1983).[37] They are also concerned that present surplus labour supply might turn to labour shortage in the 1990s, owing to the lower birth rate and much smaller cohort of potential workers entering the labour market then; they fear an adverse effect on labour supply behaviour then from too generous a basic income, which is one reason why they oppose the idea of a universal basic income paid at a minimum subsistence level.

Yet there are also some odd features of the Dutch proposals. While their long-term fear is of choking off the labour supply (even though they acknowledge that research in the United States and in their own country points to little such effect[38]), their short-term concern is to increase demand for labour, especially in labour-intensive industries and services, by reducing labour costs. This amounts to an artificial encouragement of low wages and a wasteful use of labour which, in the absence of a full basic income, is really an encouragement of exploitation, since workers cannot rely on their basic incomes for subsistence. It also reflects a lack of confidence in the market as a mechanism for adjusting supply to demand, since one of the attractions of the basic income principle would be that it would allow whatever demand existed to clear the market of the current supply. The proposal to finance the PBI partly out of a medley of taxes on consumption, imports and diswelfares destroys much of the simplicity and self-adjustment of the idea of an integrated income tax and social security system.

It would be more logical to see the Council's proposals as transitional ones, a first step on the road to a fully fledged basic income scheme, such as the one I am about to outline. Their fears about disrupting the labour market appear irrational if the scheme was introduced by way of starting with a PBI, and gradually increasing it up to subsistence level. In the short run more variable wages and more flexible hours and terms of employment would be enabled, because the PBI would encourage potential multi-earner house-holds to do bits and pieces of work, while the national assistance scheme would give a fall back if they failed to clear the national minimum level for any period. But in the longer term, even if demand for labour did begin to overtake available supply, this could occur only under conditions of sustained growth of per capita incomes, and presumably also of profits, so industry would have to offer higher wages and increased hours to workers – and it could afford to do so.

A Basic Income Scheme

The basic income principle establishes quite a different linkage between economic life and households, but one which returns to the notion of social rights of citizenship. The Dutch example shows that a linkage based on social insurance and the minimum wage can lead to very high rates of unemployment and exclusion from economic life without preventing poverty. The British example shows that a return to the social assistance approach to income maintenance involves the creation of a large permanent underclass, whose members are less than full citizens. Neither approach addresses the issue of women's role in the economy and the household, and neither provides the kind of equal autonomy which every individual should enjoy – both in the labour market and in domestic life – before he or she can negotiate about roles and resources, and reach a fair distribution of welfare.

I have argued before[39] that a universal basic income would be the best cornerstone of this kind of equal autonomy in an advanced economy. This is because the alternative basis – redistribution of productive resources to give everyone enough to produce their own basic subsistence – is no longer practicable. It is perhaps conceivable that a peasant economy might achieve such widespread holdings of land and equipment as to make this possible,[40] particularly if there were also extensive common rights and an infrastructure of public services.[41] However, in advanced countries – both in the Western and Eastern blocs – people have become more dependent on waged labour for subsistence than at any previous time in history. What is particularly problematic is that in the West they have become dependent on the waged labour of male adults in a single full-time occupation; household norms and income maintenance systems were gradually adapted to this pattern in the first half of this century. Yet meanwhile the labour market has changed, so that full-time male jobs cannot sustain households, and household patterns and roles have changed also. The income maintenance system is now the most maladapted feature of the whole system; yet it also can provide the key to equal autonomy, which would allow both the economy and the household to develop towards a fairer distribution of welfare in society, and a better reconciliation between individual and communal welfare.

The basic income principle starts from the idea that, in order to guarantee the basic needs of all citizens, it is necessary to give each individual enough income for subsistence before he or she enters the labour market or the family. This would be the only way of simultaneously preventing poverty and giving all an equal chance to participate and co-operate in the economy and in the household. It would mean that each individual would have an independent income as the basis for negotiating a paid and an unpaid work role – that no one could be coerced into a job or a domestic responsibility out of dependence on another for his or her basic resources.

The technical way in which this could be achieved is by giving each individual a tax-free sum sufficient for subsistence. Children would get a slightly reduced basic income; invalids, disabled, handicapped and retired people would get substantial supplements to meet higher living costs associated with extra health and welfare needs. The basic income would be financed by amalgamating all present personal income tax allowances and reliefs with all social security benefits, together with student grants and other subsidies and supplements. It would thus give equal social rights to all citizens, giving all enough income to reach the same living standards, but leaving all free to pursue their projects and commitments through the labour market and through domestic life and voluntary associations. It would abolish distinctions between workers and claimants and between men and women, because it would be the same for all, whatever their employment or marital status.

This would allow people to make much fairer and more rational decisions about paid and unpaid work roles. It would mean, for instance, that couples could negotiate about individual and shared projects, about work careers, care-giving roles and so on on a more equal footing. It would allow both partners to do part-time paid work and to share domestic tasks, while providing the security of a basic income for subsistence needs.

The concept of a basic income requires a major change in social attitudes – one which would be particularly difficult to achieve in institutions based on the roles of industrial employment. For instance, it requires that people think primarily of what is a fair *income* for an individual, or a household, rather than a fair *wage* or salary. People would think of wages no longer in terms of subsistence, but in terms of their additional income potential above the subsistence that would be provided by the basic income. This is an especially large change for trade unions, which have always bargained as if the subsistence needs of their members were at stake – even when in fact many of their members were receiving below-subsistence earnings, and were having to claim means-tested supplements. In reality, the basic income would only ratify a situation where (in Britain and Western Europe) a large proportion of disposable incomes are determined not by collective bargaining, but by either state benefits or statutory minimum wages. Under a basic income scheme this state determination of minimum incomes would be overt, and trade unions would have overtly to recognize that they were not bargaining about subsistence. But their members would be far more immune from exploitation because their basic incomes would be unconditional, and they would therefore have a guaranteed subsistence before they entered the labour market.

Indeed, a basic income would imply that wages and salaries no longer distributed the benefits of social and economic co-operation, but were instead simply the reward for individual effort. I argued in chapter 4 that the promise of industrial development was that the higher productivity achieved through new forms of co-operative production would be distributed in higher wages as well as through profits – it was this that persuaded peasants and handcraft workers to give up their means of family or communal production to become waged employees. A 'fair wage' was therefore both the share of the final product's price that was due to labour and the reward due to the worker's skill – a composite dividend of co-operative and individual effort. The basic income is really a universal distribution of the higher productivity made possible in complex industrial societies, sometimes referred to as the 'social dividend' or 'social wage', and representing a sharing among all actual and potential workers of the benefits of economic development; logically, it should increase in proportion with the overall increase in the general productivity of labour in the community. Hence wages and salaries become in effect the specific rewards to individual effort, skill and productivity.

Since trade union definitions of fairness, both in terms of the overall reward due to labour in the whole economy and in terms of comparative pay between groups of workers, are founded on a complex mixture of market factors, organizational power and collective self-defence, it is not surprising that this new approach is unwelcome.[42] In a sense the trade unions, as much as capital itself, have derived their justification of their functions from an understanding of industrial society in which what was to be shared out was the collective co-operative product, and their role was defined in terms of giving labour its fair share of the fruits of economic co-operation. Yet increasingly, the trade unions in advanced capitalist countries have encountered the paradox discussed in chapter 1, that with a shrinking industrial workforce their economic role – representing the exclusive interests of their members, and especially of organized, regular workers against disorganized, casual ones – is difficult to reconcile with the collective, political goal of promoting the interests of a united working class. Both mass unemployment and the increase in short-term, sub-contracted, part-time and self-employment have heightened the tensions between these two objectives, and have undermined the ideals of fairness represented by a structured, stratified labour market, with full employment and high rates of union membership. Instead (especially in Britain), there is a dual labour market, with no common standards of fairness over pay linking regular organized with casualized unorganized workers, and a politically divided working class.

One aim of the basic income approach would be to remove this potential conflict of interests, and to heal divisions in the working class, by ensuring that the benefits of higher industrial productivity could be shared equally among all citizens, even though the industrial workforce might continue to shrink. This would not imply a diminished role for trade unions, in fighting for a fair reward for the efforts and skills of all their individual members and for their trade or profession, though it would imply an end to battles over a very substantial share of the social product. In effect, it represents an alternative to the corporatist approaches adopted in the Scandinavian countries, and especially in Sweden, where unions have promoted 'social citizenship' through negotiating reduced differentials and high minimum wages, as well as generous social security benefits. It recognizes that security over the meeting of basic needs is an issue of citizenship and the business of the state, and that, where this cannot be achieved through corporatist co-operation between the 'social partners', it must be guaranteed by a universal division of the fruits of economic development.

Within the domestic economy, it is unlikely that traditional roles or expectations would change during the first generation after a basic income scheme was introduced, but the marginal changes already evident in surveys of household patterns would certainly be accelerated if married women had an independent income of their own and part-time work for men was facilitated. It is possible that, given a state-guaranteed basic income equivalent to the low wage paid in many part-time jobs, some women would withdraw from the labour force in the short run, finding that their current wages were inadequate when compared with the equivalent hourly benefit of unpaid work. Hence in the short term there might appear to be a return to more traditional patterns, with fewer married women in employment and more men (though more of these would be part-time). In the longer run there would be likely to be a rise in the wages of married women, and of part-time workers generally, as demand for labour increased. In other words, married women's wage rates could become much more nearly equal to men's, and they would again be drawn back into the labour market. This would be particularly obvious in Britain, where the combined effects of tax allowances and exemption from national insurance contributions give an effective premium of 40 per cent on earnings below about £40 per week, and where married women under a basic income scheme would have to pay tax from the first pound they earned.

What would the cost of a basic income scheme be? Hermione Parker has worked out a formula for costing a scheme,[43] by adding together the costs of the basic incomes (*BI*), the costs of administration (*A*), and the costs of abolishing existing income tax, advanced corporation tax and national insurance contributions (*IT, ACT, NIC*), then deducting the anticipated savings on existing public expenditure (*S*), dividing the balance by the estimated new income tax base, and multiplying by 100. The formula is therefore:

$$Tax \ rate = \frac{BI + A + (IT + ACT + NIC) - S}{new \ IT \ base} \times 100$$

(The costs of abolishing the various taxes are included because of the continued need to fund all other programmes from tax revenues.) On this basis, Hermione Parker has calculated the costs of providing basic incomes at various levels for the whole British population (44 million adult citizens, 12.3 million children). Her main conclusion is that it is difficult or impossible to reconcile the *prevention of poverty* with the *pure* basic income principle (paying the same to each adult citizen); for instance, a basic income of £50 per week for each adult and £15 a week for each child under 16 – which would not eliminate poverty among some single pensioners and disabled people – would require a tax rate of 86 per cent. While it can be pointed out that present means-tested programmes for low-wage-earners produce even higher effective marginal tax rates in the bottom quintile of earnings, and that both the British government's White Paper on social security reform and proposals for a negative income tax scheme involve similar tax rates across a wider range of below-average earnings, this would not be considered a politically feasible level of taxation in a strongly liberal and market-orientated society like Britain. Furthermore, its effects on labour supply behaviour would be difficult to predict if it were suddenly imposed.

Parker's compromise suggestion is a scheme which pays all adult citizens a rate of basic income equivalent to present ordinary non-householder rates of supplementary benefit (£21.50 in 1984–5; hence the total costs of the adult universal basic income would have been £42.5 billion) and a child rate of £15 per week[44] – but to supplement this with two additional elements. The first would be substantial additions to the basic income for elderly and disabled/handicapped people, the former relating to their age and the latter to their additional living costs.[45] The second would be housing benefit, which would be means-tested, a feature included as a regrettable necessity, in order to stay within currently accepted tax rates. This would take the form of a householder addition plus amounts for rents and rates, heating and water rates. With a taper which phased out benefit at 33 pence in the pound, this would give maximum marginal tax rates of 73 per cent, a big improvement on other schemes. Using figures based on the tax year 1982/3,

Parker has produced an illustrative costed basic income scheme for the United Kingdom which requires tax rates of 40 per cent up to average earnings, rising to 60 per cent at four times average earnings.

Like the Netherlands scheme, this can be regarded as a practical proposal for transitional reform, which introduces a radical new principle but stays within the parameters of traditional policy constraints. True to the British history of parsimony towards poverty programmes, Parker's basic income rates are actually well below the ones given in the Netherlands scheme – even though the latter are clearly described as partial basic incomes, and are supplemented for almost all those receiving no earnings. But her scheme is much simpler and more internally consistent, especially in its financing, than the Dutch proposal. It illustrates that the basic income principle is not a pipe-dream but a practical possibility, and that moves towards a society which would give equal autonomy to all citizens *before* they entered the labour market or the family are possible, even within the limits imposed by existing attitudes and economic orthodoxies.[46]

Conclusions

The basic income principle cuts across present class and political divisions because it replaces traditional social democratic and trade union struggles over maintaining full employment and subsistence wages with the notion of a subsistence income as a citizenship right. It would have least appeal in Scandinavia (especially Sweden), where the labour movement seems to have been able to achieve the same goal through maintaining class solidarity, sharing employment and redistributing income.[47] It would not have much appeal in Japan, where a surprisingly egalitarian distribution of income has been achieved despite the slow development of social security, or in Australia, where high wages have also given an egalitarian distributive pattern, and where income maintenance has traditionally been means-tested.

But in most of Western Europe, with labour movements divided between relatively prosperous unionized sectors and secondary casualized ones, it seems to offer a possibility of reintegration and regrouping. From the trade union point of view, fears about intensified exploitation might be offset by the greater ease with which workers could withold their labour if pay and conditions were unsatisfactory.

From the employers' point of view, it would offer increased opportunities for flexibility in labour utilization, which seems to be the key to profitability in the foreseeable future. This might be a more important factor in encouraging them to support the idea than the slight anxieties about the total quantity of labour supply that it engenders. Even the political right, which has gained by dividing the working class, and setting taxpaying workers against social security claimants, might come to recognize the need to reduce conflict and rebuild social harmony through such a measure.

This income maintenance policy would be consistent with a wide range of employment policies, and of public–private mixes. It would shift the focus of economic management away from demand-side Keynesian measures, and from the idea of job creation, towards issues of efficiency and product choice. The question would not be 'How can we get our people back to work?' but 'What can our people most effectively make and do?' Answers to this question might be sought primarily through the market, or by a combination of research and planning. Certainly in the public sector it would require a series of decisions about the infrastructure, environment, public utilities and social services, based on a clear philosophy of what central and local government was aiming to provide in these spheres.

There would also be scope for a wider range of employment opportunities than at present. Because of the constraints of income maintenance systems, schemes for improving local environments, meeting new social needs and so on have either to come within the range of full-time employment wages and conditions, or else to be carried out under special programmes which pose as retraining. The same is true for new businesses and co-operatives; in Britain only self-employment readily attracts the kind of unconditional income support offered by the basic income, in the form of the enterprise allowance. But the new principle would enable schemes to be set up which offered opportunities both for voluntary effort and for future-orientated initiative, based on the security provided by the basic income. Governments could thus encourage small businesses, co-operatives or local authority schemes – rather as Regional Enterprise Boards do in Britain at present, but within a more favourable framework.

The basic income principle would indeed define new terms of citizenship. It is sometimes objected that it would give new unconditional rights to income security without laying down corresponding duties – that citizenship is an *active* concept, and that this allows passive non-participation. There are two answers to this. The first is that the present terms of citizenship in advanced capitalist countries are unequal and anomalous. Property-holders get the protection of the law, but their only obligation is to pay taxes – they are not required to work or participate in any other way. All other working-age men are required to take full-time employment (if it is available), in exchange for rights to income maintenance. Married women have no such obligations, but equally they have no such rights – they must claim from their husbands. Claimants are obliged *not* to work or earn, and often not to be educated either, as a condition of receiving benefits. There is little equality or fairness in this, and expectations of participation are highly differentiated.

Second, the basic income principle assumes that people participate in social co-operation voluntarily, and that much of this co-operation is informal. It assumes that formal systems provide opportunities and incentives for the production and distribution of social goods, and that people choose how to use these formal systems and how to combine them with informal ones. Decisions about who works, for how long and on what terms are not made on the basis of pure maximization, nor can they be coercively imposed; they are – like any other decisions – the result of complex negotiations and decisions concerned with welfare shares. People link what they get from the market and from the state with what they do for themselves in their own way. This process is in itself a form of participation, in the co-operation that underlies all social systems. The aim of social policy should be to enable and enhance the fairness of the informal moral order; under present economic circumstances, the basic income principle looks the most promising way of doing this.

Notes

1 See for instance F. F. Piven and R. A. Cloward, *Regulating the Poor*, Tavistock, 1972, and Bill Jordan, *Poor Parents: Social Policy and the Cycle of Deprivation*, Routledge & Kegan Paul, 1974.
2 See Albert Weale, *Political Theory and Social Policy*, Macmillan, 1983, pp. 42–6, and Bill Jordan, *The State: Authority and Autonomy*, Basil Blackwell, 1985, pp. 11–15.
3 Gerald Caplan, in *Principles of Preventive Psychiatry*, Tavistock Press, 1964, p. 31, argues that people's basic needs are physical (goods needed for sustaining life and health), psychosocial (goods needed for cognitive and emotional development) and sociocultural (those needed for sustaining participation in social and economic activity).
4 See Jordan, *The State: Authority and Autonomy*, part III; Weale, *Political Theory and Social Policy*, chapter 3; Hermione Parker, *Action on Welfare: The Reform of Personal Income Taxation and Social Security*, Social Affairs Unit, 1984, and Keith Roberts, *Automation, Unemployment and the Distribution of Income*, European Centre for Work and Society, Maastricht, 1983.
5 DHSS, *Reform of Social Security* (The Fowler Report – Green Paper), Cmnd 9517, HMSO, 1985, vol. 3, tables 2.1 and 2.2, p. 27.
6 Ibid., vol. 1, figure 4, p. 11.
7 Ibid., vol. 1, figure 3, p. 10.
8 Ibid.
9 Ibid., vol. 3, table 2.3, p. 27.
10 Ibid., vol. 2, figure 3.2, p. 35.
11 Ibid., vol. 3, p. 68.
12 Ibid., vol. 2, p. 13.
13 Ibid., vol. 2, figure 2.1, p. 13.
14 Ibid., vol. 3, table 2.4, p. 29.
15 Ibid., vol. 3, table 2.5, p. 29.
16 Ibid., vol. 1, p. 1.
17 Ibid., vol. 1, p. 2.
18 Ibid., vol. 1, p. 19.
19 DHSS, *Reform of Social Security: Programme for Action* (White Paper), Cmnd 9691, HMSO, 1985, p. 21.

20 *Reform of Social Security* (Green Paper), vol. 1, figure 6, p. 30.
21 A. Dilnot, J. Kay and N. Morris, *The Reform of Social Security*, Oxford University Press, 1984. For a demonstration of the effects of the proposals on the income of typical households earning less than £140 per week in 1986, see Hermione Parker, 'Off Target', *New Society*, vol. 75, no. 1206, 7 February 1986, p. 232, and 'Fowler's Reform of Social Security: Facts and Figures', *BIRG Bulletin*, no. 5, spring 1985, pp. 12–17. Parker showed that a couple with two children, one aged under 5 and the other 5–10, with a rent of £16.55 per week and rates of £6.40, would end up with £85 on no earnings, £88 on earnings of £100, and £95 on earnings of £140. Under the existing system the figures are £91, £92 and £95.
22 The Green Paper itself shows that the number of single payments for exceptional needs dropped to almost half its previous levels in 1981, the year after a system of regulations prescribing *entitlements* to these payments was introduced – as had been the intention of the 1980 Social Security Act. But the following year they rose again to their previous levels, and resumed the upward trend that they had been on since the early 1970s, exactly on the same path as before. The Green Paper argued that a return to the pre-1980 system of discretionary decisions would be more appropriate, but still wanted to reduce the number of payments. In practice, between 1948 and 1980, while the discretionary system was operating, the vast bulk of payments were for items supposedly covered by the scale rates, especially clothes and fuel, indicating that a substantial minority of claimants could not meet *ordinary* recurring expenses out of their weekly benefits.
23 Robert Walker, 'Resources, Welfare Expenditure and Poverty in European Countries', in Robert Walker, Roger Lawson and Peter Townsend (eds), *Responses to Poverty: Lessons from Europe*, Heinemann, 1984, table 2.12, p. 47.
24 Netherlands Scientific Council for Government Policy, *Safeguarding Social Security*, WRR, The Hague, 1985, table 2.8, p. 23.
25 Walker, 'Resources, Welfare Expenditure and Poverty', table 2.14, p. 50.
26 Ibid., table 2.15, p. 51.
27 Ibid., table 2.16, p. 52.
28 *Safeguarding Social Security*, p. 17.
29 A. A. M. van Amelsvoort, 'The Netherlands: Minimum Wage and Unemployment Policies', in Walker, Lawson and Townsend, *Responses to Poverty*, p. 123.
30 Ibid., p. 125.
31 Ibid., p. 124.
32 *Safeguarding Social Security*, table 2.1, p. 16.
33 Ibid., table 2.5, p. 19.
34 *Safeguarding Social Security*.
35 Ibid., p. 22. The Report found that, in the multi-person households which form 79 per cent of households in the Netherlands, an average of 1.8 persons brought in an earned income; the average number of incomes per couple without children was 1.4, and for couples with children living in, 1.9. But the number of second incomes from children living at home was greater than the number of second incomes earned by married women in work (in 1981). The participation rate of married women increased from 24 per cent in 1960 to 36 per cent in 1983, still low by European standards. On average, working women contributed around 25 per cent to family income, and three-quarters earned no more than the minimum wage.

36 *Safeguarding Social Security*, p. 27.

37 Ibid., table 2.9, p. 24.

38 Ibid., p. 27.

39 Jordan, *The State: Authority and Autonomy*, part III, and 'The Social Wage: A Right for All', *New Society*, vol. 68, no. 1118, 26 April 1984.

40 This was the kind of society advocated by radicals in seventeenth-century Britain and eighteenth-century America.

41 Attempts at this kind of development, using rural co-operatives, can perhaps be recognized in present-day Nicaragua and Tanzania.

42 See Jordan, *The State: Authority and Autonomy*, ch. 16.

43 Hermione Parker, 'Costing Basic Incomes', *BIRG Bulletin*, no. 3, spring 1985, pp. 4–13.

44 Illustrative child rate of basic income was £15 for all children in Parker's 1984–5 scheme. Her adult non-householder rate is slightly lower than the rate for supplementary benefit for non-householders over 21, but all other rates (couples and families) work out higher.

45 Supplements to be added to the universal basic income were £27.50 for each person aged 64–84, and £32.50 for each aged 85 and over. Invalids and handicapped people were to receive the same supplement as those over 65 for income maintenance, and a disability costs allowance which would vary with their degree of disability – budgeted to cost an around £1.75 billion. There could also be slightly lower supplements for expectant mothers, widows and lone parents. Parker, 'Costing Basic Incomes', table 1, p. 8.

46 For other proposals of basic income schemes for advanced capitalist countries, see *The Royal Commission on the Economic Union and Development Prospects for Canada* (Macdonald Commission), 1985, summary of conclusions and recommendations, pp. 31–41; Ronald Mendelsohn, 'Creating a Fairer Future', *Australian Society*, November 1985, pp. 8–13; C. Offe, *Disorganised Capitalism: Contemporary Transformations of Work and Politics*, Polity Press, 1985, ch. 3; R. van der Veen and P. van Parijs, 'A Capitalist Road to Communism?', *Theory of Society*, March 1985, For recent British political interest in the subject see Francis Pym, 'How More Give and Take Would Help Us All', *The Times*, 16 October 1985; Michael Meacher 'What Next for the Welfare State', *National Student*, February 1986; and Philip Vince, 'Basic Incomes: Some Practical Considerations', *BIRG Bulletin*, no. 5, spring 1986, pp. 5–7.

47 G. Esping-Andersen and W. Korpi, 'Social Policy as Class Politics, in Post-War Capitalism: Scandinavia, Austria and Germany', in J. H. Goldthorpe (ed.), *Order and Conflict in Contemporary Capitalism*, Oxford University Press, 1984.

10

Housing and the Environment

Shelter is a basic human need, and it is part of a wider need for a benign social environment. The disaster at the Chernobyl nuclear power station served as a reminder of how interdependent all human beings have become, and of the vulnerability of all species to human error. Fortresses, bunkers and even fall-out shelters would be rendered pathetically inadequate by the ultimate nuclear catastrophe. Because of the counter-claims of private and public space and resources, housing policy is a clear example of the balancing of individual and communal welfare. In liberal capitalist societies this balancing act has been much more difficult because people use houses as a way of accumulating personal wealth.

The attention given by public policy to housing needs and that given to environmental issues have always been in tension, if not in conflict. On the one hand, there has been pressure on the state to guarantee an adequate supply of basic housing, and to reduce or eliminate overcrowding and homelessness. On the other hand, rapid building programmes have often been a major source of environmental *diswelfares*, whether in the form of Victorian back-to-back urban terraces, interwar ribbon development of private housing or postwar tower blocks and problem local authority estates.

Environmental sources of welfare and diswelfare are far wider than housing. They include the planning, siting and upkeep of industrial buildings; all forms of pollution control; the provision of parks, sports grounds, leisure amenities and children's play areas; the layout of highways and alleyways; street lighting; shopping facilities; transport; and access to the countryside. The question is really one of how policy in the field of housing can be co-ordinated with these environmental considerations, so that the basic needs of households for shelter can be reconciled with communal needs for pleasant and convenient surroundings.

Housing policy analysis traditionally starts from housing shortages. At any point in time there never seem to be enough houses to meet household demand, and the construction of new houses always seems to be falling short of whatever targets have been set. Yet there have been dramatic increases in the housing stocks of all the Western European countries, and of Eastern European ones also, since the Second World War.[1] The slowing down in this rate of growth has coincided with the slower growth of national economies and also with a general decline in the birth rate – but not in the number of new households being formed.

In Britain at present there are actually just over a million more houses (defined as separate dwellings with their own front doors) than there are households (defined as individuals or groups living as units).[2] This surplus is made up of a quarter of a million second or third homes standing empty for much of the year (often in inconvenient locations for all-the-year round living) and three-quarters of a million vacant dwellings, some of them uninhabitable buildings and some rented accommodation standing unlet (including a high proportion of local authority property, at least enough to eliminate waiting lists). The latter is partly a problem of management – local authority housing departments are essentially paternalistic bureaucracies, so letting is rather a slow process – and partly due to the fact that certain properties or areas are very unpopular, or dilapidated, or both. The special difficulties of local authority housing will be discussed in the second part of this chapter.

An overall policy for housing and the environment would take account of all forms of housing tenure, housing finance and the different processes through which houses are constructed; it would also take account of common environmental needs. Clearly, it is difficult to find or pursue such a policy in societies where there is a mixed and shifting economy of housing (as for instance in Western Europe, where owner occupation has rapidly increased during the period from 1960 to the present)[3] and where most of the physical environment is privately owned. It is interesting that in the USSR and Eastern Europe, where such a policy is in principle easier to pursue, more dwellings have been constructed during the same period, but a much smaller proportion of GNP has been devoted to housing.[4] These dwellings are much smaller, in terms of both space and numbers of rooms, and they occupy much less land, which makes them more economical of resources.[5] But even Singapore, an aggressively capitalist society, has 80 per cent of its inhabitants living in state housing, most of which consists of high-rise flats.

One of the issues that will be considered in this chapter is the process by which the proportion of national resources going to private dwellings is determined. In all countries, the state influences this process, by direct intervention in the housing market, by legislation, by subsidies, by housing benefits and by tax concessions; but in capitalist countries it is also strongly influenced by forces not directly connected with the supply of accommodation. Under certain circumstances, I shall argue, there are strong inducements for people to accumulate larger holdings in land and dwellings than they need for their immediate use or to accommodate others, and this is one of the main obstacles to a coherent housing policy in such societies.

The other characteristic of housing as a sphere of policy is that the household is by definition the unit of account. Whereas I have argued that in the field of income maintenance there are very strong grounds for basing state provision on the individual, in housing this can scarcely be achieved. What can be done is to monitor the kinds of housing units demanded, in terms of both size and facilities, and to ensure that these needs are met as far as possible. In Britain – but to a much less extent in some Western European countries – the demand for smaller living units has largely been left to the private rented sector.

In each section I shall try to relate issues of housing demand and supply to environmental ones, so that the overall issues of environmental welfare can be taken into account in considering public policy.

Owner Occupation and the Privately Rented Sector

The most important thing about owner occupation as a form of tenure is that, like landlordism, it makes housing a form of wealth. The purchase of a house becomes both a way of providing for a basic need of household members and a way of storing wealth; it is usually also a way of transferring wealth from one generation to another. This creates a serious problem for public policy, since it is usually impossible – except in the case of second and third homes – to disentangle the function of meeting basic needs from that of storing (and increasing) wealth through home ownership.

Owner occupation is a twentieth-century phenomenon. Before the First World War only about 10 per cent of houses in Britain were owner-occupied, and these were spread across the range of social classes from the nobility to skilled workers. Between the wars the proportion of owner-occupiers grew to one-third, as a result of the massive speculative building drive, particularly in the Home Counties, and the growth of mortgage finance. By 1971 it had increased to 53 per cent, and since then it has grown more slowly – to 56 per cent in 1981.[6] In West Germany the proportion of owner-occupiers in 1948 was still only a quarter; now it is almost a half.[7]

People have strong motives to become owner-occupiers when rented property is scarce and rents are high, and conversely when there is a plentiful supply of housing for purchase and prices are relatively low. This was the position in Britain between the wars, when builders were able to get development land fairly cheaply (partly because of the agricultural slump), when interest rates were low, and when building for direct sale was far outstripping building for sale to landlords or by local authorities.[8] The characteristic housing development of this period was suburban, linked with large cities by new electric railways and buses.

The other set of circumstances in which people have strong motives for becoming owner-occupiers is when house prices are rising at least as fast as other prices in a generally inflationary situation, and when opportunities for improving the value of houses by repairs and improvements outstrips opportunities for earning extra income by employment. This describes the situation in Britain since the mid-1960s. Although interest rates were high in the 1970s and 1980s, favourable tax treatment of mortgage interest repayments offset this, making house purchase very attractive, even for people on quite modest incomes.[9]

Indeed, once people were able to get into the housing market, they could hardly lose, barring the disaster of not being able to keep up their mortgage repayments through a sudden fall in income. For much of the 1970s the rate of inflation of house prices was actually higher than the net interest rate, after mortgage interest tax relief, so owner-occupiers were effectively getting their houses for less than the repayment of the capital sum.[10] Once they became outright owners they were then in possession of a very considerable asset; they could keep moving up the housing market for as long as their earnings allowed and their family needs required, and then move down the housing market when they chose, realizing some of their capital as they did so.

People on the outside of this rewarding board-game were less fortunately placed. For first-time buyers in Britain, the situation was at times very difficult. Most new purchasers earn less than average household incomes, yet in 1974 and 1980, during boom conditions in the housing market, initial repayments on an ordinary house were 45 per cent of average earnings before tax.[11] Hence the owner-occupied market was dominated by existing owners, and demand by new purchasers was highest during relative slumps. New building provided too small a proportion of the market for extra supply to influence prices significantly, as economic conditions for housebuilding became less and less favourable.[12] Meanwhile rents, especially local authority rents, were rising rapidly under the Conservative government in the early 1980s.

Academic discussion of housing finance usually centres on the apparent inequity in the system of mortgage interest tax relief – that the bulk of this goes to people on higher-than-average incomes.[13] By contrast, subsidies on rented property (including housing benefit) go mainly to poorer people.[14] But this is really an issue for income maintenance and income distribution, not primarily one of housing. While mortgage interest tax relief has become a political sacred cow in Britain, and no party dare suggest that they intend to tackle its inequities, this really reflects the way in which the tax system distributes hidden benefits (fiscal welfare) while the social security system (including housing benefits) distributes ones which are all too visible. One of the main advantages of the basic income scheme discussed in the last chapter is that it would end this false and misleading distinction. For the past two decades, people with mortgages have been getting a disguised basic income, and have been able to make large sums of money through unpaid work on home improvements.

A much more important point is whether the proportion of national income going into housing is the right one, and whether the present massive conversion of income into housing *wealth* is producing a distribution of environmental welfare which is fair and meets basic needs. If people are using the opportunities provided by the tax system and the state of the housing market to accumulate wealth through house purchase, but this same process is restricting the supply of houses for basic housing needs, then policy should aim at reducing the finance available to individuals for accumulating housing wealth, and at increasing the supply of housing for rent and for new purchases.

The example of Italy illustrates very clearly the tendency of better-off people to invest in housing when other profitable opportunities become less available, and how this can worsen the housing situation of the poor. Unlike Britain, Italy has maintained a high rate of construction, even after the boom of the 1960s – around 6 new dwellings per 1,000 inhabitants in the 1970s compared with less than 2 in Britain, and an investment in housing of around 6 per cent of gross national revenue, nearly 30 per cent of total investment, in the same period. Yet overcrowding, waiting lists for public housing and disrepair are widespread – house-sharing has actually increased in recent years. The main explanation is that since about the mid-1960s there has been an enormous increase in the numbers of houses used as second homes or temporary residences, or left unoccupied; the rich have increasingly 'over-consumed' housing, or have used it to store wealth, leaving the poor under-housed. Table 2 illustrates this trend.

Table 2 Italy: average annual increase in housing stock and households, 1951–1981

	Total dwellings	Occupied dwellings[a]	Non-occupied dwellings[b]	Households
1951–61	280,298	227,550	52,748	203,381
1961–71	322,030	226,981	95,049	241,189
1971–81	441,875	220,763	221,111	255,539

[a] Dwellings occupied as first residence.
[b] Dwellings temporarily occupied for study, work or second homes, and unoccupied dwellings.
Source: Wynn, *Housing in Europe*, table 9.1

The extraordinary result of the massive Italian building programme since the mid-1960s, therefore, has been that the number of new 'occupied' dwellings has actually fallen, while the number of new, 'non-occupied' dwellings has more than doubled, to the point where over half of new houses are being sold for 'non-occupation'. Whereas there were more new occupied dwellings than new households created in the 1950s, in the 1970s there were considerably more new households than new occupied dwellings. The total housing stock in 1981 was nearly 22 million dwellings and the total number of households was only 18.5 million, but the number of non-occupied dwellings had increased from 645,000 in 1951 to 4.3 million.[15]

This tendency is particularly a problem if the economy is moving from a long wave of slow growth and low rates of profit to one of faster growth and expanding employment possibilities.[16] During a prolonged recession, when employment is contracting, it makes good sense for people at all levels of income to devote a considerable proportion of their energies to self-servicing in their homes, and especially for home improvements. As Pahl has shown, this is what has happened in Britain in the 1970s and early 1980s; the return on owner-occupiers' unpaid labour has been at least as favourable as what they could earn on the labour market at a time when overtime was scarce, and opportunities for second jobs limited.

But if economic conditions change in favour of expanded employment, or if government policy found a way of promoting it, then one aim of policy might be to shift some of people's time and energy out of do-it-yourself home improvements and back into the labour market. At present in Britain very large sources of finance are tied specifically to housing through mortgages and mortgage interest tax relief, so policy could move in this direction simply by ceasing to give these funds specially favoured tax status; this in turn might lead to a reallocation of both housing resources and productive energies.

The history of mortgage of mortgage interest tax relief in Britain is one of policy drift. Prior to 1969, interest payments on all personal borrowing were exempt from taxation. Before the Second World War, few owner-occupiers paid income tax, so this concession was of little real significance, but by the 1960s its importance had increased as home ownership grew, prices rose and the tax net widened.[17] Up to 1963, owner-occupiers paid schedule A tax on the imputed increase in value of their properties, a measure originally designed to tax landlords. With the abolition of schedule A in 1963 and the special treatment of mortgage interest after 1969, tax conditions not only favoured owner occupation compared with other tenures, but they also favoured the conversion of income into housing wealth over other forms of saving and investment. This was never declared government policy, but subsequent events have consolidated the trend.

During the 1970s, the balance between the sums dispensed through mortgage interest tax relief and those spent on local authority subsidies was about even; in the early 1980s it shifted strongly in favour of owner-occupiers. By 1980/1 the value of mortgage interest tax relief was five and a half times higher in real terms than it had been in 1970/1.[18] Throughout this period, people with mortgages were roughly equal in number to people in local authority rented housing, as the proportion of outright owners (who had paid off their mortgage) was rising.

This period also saw a remarkable shift in personal wealth from other assets into housing. Table 3 compares the asset composition of gross personal wealth in the United Kingdom for 1960 and 1975.[19] While the shift away from company securities and into houses represents a dispersal of personal wealth to a great many small property owners, it has not greatly shifted the highly uneven overall distribution of wealth in British society. The top 1 per cent of the UK population still owns 21 per cent of personal wealth, and the bottom 95 per cent only 59 per cent.[20] What it has done, as we saw in the chapter on households, is to polarize the life-chances of households on average and below-average incomes between those who are owner-occupiers and those who are not: the former have access both to special tax concessions and to opportunities to improve their relative status and stock of wealth by their unpaid labour; the latter do not.

Table 3 Asset composition of gross personal wealth in the United Kingdom, 1960 and 1975 (%)

	1960	*1975*
Land	1.9	3.6
Building society deposits	5.0	6.8
Life policies	11.0	13.8
Other physical assets	7.0	6.5
Other financial assets	34.7	21.7
Company securities	21.2	8.7
Dwellings	19.1	38.9

Source: *Social Trends*, 1976, table 5.37

The distribution of owner occupation is not primarily a matter of choice; increasingly, the vast majority of people who can afford to buy their own houses. In 1983 the mean and median weekly incomes of households with mortgages were £243 and £219, while those of council tenants were £110 and £81[21] – a gap that has been steadily widening since the 1950s.[22] Ninety-five per cent of those households with mortgages have economically active 'heads'; unskilled and semi-skilled workers are under-represented, as are single parents.[23] Among council tenants, only half the heads of households were in employment, 68 per cent were 45 years old or older, and most were manual workers.[24] Local authority rented housing has become (increasingly with the sale of council houses, but as a long-term trend) a residual form of housing tenure, for those who cannot afford to be owner-occupiers, and especially for people with irregular employment. It is also an expensive form, for those households that do not qualify for rebates.

Another important group are outright owners – people who have paid off their mortgages – who make up 24 per cent of all households. They are predominantly older – over half were 65 or over in 1983[25] – and represent a broad spread of occupations (37 per cent were manual workers in 1978).[26] As so many are retired, it is not surprising to find that their average incomes are little higher than those of council tenants – mean incomes £145 per week and median incomes £105 per week on average in 1983.[27] This implies that a fairly high and growing proportion of retired people will have lower regular housing costs in old age, though many houses belonging to pensioners are old and in need of expensive repairs which the owners cannot afford.

All this means that a great many of the current generation of people in Britain aged between 40 and 65 stand to inherit all or part of a house now occupied by an outright owner, and this makes the whole question of inheritance of wider significance in issues of welfare than it has ever been in the past. Once again, at a time of stagnation or recession it may make quite good sense for a large proportion of elderly people to be outright owners, for a large middle-aged mass of people with fairly secure jobs and relatively high incomes to have mortgages, and for another large group of young people, with high rates of unemployment, insecure jobs and very low earnings, to be living mainly in rented accommodation, often on means-tested housing benefit. This is one way in which housing costs can be related, in a very rough-and-ready way, to earnings and life stages, and it also provides a kind of rationale for why the middle-aged should dominate the secure and better-paid sector of the labour market.

But this makes much less sense when, in the next generation, and with an ageing population, we can foresee that people who will be outright owners themselves, will inherit houses from their parents and become multiple owners (or just wealthier). We need to be sure that there is some reliable mechanism by which they will then put these houses back on the market, or rent them out, at prices which make them available and affordable to the younger generation. If this does not happen, then the housing market will increasingly become distorted away from supplying the basic needs of young people, and towards providing a store of wealth for the middle-aged. And even if we could imagine (as seems rather unlikely) that the middle-aged would release their inheritance to their offspring at little or no cost to the latter, there would be an important issue of fairness between those who stand to benefit from this chain and those who do not.

There is plenty of evidence that no such mechanism exists at present. If we compare the current housing situation with the one which existed in Britain in the 1950s, for instance, it is clear that the availability of small, inexpensive units (to rent or buy) is now extremely limited. At that time there was very little demand for larger, older houses for owner occupation, and many of these were being converted into flats. In the 1970s the move was in the opposite direction – large houses were coming back into the owner-occupied sector, and the supply of privately rented houses and flats was falling. Britain now has the lowest number of persons per room in Western Europe. The example of Italy just quoted shows how a move in this direction can coincide with a severe shortage of smaller, less expensive dwellings.[28]

The market-minded blame the restricted supply of rented housing on changes in the law which have given tenants greater security and protection, and the decline in the numbers of private dwellings for rent has certainly coincided with these changes. However, it is difficult to disentangle the effects of changing legal rights from the very long-term shift out of landlordism and the more recent shift of personal wealth into housing. The better protection of tenants' security and rights would not be such a threat to owners if they did not perceive houses primarily as a store of wealth rather than as a source of income. It seems that in the past two decades it has become more advantageous for owners to live in half-empty houses which they have improved to luxurious standards, or to own holiday cottages, than to let parts of their property as flats. Thus the enormous sums of money disbursed as mortgage interest tax relief (far greater as a proportion of national income than the council house building programmes of the 1950s) serve only to encourage people to hoard their houses like gold, while others remain overcrowded or homeless. The examples of France and Germany, with very different systems of housing finance and taxation, suggest that government policy can act to ensure that more of the housing stock becomes available as dwellings.[29]

The basic income scheme which was set out in the previous chapter would provide one simple remedy for this situation. If people's income needs were met in this way, and mortgage interest tax relief were abolished, then the tax treatment of housing would become neutral. (A means-tested housing benefit system could subsidize rented housing as an interim measure, partly to accomplish the swing of the pendulum required by decades of rewarding house-hoarding.) Under this scheme, people would have every inducement to increase both their earnings and their savings, since both the poverty trap and the pensioners' savings trap would have been eliminated. The aim of the scheme would be to increase overall levels of employment and to encourage people to offer themselves on the labour market – though not necessarily in full-time jobs; above all, it would be to end the polarization between active, earning households and passive unemployed ones. Taxpayers could then perhaps be offered tax relief for any five-year period of their lives on interest paid for loans, not necessarily for housing, as a way of helping new buyers.

At present, it is active households that also have the best access to favourable housing finance, and to the income needed for self-servicing home improvements; they alone are in a position to indulge in house-hoarding. The change in the tax-benefit system required by a basic income scheme would lead to inducements for potential house-hoarders to see their property more in terms of potential income, and less as a store of wealth. Its redistributive effects, and the resulting greater earnings opportunities for poorer households, should ensure that the position of these households in the housing market was improved, and that they had better access to house purchase and to rented property.

However, this would certainly not be the only change required by fairness and need in the field of housing and the environment. Direct action in issues of planning, housing supply and the management of local authority estates is an obviously urgent priority.

State Intervention and the Rented Sector

The period after the Second World War was one in which West European governments intervened directly in the housing market, controlling rents, making planning orders, allocating resources and in many cases becoming directly involved in new construction. For instance, the French state was engaged in a whole range of measures, including rent controls, direct building programmes, subsidization of buildings for sale, planning and influencing housing finance, which blurred distinctions between a 'private' and a 'public' sector of housing.[30] In West Germany the desperate housing shortage after the war led to a massive building programme – an average of over 500,000 houses a year from 1950 to 1974 – achieved mainly by means of public grants to private investors, who then leased the accommodation at controlled rents. In spite of financing over half the postwar building programme, the West German state owns only about 3 per cent of housing, a proportion that has been declining in the past 15 years.[31]

A number of factors caused changes in policies in the later 1960s and early 1970s. All over Europe, groups began to protest against the demolition of old areas of cities, poor planning and sub-standard construction of new projects, and the failure of new provision to create an environment suited to convivial social life. The greater stringency that accompanied slower economic growth slowed new building, and encouraged governments to concentrate on rehabilitating older dwellings. Recently there has been increasing evidence of the rapid structural deterioration of much of the housing constructed in the 1960s – especially large system-built units – and of social problems associated with their design.

Both these factors have been very marked in the British public sector (local authority housing). In the spring of 1986, the Audit Commission found that 85 per cent of local authority dwellings required major repairs, at an average cost of £5,000. These figures reflect the plight of Britain's increasingly run-down council housing stock. It is not simply that council house building virtually stopped in the early 1980s; it is also that flats and houses have been neglected to an alarming extent, so that the diswelfares of often bleak estate environments are compounded by the diswelfares of damp, dilapidated or damaged dwellings.

Council housing was the growth area of British housebuilding in the period of reconstruction after the Second World War; between 1945 and 1950, 113,000 of the 141,000 new houses constructed annually were for local authorities. As house construction continued to accelerate during the 1950s and early 1960s, the proportions of new council and private houses first became equal (around 1960) and then shifted, so that by 1964 almost 60 per cent were for owner occupation.[32] In the 1970s, the local authority housebuilding programme was the first major casualty of public spending cuts, and since 1979 the Conservative government has virtually put an end to local authority construction.

There is ample evidence that in the postwar period council housing was the preferred form of tenure for a large section of working-class households – it gave security; standards of construction were reasonably high; floor space was quite generous; the new estates were seen as pleasant environments. A great many factors have contributed to the progressive downgrading of council housing since then, and all have made it both economically a less desirable tenure and socially a less attractive environment. Failures of planning and management have compounded political and economic factors, leaving the whole local authority sector in a sorry mess.

The postwar Labour government used the apparatus of wartime controls to build good-quality housing at low cost on compulsorily purchased land. By squeezing out the development profit extracted by landowners and speculative builders, it was able to avoid the problems of the first wave of local authority building which followed the First World War.[33] With the re-emergence of building for the private market and rising costs, the local authority building programmes of the mid-1960s onwards (and especially the disastrous experiments with tower blocks and deck-access systems) departed from traditional plans and designs, and created environments with enormous unforeseen problems. Poor construction and design, along with the adverse reaction of tenants to compressed high-rise living, created tensions and conflicts which a bureaucratically organized and trained management was quite unable to tackle. In a recent survey in the West Midlands, it was reported that a high proportion of contacts with housing departments in the region take the form of complaints about neighbours; yet the staff have no training in such problems, and resort to a standard threatening letter which is neither credible nor helpful.[34]

Meanwhile, economic conditions were also transforming the social environments of many of the older outer-city council housing estates. A survey of four large estates in 1984 found unemployment rates of well over 30 per cent, with 70 per cent of households on means-tested housing benefits and 70 per cent of households with no car, but needing to travel into the city for many shops and services. The director of the research agency commented:

Here we are seeing the emergence of whole communities which have sunk into a kind of subsistence economy. There is less and less cash circulating, no land market, little or no market for consumer goods, and no competition. . . . What we are seeing is not simply inequality. It is the emergence of two entirely different socio-economic systems, with a local economy subsisting entirely on state provision and administrative fiat, where resentment grows in proportion to the sense of powerlessness.[35]

This survey, and others of inner-city estates, suggest an utterly bleak social environment. The surprising thing is that people do sustain supportive networks and informal organizations, even under such adverse conditions; with a bit of encouragement, and the opportunity for dialogue with planners and housing officials, they can do a good deal to improve the quality of their neighbourhoods, despite their lack of material resources.[36] To quote just one example, on the Sholver estate in Oldham (40 per cent male unemployment, with vandalism alone costing £10,000 per month) a 50-strong group of young volunteers (the Sholver Rangers) has undertaken to try to improve the environment, clearing up litter and rubbish, planting trees, and even trying to create a wildlife sanctuary.[37]

Clearly, future policy must combine the regeneration of the local authority housing sector (programmes for redesigning access, refurbishment, repair and new building, and especially for building more smaller units) with measures for local participation and control. Tenants and residents should not merely be consulted by politicians and officials; they should be allowed far more day-to-day involvement in the running of their neighbourhoods. This requires a different form of local politics as much as it does different training and attitudes from housing officials. The council must be seen to be concerned about the whole social and physical environment, and about developing the community, not simply with the management of its assets.

It is ironical that by far the most vigorous, and in many ways the most successful, housing policies should be found in Liverpool, which in 1985 built more houses than the other councils in England put together. Furthermore, experts judge the planning and design of the new building in Liverpool to be among the best in the country; the council has listened to tenants, and responded to what they want by way of privacy, access, communal areas and a rather traditional urban residential environment. Unfortunately, the City Council's political style leaves something to be desired in other aspects of public relations; aggressively paternalistic and service-delivery-orientated, it pursues its policies in the name of its employees' jobs and wages, of state provision and political orthodoxy, rather than in terms of local participation or control. But there seems to be no logical reason why a similarly committed programme of building and repair should not be combined with a willingness to involve local people in the management and development of their social environments.

If not, then the dismal views of the market-minded will have been borne out – that state ownership and state provision are always and necessarily correlated with bureaucratic controls and the dead hand of officialdom, stifling both freedom and participation. The failures of British local authority housing seem to reflect arrogant political assumptions and lack of official imagination and skill rather than any iron law of social welfare. Until the 1960s, ideas about participation in social provision were very little developed, and when they started to receive attention (in the era of the community development projects) they were based on the notion of tiny adversarial agencies (without a political base) waging war with giant bureaucracies (which enjoyed the full support of local political elites). The changes required by the local authority housing sector are more thoroughgoing than this model would allow, and they need strong political leadership, of a kind that seems to have emerged in some local authorities in the adversity of a punitive Conservative central government.

In a strange way, the phenomenon of large-scale purchase by tenants of their council houses offers encouragement; to buy a house in such an environment is not simply an economic act, but some kind of vote of confidence in the community. Some whole estates have been sold to residents, who plan to manage them corporately. The notion that ownership and control are not necessarily synonymous, and that negotiations about welfare require partnership and participation by people with different interests, is nowhere more relevant for social welfare than in the field of housing.

Conclusions

In British society, the divided economic interests of the sectors, reinforced by income maintenance policy, is largely reflected in the physical segregation of residential environments, and in the division between housing tenures. The market sector is predominantly one of owner-occupiers; the state sector (those dependent on means-tested benefits) coincides closely with local authority housing. The values and principles which inform policy in these two spheres under a market-minded government are entirely different, and continue to diverge.

If policy on housing and the environment is to change, there will be a long period in which the distortions associated with this split will have to be tackled by different means, which will involve a rather artificial dual approach. I do not want to imply that there are not important environmental and social problems in private residential areas, or that the tangled mess of local authority housing finance can be easily resolved by a shifting of political will. What I am suggesting is that the excessive wealth-storing orientation of the private sector will have to be tackled before a better balance between housing stock and occupation is established in that sector; that this in itself will create a rather different social environment in many areas; and that measures to correct the appalling neglect and mismanagement of the local authority sector would in themselves restore some economic vitality to many depressed council estates, in turn changing their social systems.

Housing and environmental policy in other West European countries suggests that Britain's dualism is not inevitable, and that the state can contribute to the supply of inexpensive accommodation (including units for single people) by a variety of interventions, including (but not necessarily mainly) ownership and management. The problem of the economic power of home-owners, and the tendency of liberal capitalist societies to divert excessive resources into housing under certain conditions, do seem to be very widespread. Housing policy should aim to counteract these forces, not to reinforce them.

The environmental dilemmas of advanced capitalist countries are in some ways the obverse of 'the tragedy of the commons'. Exclusive property rights lead people to hoard private space, to accumulate wealth and to pollute the public environment. The problem is not so much overuse of common resources as undervaluation of the shared environment; political processes provide little opportunity for people to participate in planning, or to show direct concern for their social milieu. It is just as important that local authorities find ways of enabling common environmental concerns to find active expression as it is for household shelter needs to be met.

Notes

1 David Donnison and Clare Ungerson, *Housing Policy*, Penguin, 1982. All over Europe, including Eastern Europe, the supply of housing has been increasing at around 2 per cent per year since the war – in Spain at about 2.7 per cent. But in Britain it fell to around 1 per cent from 1969, and even lower in the 1980s. If dwellings are defined as structurally separate living units with their own entrance to places of public access, in 1960 Britain had more dwellings (315) per 1,000 inhabitants than any other Western European country except Sweden, Denmark and Belgium; by 1975 nearly all others had more, as did East Germany, and the other eastern and southern European countries were catching up (ch. 3).
2 Central Statistical Office, *Social Trends 15, 1985*, HMSO, 1985, chart 8.2, p. 124. In 1983 there were 22.2 million dwellings, compared with 14 million in 1951, and just under 21 million households. This gap has been roughly the same since 1980.
3 In the United Kingdom owner occupation as a proportion of all housing tenure rose from 35 per cent in 1961 to 57 per cent in 1983; in France from 41.3 per cent in 1962 to 46.7 per cent in 1978; in West Germany from 33 per cent in 1960 to 48 per cent in 1980; even in Yugoslavia almost two-thirds of the houses built in this period were for owner occupation. Martin Wynn (ed.), *Housing in Europe*, Croom Helm, 1984.

4 Martin Wynn, 'Introduction' to Wynn, *Housing in Europe*, table 1.2, p. 4. In Western Europe average investment in housing as a proportion of total fixed capital investment in 1976 was 20.25 per cent, compared with 10–15 per cent in Eastern Europe, but dwellings per 1,000 inhabitants in East Germany, Hungary and Czechoslovakia are comparable in numbers to those of West Germany, Austria and Italy, or Canada and the United States.

5 Ibid. Average usable floorspace in Denmark in 1976 was 122 square metres, in the United States 120 square metres, but in USSR and East Germany only 49 and 60 square metres. Average number of rooms per dwelling in Britain and the Netherlands was 5, compared with 3 or less in Eastern Europe. Donnison and Ungerson, *Housing Policy*, p. 44.

6 Michael Ball, *Housing Policy and Economic Power: the Political Economy of Owner Occupation*, Methuen, 1983, table 1.1, p. 2.

7 Declan Kennedy, 'West Germany', in Wynn, *Housing in Europe*, pp. 64–5.

8 Ball, *Housing Policy and Economic Power*, ch. 2.

9 Ibid. ch. 11.

10 Donnison and Ungerson, *Housing Policy*, p. 186.

11 Ball, *Housing Policy and Economic Power*, ch. 11.

12 Ibid., p. 335.

13 Donnison and Ungerson, *Housing Policy*, table 13.9, p. 226. In 1974–5 the total tax relief and subsidy going to households with an income of under £1,000 a year was £6 million, at an average of £59 per year, and that to those earning over £6,000 was £139 million, at an average of £369 per year.

14 Ibid., table 13.8, p. 225.

15 Liliana Padovani, 'Italy', in Wynn, *Housing in Europe*, pp. 248–51, tables 9.1 and 9.2.

16 As part of his analysis of the tendency of the propensity to consume to decline, Keynes suggested that owner-occupiers might reduce aggregate demand by repaying their mortgages more quickly than the house actually deteriorates, hence diminishing their propensity to consume. Because there were few owner-occupiers at the time, Keynes did not treat this as important, and gave more attention to the creation of large sinking funds by local authorities in relation to their building programmes. However, the large sector of owner-occupiers who are now outright owners indicates the number of people who have recently behaved exactly as Keynes anticipated during the recent recession. See J. M. Keynes, *The General Theory of Employment, Interest and Money* (1936), Macmillan, 1957, ch. 8, pp. 101–2.

17 Ball, *Housing Policy and Economic Power*, ch. 12.

18 Ibid., pp. 8–9.

19 Donnison and Ungerson, *Housing Policy*, table 13.6, p. 219. Since then, the proportion held in dwellings has fallen slightly to 35 per cent in 1982, and that in other financial assets has grown to around 25 per cent. *Social Trends*, 1985, chart 5.23, p. 90.

20 *Social Trends, 1985*, table 5.22, p. 90. In 1971 the comparable proportions were 31 and 48 per cent. When occupational pension rights are included, the 1982 proportions are 17 per cent for the top 1 per cent and 66 per cent for the bottom 95 per cent.

21 Office of Population Censuses and Surveys, *General Household Survey, 1983*,

HMSO, 1985, table 6.14(a), p. 75. In 1978 the comparable figures in terms of *annual* incomes were £7,192 and £6,573 for mortgagors and £4,186 and £3,582 for council tenants. In 1953 median household incomes of council tenants were 83 per cent of owner occupiers'; in 1983 it was 35 per cent.

22 *General Household Survey, 1983*, table 6.13(a), p. 74. Only 10 per cent of owner-occupiers with mortgages are semi-skilled manual workers, personal service workers or unskilled manual workers, and only 5 per cent economically inactive.

23 Ibid.

24 Ibid. and table 6.9, p. 70.

25 Ibid., table 6.9.

26 Ball, *Housing Policy and Economic Power*, ch. 9.

27 *General Household Survey, 1983*, table 6.14, p. 75. In 1978 the mean income of outright owners was still only just above that of council tenants, and the median slightly lower.

28 In Italy the number of rooms per person in the population is now almost 1.5, compared with about 0.8 in 1951; but the number of occupied dwellings is now 1 million less than the number of households, whereas in 1951 it was only 750,000 fewer. Padovani, 'Italy', table 9.1, p. 249.

29 In France since the Second World War the state has been much more involved in the building of subsidized housing for sale to lower-income households, in construction itself and in planning the output of dwellings, as well as in a more conscious attempt to influence the finance of this sector of the housing market. In West Germany the state-financed building programme (Social Housing) produced about 300,000 low-rent houses a year between 1950 and 1974; about half of all West Germany still live in rented housing. Wynn, *Housing in Europe*.

30 Jon Pearsall, 'France', in Wynn, *Housing in Europe*.

31 Kennedy, 'West Germany', in Wynn, *Housing in Europe*.

32 Donnison and Ungerson, *Housing Policy*, p. 148.

33 Ball, *Housing Policy and Economic Power*, ch. 12.

34 BBC Radio 4, *Today* programme, 6 March 1986.

35 CES Ltd, *The Outer Estates of Britain: Preliminary Comparison of Four Estates*, CES paper 23, Interim Report, 1984. The director was quoted in *Guardian*, 24 October 1984.

36 See for instance Brian Sabel 'Community and Social Services', in Bill Jordan and Nigel Parton (eds), *The Political Dimensions of Social Work*, Basil Blackwell, 1983.

37 *Guardian*, 5 June 1986.

11

Health

It seems very obvious that health should be one of the items in any list of basic needs that the state should meet, without reference to the citizen's social position. After all, we all need a certain standard of physical functioning to be able to form and carry through life plans. Poor health narrows opportunities to choose from the range of projects and commitments available to members of any society; hence equal access to health care should be one of the basic rights of citizenship.[1] It should not depend on income, occupational status, marital status, race or any other distinguishing feature of individual citizens.[2]

But things are not as straightforward as this. While some physical impairments and illnesses are entirely random in their social distribution, most are not. Most common ailments and injuries and many serious ones are caused by identifiable – and often avoidable – stress, carelessness, indulgence or excess. Death is inevitable, but the risks of most illnesses and injuries can in theory be greatly reduced by regimes of self-care, diet, exercise and stress-reduction. Does this imply that people have a duty to care for their own health, and if so, what does this entail for the state's policies in health care provision?

Risks are not merely related to self-care or self-neglect; they also vary with occupation, gender, income, environment and many other social factors. Even if the state equalizes access to medical services, this will not equalize people's vulnerability to illness and injury. Some people choose careers or life-styles with high material rewards but which they know carry high health risks; others have little choice about taking roles which are bad for their health (such as caring for elderly relatives), or living in unhealthy environments.

Because of all these factors, what we might mean by a citizenship right of equal access to basic health care consists of a rather diverse list of needs to be met. First there would be adequate diet and shelter; then safe, sanitary, unpolluted living and working conditions; then opportunities for exercise, rest and leisure pursuits; then preventive (e.g. vaccination and inoculation), curative and rehabilitative personal medical services; and finally non-medical support services.[3] In this list, the services of doctors, nurses and hospitals play a very small part – a subdivision of one section of what we might mean by basic health needs. Yet this sector is what most people think of as a health service; it consumes up to 10 per cent of GNP in advanced capitalist countries, and it raises many acute moral dilemmas about fairness and need.

The central dilemma of health policy might be seen as how to encourage everyone to take the best possible care of their health, and how to combine this self-care with the expertise of medical science so as to produce the healthiest possible population. But the question of fairness in the distribution of health and illness requires us to consider how both self-care and medical care opportunities could be equally available to all citizens, rather than simply to leave self-care as a duty of citizenship, which it is assumed all have equal opportunity to fulfil.

In chapter 9 I argued for a basic income as a citizenship right – this would give everyone a guaranteed income as a way of meeting their dietary needs, while the allowances for disability costs, age and so on should also provide for non-medical social support. In chapter 10 I argued for measures that would enable a fairer sharing of accommodation and a healthier, less stressful environment. Given that the basic income would allow work (both paid and unpaid), earnings and leisure to be more fairly shared, it could be argued that this represents the best way of making self-care equally available to all citizens, consistent with the principle that people should be allowed autonomy and self-direction in their choice of projects. Following the logic of this approach, why should medical services not then be provided through private insurance? Why should the basic income not include an element sufficient to cover insurance against all reasonable medical care needs, leaving individuals to make their own arrangements through insurance companies, whose interests would be in securing cost-effective services?

The present argument against this approach lies in the fact that insurance cover is not available against certain widespread risks except at exorbitant prices, and that the groups most vulnerable to these hazards are least able to afford them. Proposals for adopting American-style private or occupational health insurance in Britain or Western Europe all rest on an assumption of a residual state scheme (like the US Medicare and Medicaid) to cover people who cannot afford commercial schemes; the rather attractive figures they quote for the 'normal' insured person are possible precisely because certain risks and groups are excluded.[4] The US system is clearly unfair, not merely because some people are left out of both private and public schemes, and because the public one gives inferior services, but also because evidence shows that poorer people are deterred from getting the service they need, and suffer more illness.[5] But under the proposal I am investigating, we could assume that state-approved insurance companies were required to offer a good-quality service covering all these eventualities, and that no one would be excluded from this basic coverage.

Yet once these stipulations are made, the point of leaving the whole thing for individuals to arrange is really lost. Before an adequate sum for 'reasonable' coverage can be included in the basic income, a definition of what reasonable health care needs are must be decided. While it would be permissible for people to spend more than this sum on health insurance, the state could scarcely allow people to spend less without defeating the whole object of the exercise. And once they had also approved the insurance companies' coverage, they would in effect have completed a compulsory, national, insurance-based scheme, providing a universal level of medical services. The only question which would then remain would be whether this insurance basis was more efficient, and caused people to use services more rationally, than one provided free or at reduced cost out of taxation. Evidence from the United States and some Western European countries suggests it might not be; the British national health service, paid for out of general taxation, is widely recognized as being one of the most cost-effective in the world.

So we are left with the problem of how best to combine an expert service for curative medicine with informal systems for self-care and mutual care. Does the professionalization of medical treatment weaken people's commitment to self-care, and perhaps even their sense of responsibility for their own physical and psychological wellbeing? Does the pursuit of scientific cures for diseases consume an ever-larger proportion of resources, and put societies at risk of what Illich calls 'medical nemesis'?[6] Do doctors arrogate to themselves powers (including moral decision-making) which should be left with individuals? Does the medicalization of problems distort their nature, and distract us from more important issues of fairness?

The Medical Profession

Medical services are dominated by doctors; other medical occupations define their legitimacy and their roles largely in relation to those of the dominant profession. Most studies of professionalism take medicine as their paradigm, and consider how doctors have been able to control the nature of their work, to limit entry into their occupation, to claim the exclusive authority to practice medicine, to legitimate their body of knowledge and to be accountable only to each other for professional standards and ethics.[7]

In the advanced capitalist countries, all this was accomplished before scientific developments allowed modern medical achievements. The main causes of improved health in the late nineteenth and early twentieth centuries were better nutrition, housing, sanitary engineering and personal hygiene; immunization was a scientific advance that needed little medical skill to implement, and the other major breakthrough – the use of antibiotics – scarcely requires enormous sophistication of practice.[8] Yet doctors have consolidated their professional status and power and have gained a pre-eminent place, not merely clinically, but to a large extent administratively, and in the planning of services, within state schemes for health care.

The processes by which this occurred have been similar in most capitalist countries. Doctors made a living by combining services to fee-paying private patients (either directly or through insurance schemes) with services to the state. For instance, in Britain during the Poor Law era, doctors contracted to work in public assistance hospitals in addition to their private practice. In Spain as recently as the early 1970s, most doctors were primarily private practitioners, who also worked part-time in a public hospital, even when more than 80 per cent of the population was covered by a state health insurance scheme.[9] But as extensions of state provision drew them more into the public sphere, their monopoly power allowed them to retain professional autonomy, as well as to gain control over decisions about resources, priorities and plans for state health services.

Doctors achieved this position of power in the distribution of health care without showing conspicuous concern about unfairness in this distribution before state schemes were established. Only in Portugal can they be seen to have played a positive role in the political process of widening access to medical services and redistributing resources.[10] Elsewhere their main concern was to retain their autonomy and dominance, their relative status and earning power.

Since the Second World War there has been a rapid growth of expenditure on medical services in all the advanced capitalist countries. In the 25 OECD countries the proportion of total GDP spent on these services rose from 2.5 per cent in the early 1960s to 4.5 per cent in the mid-1970s;[11] this led to some alarm, and attempts to limit increases and make spending more cost-effective in a period of slower overall economic growth. But there continues to be strong upward pressure on health service expenditure, arising from demographic change (old people are an increasing proportion of populations, and consume more medical care), and new technology in diagnosis and treatment.

At a policy level, it is difficult to demonstrate the effects of all this extra spending on medical services. McKeown, in his review of the impact of medicine on mortality rates, concluded that 'medical intervention has made, and can be expected to make a relatively small contribution to prevention of sickness and death'; and, in relation to the relief of sickness, 'a successful operation which restores the patient to health is not typical of the work of hospitals, much of which is palliative or unproved.'[12] In recent years most of the great increase in spending on medical services has gone to expensive acute hospital care, with small returns for additional expenditure. Methods like open heart surgery and transplants are vastly expensive and achieve only a small prolongation of life. Research on coronary-artery bypass operations found that, although they gave considerable relief, five years later the original symptoms had returned.[13] During the period when spending on medical services was rising fastest in Britain (1960–75) there was little change in numbers absent from work for sickness or numbers claiming sickness and invalidity benefit, and the expectation of life at most ages improved by about a year.[14]

British surveys in the 1960s and 1970s suggested that the prevalence of many conditions is much wider than the number of people receiving medical treatment. One in 1963 found that, for every case of diabetes, epilepsy or rheumatism known to the general practitioner, there was another case undiagnosed;[15] another in 1970 suggested that, for every known case of bronchitis, urinary infection, high blood pressure and glaucoma, there were four unknown.[16] Other surveys have found that up to half of a population have conditions sufficiently serious to warrant referral to a general practitioner.[17] But a five-year follow up of 200 people found to have unexplained abnormalities in medical tests discovered that only three had developed clinical disease that could be predicted from the earlier survey.[18] This suggests that physical conditions which are 'abnormal' in the sense of diverging from the statistically average occur in most people from time to time, and generally right themselves without bringing serious illness, which casts doubt on the value of diagnostic and treatment methods. However, it is also clear that with advancing age most people suffer from chronic sicknesses of various uncomfortable or debilitating kinds – the General Household Survey reports rates of around 60 per cent for those aged 65–74 and nearly 70 per cent for those aged over 75.[19] It is these conditions, such as arthritis, back pain and bronchitis, that are least susceptible to medical treatment, and receive least attention from hospital specialists.

With psychological disorders this is even more strikingly the case. In Britain, research suggests that about a quarter of any population suffer from psychological symptoms sufficiently disturbing to cause them to consult a doctor in any year.[20] But of these, only just over half will be recognized by their general practitioners as having psychological symptoms. Although doctors report that they regard the appropriate treatment for such conditions as psychotherapy, what they actually give is almost always reassurance or sedatives.[21] Most patients stopped taking their tablets before the course was over, without telling their doctors, and few regarded the advice they were given as helpful.[22] Recovery rates were high, but those who failed to recover were mainly suffering from unsolvable *social* problems. About 2 per cent of the population are referred to psychiatric outpatient clinics in any year, and a study of these showed that the improvement in a group treated by psychiatrists on this basis was no better than a matched group treated by general practitioners.[23] Research in both Britain and the United States has shown that social factors are more important influences on recovery rates than clinical factors; the most important predictive variables for non-psychotic psychiatric outpatients were the patient's material and social circumstances, including poverty, isolation and lack of leisure opportunities.[24] In other words, social rather than clinical factors were the most important elements in prolonging psychological disorders, and the most important influence on chances of recovery.

Finally, there is the evidence that in all advanced countries, although age of death is lower and prevalence of chronic illness is higher among the lowest socioeconomic groups, medical services, and especially expensive hospital care, go disproportionately to people in higher-income groups[25] – this is true even in Eastern European countries, it appears.[26] Some countries have tried to tackle this directly, with limited success, but it seems to relate to cultural traditions as well as to the organization of health care. These traditions may include variations in the ways in which doctors react to people according to their class position, and a longstanding medical neglect of conditions which are most common among working-class patients.

In answer to all these criticisms of recent medical developments, it could certainly be argued that even highly successful treatment of a small number of serious illnesses would not show up prominently in large-scale statistics, and that many advances in recent years have been of this kind. Even supposing that other hospital treatments could not be shown to prolong life or allow a full recovery to any significant extent, in so far as they relieve suffering and improve the quality of life, even for a limited period, they serve a humanitarian purpose. Above all, enormous numbers of people suffering from physical and psychological disorders consult doctors, request treatment and express appreciation for the help they receive. Far from reflecting dissatisfaction with medical services, increasing expenditure reflects an apparently insatiable rise in demand – people regard doctors and hospitals as having solutions to their health problems, and medicine simply responds to this demand to the full extent of its scientific ability. This in turn focuses attention on the relationships between patients and doctors, and on how health care is best provided within this relationship.

The Doctor–Patient Relationship

Doctors are in a specially powerful relationship with their patients, because of their monopoly over the treatment of illness, because they deal (among other things) in matters of life and death, because they enjoy high social status, and because the state gives them the authority to decide a number of important issues affecting people's family lives, employment roles and incomes. In addition to this, doctors tend to behave decisively and authoritatively, once they take responsibility for the treatment of illness.

Because of the dual origins of medical practice, there were really two paradigms of the doctor–patient relationship. On the one hand, there was the role of doctors who were paid by better-off patients for their services, and who therefore provided consultations and treatments within the ethos of a service offered for a fee. On the other hand, there was the role of doctors in state (public assistance) hospitals, where they were answerable to the state which employed them, usually under contract, to give basic health care to its dependants. Studies from Spain, the European country where this dual system was most clearly in evidence in recent times, show that medical ideology tended to be conservative, to reinforce the values of the Franco regime and the Catholic hierarchy, and to be authoritarian towards patients, especially those paid for by the state.[27] The doctor–patient relationship in modern West European medical care contains elements of both these paradigms. In Britain, there are still significant differences in the relationship between private and national health service patients and their doctors.

The fee-for-service model implies a diagnostic assessment followed by a discussion of the doctor's opinion; the public assistance model implies medical attention on behalf of the state, followed by 'doctor's orders' – 'being under the doctor' as the modern vernacular has it. The patient in the fee-paying model is still in charge of his or her life and is the moral agent who is being advised, not the passive, compliant receiver of treatment (which the state may require to be carried out as a condition of receiving sickness benefit).

Most treatments prescribed by doctors are self-administered, and most care is provided informally within the household. The decision to give treatment in hospital entails a dramatic change of environment, to a large institution, equipped with sophisticated technology and a complex hierarchy of professional staff. While it is often fairly arbitrary who gets treated in hospital and who at home, the differences in methods and costs are startling. Hospital regimes were originally designed to treat people who were sufficiently ill, injured or fevered to be prone, with anaesthetics to lay low those who did not arrive in this condition. Medical ethics mainly prescribe what doctors may or may not do to people's bodies once they lose consciousness and agency; hospital routines impose passivity and dependence even on people who are in full possession of their faculties. Doctors get most of their training in hospitals, and the majority practise there. They therefore meet patients in a setting which discourages a dialogue about shared responsibility for health care.

The most spectacular examples which illustrate this problem concern operations whose consequences have not been properly explained to patients. Recently in Britain cases came to light of elderly men who, in the process of treatment for prostate gland cancer, had been castrated without their informed consent.[28] But the more general, and perhaps more serious, problem is how medical services which are characteristically delivered in this way can engage with ordinary people to combine effective, active self-care with medical treatment.

Perhaps the best illustration of the problem concerns illnesses which are progressive and incurable, and result in paralysis and eventual death. Doctors are faced with a situation where various palliative treatments are possible but there is no cure, and the outcome is very unpleasant and inevitable. Medical wisdom has conventionally been to shield patients from the truth (though sometimes to tell relatives), in order to avoid distressing them and causing them to lose hope; when patients do not ask directly for information about outcomes, this is taken as evidence that they do not wish to be told.[29] The result is that patients lose all control over the processes of their remaining life and death, and are surrounded by a conspiracy of silence or untruth, in which their immediate care-givers may be included. The alternative approach is to give the patient full information about the illness and its progress, not in one solemn announcement, but continuously over the period of deterioration, through the whole team of medical and paramedical workers – including physiotherapists, social workers and nurses – in order to allow the patient and family to face and manage their fears and feelings in full knowledge, but with full support.[30] The result appears to be a much more effective and humane process, which allows patient and relatives the opportunity to retain some autonomy and dignity in their sufferings (and, paradoxically, some realistic hope), as well as enabling medical staff to share responsibility and care rather than usurping it.[31]

The same principles apply to the treatment of other diseases, where the outcome is less certain, and both prognosis and treatment are necessarily speculative. It seems far better for doctors to share with patients their knowledge *and* their uncertainties, to explain the nature of the disease and treatment, to try to understand the ways in which families deal with the problem and support them, consulting them at each step of the process, rather than taking all control and responsibility away from them. Many of the most difficult ethical problems concerning whether or not to use drastic treatments, or how to allot very expensive resources, arise because doctors insist on agonizing about such issues among themselves, rather than entering into a dialogue with fully informed patients, who are given time to think about the implications of the alternatives for them.

In primary health services, the issue is not so much one of the powerlessness and passivity of the patient as of the possibilities of dialogue and sharing within the very brief and ritualized terms of the consultation – usually a few minutes' prelude to the writing of a prescription.[32] Increasing interest in self-care by middle-class people, starting in America and spreading to Western Europe, has extended from exercise, diet, posture and the environment to holistic and alternative methods, which tend to emphasize patients' participation in and responsibility for their wellbeing. One problem for the future of primary health services is how this trend can be accommodated within the doctor–patient relationship; better self-care has advantages for doctors, but holistic medicine and alternative therapies do not fit into the scientific paradigm of traditional treatment, nor do they accord with the norms of medical responsibility and professional monopoly.[33] An awkward era of renegotiating boundaries in health care seems inevitable. A second problem is how those groups that have not yet begun to take an interest in self-care can be introduced to the concept, especially when unhealthy customs (such as smoking) are very much part of class or occupational culture, or represent a defence against stress or a protest against adversity.

If we are indeed in a phase of renegotiating boundaries in health care, in which some patients are reclaiming control over their physical functioning and some doctors are encouraging this (even in the face of resistance from some of their patients), then a very significant drama in this process is represented by the Wendy Savage court case in Britain.[34] Mrs Savage, a consultant obstetrician, was suspected from duty for misconduct and accused of incompetence over five deliveries of babies. She appealed against suspension, arguing that her colleagues were making excessive use of caesarian sections and other technology in their work, and that her professional stance on childbirth was made quite explicit to her patients, and was generally supported by them, both as a general position and in their individual cases. She insisted that the scientific evidence about the risks to babies from prolonged labour was ambiguous, and that the issue was really one of professional ideology and the doctor–patient relationship. She argued that she explicitly upheld the rights, wishes, feelings and dignity of women as mothers, championing their control over and participation in childbirth. The case directly raised issues of moral agency, and doctors' right to arrogate to themselves wider social decisions, turning them into matters for scientific expertise. But the re-emergence as moral and political issues of questions which had seemed to be 'medicalized' – such as contraceptive advice for girls under the legal age of consent – can be an uncomfortable and contentious process.

Conclusions

Health services meet basic needs, and hence should be part of what the state guarantees to provide equally to all citizens. This implies equal access to medical treatment; but it also implies a range of other measures which enable and encourage good health care, including education, environmental improvements, preventive measures, safety at work and public hygiene.

It is unreasonable to suppose that the medical profession will promote all (or perhaps any) of these policy goals – indeed, it may be more realistic to assume that they will try to obstruct some of them. Like other occupational groups, doctors are more likely to pursue traditional definitions of their own short-term advantages than wider long-term goals; they have to be shown the benefits of state health policies for themselves as well as for their patients. But if the state has a duty to try to meet the basic health needs of citizens, and if citizens have a corresponding duty to look after their own health, then it is a misguided policy to leave the medical profession with too much overall responsibility for meeting health needs, or for enabling good self-care. Political leadership and new administrative systems must be developed in these fields, and public participation in health service issues – which has in the past been actively discouraged – must instead be encouraged and enabled.

This is coming to be recognized even in countries like Sweden, which have very high rates of spending on medical services and a very centralized, hospital-based, doctor-dominated system. In a recent report on Swedish health service policy for the next decade, much more emphasis was given to a wider definition of policy and to more participation by the public, at political and individual health care levels.[35]

In Britain, wider participation is growing in a field from which lay people were once most powerfully excluded – mental health. As part of the process of trying to relocate services for mentally ill and mentally handicapped people in the community, joint care planning teams have in some areas included voluntary groups and the parents of mentally handicapped people. Participation must tend to involve people who are long-term consumers of health care much more than others who are not directly affected, but attempts to include patients and groups in policy-making must contribute to greater effectiveness as well as fairness in the development of services.

New technology will not necessarily always serve to concentrate resources in hospitals. It is possible that microelectronic devices will soon help people monitor their own health, or allow primary health care centres to develop methods of self-screening. The dispersal of expertise in self-monitoring and self-care would alter the doctor–patient relationship, and perhaps also that between general practitioners and specialists; it might even reverse the trend of growing proportions of hospital-based specialists, and allow more expertise to be relocated in the community.

As proportions of elderly people in the population rise, issues about the distribution of medical services become more difficult. In the United States people over 65 use about 3.5 times the value of services of people below that age.[36] The question of fair shares in health care, including the definition of the basic health needs of elderly people, is far too important to leave to a single profession. It ought to be clearly on the political agenda, for detailed debate, in all democratic countries.

Notes

1 This is the line of argument adopted in Norman Daniels, *Just Health Care*, Cambridge University Press, 1985.
2 This might be the claim of the British national health service.

3 This is in fact the list provided by Daniels, *Just Health Care*, p. 32.

4 See for instance Arthur Seldon and Ralph Harris, *Overruled on Welfare*, Institute for Economic Affairs, 1979.

5 According to the President's Commission for the Study of Clinical Problems in Medicine and Biomedical and Behavioural Research, *Securing Access to Health Care*, vol. 1, US Government Printing Office, 1983, pp. 92–3, between 11 and 12.6 per cent of the non-institutionalized population of the United States have *no* health care insurance, and about 10 per cent more have inadequate coverage. The differential between poor blacks and relatively affluent whites, all in poor health, in their use of doctors is about 250 per cent. R. Bayer, A. Caplan and N. Daniels (eds), *In Search of Equity: Health Needs and the Health Care System*, Plenum, 1983. But blacks are significantly more likely to suffer from measurable illnesses. Ibid.

6 Ivan Illich, *Medical Nemesis*, Calder and Boyars, 1975.

7 See for instance Eliot Friedson, *Profession of Medicine: A Study in the Sociology of Applied Knowledge*, Dodd Mead, 1970, and Terence Johnson, *Professions and Power*, Macmillan, 1972.

8 Health Departments of Great Britain and Northern Ireland, *Prevention and Health: Everybody's Business, A Reassessment of Public and Personal Health*, HMSO, 1976.

9 Jésus M. de Miguel, 'The Role of the Medical Profession in a Non-democratic Country: The Case of Spain', in Margaret Stacey, Margaret Reid, Christian Heath and Robert Dingwall (eds), *Health and the Division of Labour*, Croom Helm, 1977, p. 57.

10 Ibid., p. 55.

11 OECD, *Public Expenditure in Health: Studies in Resource Allocation*, no. 5, 1977. See G. Bevan, H. Copeman, J. Perrin and R. Rosser, *Health Care Priorities and Management*, Croom Helm, 1980.

12 Thomas McKeown, *The Role of Medicine: Dream, Mirage or Nemesis*, Nuffield Hospitals Trust, 1976, pp. 114 and 116. See also A. L. Cochrane et al., 'Health Service "Input" and Mortality Rate "Output" in Developed Countries', *Journal of Epidemiology and Community Health*, vol. 32, 1978, who found in 18 developed countries that, when he related indicators to numbers of doctors and nurses, health expenditure, etc., 'health service factors are relatively unimportant in explaining the differences in mortality between our eighteen developed countries.'

13 S. F. Seides et al., 'Long-term Anatomic Fate of Coronary-artery Bypass Grafts and Functional States of Patients 5 Years after Operation', *New England Journal of Medicine*, vol. 298, no. 22, January 1978. See also H. G. Mather et al., 'Myocardial Infarction: A Comparison of Home and Hospital Care for Patients', *British Medical Journal*, 17 April 1976.

14 Roger Hadley and Stephen Hatch, *Social Welfare and the Failure of the State: Centralised Social Services and Participatory Alternatives*, Allen & Unwin, 1981, pp. 39–40.

15 J. M. Last, 'The Iceberg', *Lancet*, vol. ii, no. 28, 1963.

16 British Medical Association, *Primary Medical Care*, Planning Report no. 4, 1970.

17 R. G. S. Brown, *The Changing National Health Service*, Routledge & Kegan Paul, 1973, p. 21.

18 A. R. Bradwell, M. H. B. Carnalt and T. P. Whitehead, 'Explaining the

Unexpected Abnormal Results of Biochemical Profile Investigations', *Lancet*, vol. ii, no. 1071, 1974.

19 Office of Population Censuses and Surveys, *General Household Survey, 1983*, HMSO, 1985, table 9.1, p. 158.

20 David Goldberg and Peter Huxley, *Mental Illness in the Community: The Pathway to Psychiatric Care*, Tavistock Press, 1980, pp. 6–14.

21 M. Shepherd, B. Cooper, A. C. Brown and G. W. Kalton, *Psychiatric Illness in General Practice*, Oxford University Press, 1966.

22 D. Johnson, 'Treatment of Depression in General Practice', *British Medical Journal*, vol. 2, 1973, pp. 18–20.

23 H. M. B. Murphy, 'Which Neuroses Need Specialist Care?', *Canadian Medical Association Journal*, no. 115, 1976, pp. 540–3.

24 P. J. Huxley and D. P. Goldberg, 'Social *versus* Clinical Prediction in Minor Psychiatric Disorder', *Psychological Medicine*, vol. 5, 1975, pp. 96–100.

25 Peter Townsend and Nick Davidson (eds), *The Black Report: Inequalities in Health*, Penguin, 1982, ch. 5.

26 D. S. Salkever, 'Economic Class and Differential Access to Care: Comparisons among Health Care Systems', *International Journal of Services*, vol. 5, 1975, p. 373.

27 de Miguel, 'The Role of the Medical Profession'.

28 *Guardian*, 14 May 1986, reporting the Institute of Medical Ethics Bulletin, April 1986.

29 Jonathan Carey, 'Motor Neuron Disease – a Challenge to Medical Ethics: Discussion Paper', *Journal of the Royal Society of Medicine*, vol. 79, April 1986, pp. 216–20.

30 P. G. Newrick and R. Langton-Hewer, 'Motor Neuron Disease: Can We Do Better? A Study of 42 Patients', *British Medical Journal*, vol. 289, 1984, p. 539–42.

31 Barbara Monroe, 'Breaking Bad News', paper delivered at Exeter University, May 1986, unpublished.

32 P. S. Byrne and B. E. L. Long, *Doctors Talking to Patients: A Study of the Verbal Behaviour of General Practitioners Consulting in their Surgeries*, HMSO, 1976.

33 See for instance the report on alternative and holistic medicine by the Board of Science Working Party of the British Medical Association, reported in *Guardian*, 12 May 1986, which dismissed these as being of unproven scientific benefit.

34 *Guardian*, 11 July 1986. Mrs Savage's appeal against suspension was successful.

35 *The Swedish Health Services in the 1990s*, reported in *Guardian*, 14 May 1985.

36 Daniels, *Just Health Care*, p. 86.

12

Care in the Community

If there is an underlying moral basis of society, one would expect it to show itself most clearly in the way people care for and help each other. The notion of a community suggests that people who share the social life of a small geographical area co-operate to meet certain needs; alternatively, it suggests that people who have something in common (such as ethnic origin) come together to pool their resources for some purposes, or at least to organize in pursuit of some common interests.[1]

In advanced capitalist countries, the social services (often referred to as community services) are intended to provide a framework of resources – money, buildings, staff – to enable these processes to be more effective. In partnership with voluntary agencies and self-help groups, they are meant to strengthen informal networks, neighbourly concern and local altruism, as well as to support families in caring for members with special needs. Ideally, social services should mesh with informal systems in such a way as to allow people with special needs – those with physical or mental handicaps, mental illnesses or difficult children, or those becoming frail through age – to live in the community and participate as full members of society.

In practice, like the income maintenance services, those providing care (residential homes, day centres or domiciliary services) have historically been organized to *substitute* for family care or self-care, rather than to enable it to happen, or to share with it.[2] They have assumed that people provide care for themselves or each other within informal systems, and they have tried to identify a small minority of those who are not being cared for in this way (because they lack the necessary network, or are too needy or difficult) and to set up formal systems for caring for them. Often these have consisted of residential institutions outside people's local communities, sometimes in remote rural locations; more recently, they have consisted of bureaucratically organized domiciliary and day care provision.

Under the Poor Laws, institutions – workhouses, houses of correction, reformatories, asylums and hospitals – were the major formal systems for providing alternative care for people whose needs were not met in their community.[3] The postwar social services inherited these institutions, and many of the attitudes they embodied – for instance, the notion that there are specially needy people who cannot contribute to social life, and who should be separated from the rest of society, both for their own protection and for the sake of protecting the community.[4]

When services are organized as alternatives to informal care, families and friends have to choose between sacrificing other projects to care for their neediest or most difficult members, or 'putting them away' in institutions. Families which chose to care for handicapped or elderly members sacrificed earnings, energy, leisure, cultural opportunities and other forms of mutual care to do so. Alternatively, if they chose to 'put away' their problem person, then they usually lost touch with him or her, partly because the institutions were remote and exclusive, and perhaps also through feelings of guilt and resentment on both sides.

Recently, social policy has increasingly recognized that many people who could easily have remained within communities were 'put away' in institutions because their families, friends and neighbours lacked the support they needed to cope with their demands for practical or emotional help. This way of understanding the need for care recognizes that there are no clearly identifiable groups of people who require special care; rather, there are some people who need *extra* resources of practical help or expert assistance to live an ordinary life. But the reorganization of services that follows logically from this recognition has only just begun.

It takes an enormous change of attitudes, roles and processes to provide services that enable and strengthen informal care rather than substituting for it; furthermore, centuries of institutional systems and bureaucratic services have created public expectations which are not easily altered. Radical moves to close institutions and relocate needy and demanding people in the community – such as occurred with juvenile delinquents in Massachussetts, USA,[5] or with mentally ill people in Bologna, Italy[6] – meet with resistance from almost everyone affected. The most difficult problems in every country concern people who have spent lifetimes in institutional care, and staff whose experience and training have been exclusively institutional or bureaucratic.[7]

In this chapter I want to consider three issues about the provision of care in modern capitalist societies. The first is the role and tasks of informal carers, and how best this form of care can be fostered and enhanced. The second is the form that social services should take if they are to sponsor the best possible care for people with special needs in the community. The third is the process by which welfare which consists of care and practical help is shared in communities, and how the social services can play a part in accomplishing fairness in this process.

It is a sobering thought that in Britain, although economic change and the creation of social services have led to fluctuations in the populations of particular types of institutions, the *overall* proportion of the British population in institutional care has remained constant at between 1.25 and 1.37 per cent throughout the present century.[8] The greatest part of spending on social services in kind still goes to this sector, and the least goes to people being cared for in families, even though these are much more numerous. Can all these resources be reorganized so as to give fairer shares of welfare – more support for informal carers, better-quality services for people living in the community, and more equal burdens between those households with specially needy members and those without?

Carers

Just as the implicit obligation in earlier, agrarian societies was to sustain one's own, so also it was to care for one's own – to be practically and emotionally self-supporting in household, kinship or communal groups. This obligation was carried over (somewhat uncritically) into commercial and urbanized societies, where it became an ill-defined duty of families – in practice, of women.

Nowadays the vast bulk of informal care-giving is done by married women. In Britain there are at least 1.25 million full-time carers, usually looking after elderly or physically disabled relatives. Three-quarters of these are women, the largest proportion being daughters (27 per cent) followed by wives (17 per cent) and mothers (13 per cent); but 16 per cent of carers are husbands.[9] There are another estimated 5–6 million people putting some informal support into the care of a disabled or elderly relative or friend; in addition, of course, there are all the mothers of 'normal' children.

One of the biggest issues of fairness must be the distribution of these duties. The vast majority of informal caring for all kinds of dependent people is now done on a part-time basis. Although most women's working careers are interrupted for several years by childbearing, most of these resume paid work, and each successive cohort of married women rejoins the labour market in large proportions.[10] In Britain the social services have enabled this in two ways. Although state day care for children is very limited (less is available than in the late nineteenth century),[11] day care for other dependent people has recently increased quite substantially. Second, much of the expansion of employment for married women has been in the social services – so women had more opportunity to be paid for looking after other people's dependants.

On the other hand, full-time carers – usually women caring for very disabled or disturbed relatives, or for several children – are denied opportunities of employent and earnings. In Britain their situation was made even more disadvantageous by the fact that before June 1986 the only benefit payable to those who provide unpaid care on a full-time basis – the invalid care allowance – could not be claimed by married women. This rule was successfully challenged in the European court and has been revised.

The obvious remedy for this injustice is to pay a benefit to carers to compensate for the opportunity costs of their role. But this is not as good an idea as it sounds. It would consolidate the role of full-time carer, actually encouraging some people to occupy it in order to qualify for the benefit. But it is well-known that full-time caring carries risks of physical and mental breakdown that are around six times the average. Part-time care is far less damaging to physical and mental health.

Second, because women at present earn less than men, women would be under pressure to take the carer's role, even if men wanted to share it. Then the notion of 'full-time' would have to be defined (at present it is 35 hours a week for invalid care allowance), together with earnings rules prescribing amounts that could be earned from part-time employment. If there were an earnings taper, it would create administrative complexity.

Third, the carers' benefit would presumably not be available to women with several 'normal' children; it would therefore discriminate not only between part-time and full-time carers, but also between categories of the latter. It might also happen that support services, such as day care, would be withdrawn from households receiving a carer's benefit, to the detriment of the dependent person, who might well prefer to receive some care outside the home, and get the stimulation of other company and contacts.

The only system which would avoid these difficulties would be the basic income scheme, described in chapter 9. This would treat everyone as a part-time carer – for themselves or each other – by giving all a weekly income which was enough to meet living costs. By providing disabled and frail elderly people with a benefit to meet the costs of care in addition to this, it would allow them to decide whether to get care from outside the household, or to give other household members part of this income to compensate them for lost earning opportunities. There would be no reason why family care should all be given by one member – it could be shared by them all, since all would get the basic income, and none would be disadvantaged by working part-time.

But what about support services? How could they be meshed most advantageously with informal care, and provide the best support to isolated people?

The Provision of Services

Service provision has been made in ways that reflect the institutional origins of the social services. Residential care provides the basis of the system, with a gradual increase in services aimed at supporting people in the community and preventing admissions to institutions. But these services have tended to be rather standardized, and not carefully designed to meet the needs of their consumers. Most went to individuals who had lost family support, but even these did not make best use of their capacities to help themselves.

Yet there are many people with equally demanding special needs who are either being cared for by members of their households, or are buying care (either domiciliary or residential) from commercial sources. Hence people with similar needs are getting different forms of care from different systems – state services, unpaid household labour and the commercial market. In Britain in recent years financial support has been made more readily available for elderly, handicapped and mentally ill people to take up residence in commercially run homes, whose numbers have grown rapidly, while local authority homes have been closing as a result of financial stringency by central government. So the British state has been paying a means-tested premium (of £110 for an elderly person and £170 for a younger disabled one) to commercial carers, while unpaid family carers have been getting less and less support from local authority services.

At present, both dependent people and carers are faced with fundamental dilemmas of mutual responsibility by this situation, because the extra resources available for people who opt for commercial residential care, and are eligible for supplementary benefit, are considerable. If *all* disabled people were eligible for a disablement costs addition, which covered not only such widespread extra costs as heating and diet but also the realistic cost of care for someone of their degree of disability, then a fairer system could emerge. Disabled people could choose whether to transfer this income to family members (or friends) providing unpaid care, or use it to buy commercial services (either domiciliary or residential), or to contribute to the costs of local authority services consumed.

It may seem strange that I am advocating this solution to the problem of care when I explicitly rejected it in the field of health services. After all, it sounds very like the standard market-minded solution to all problems of resource allocation in the public sector – to try to give individual consumers the power of the purse, to allow them individual choice. Yet there are very important differences between care services and health services which lead me to this conclusion.

1 In issues of care the informal services of household members are almost always potential substitutes for paid services (either of commercial or local authority employees). In the case of medical services this is not the case – the expert part of what doctors and nurses do cannot be done by ordinary people.
2 The cost of care is composed largely of labour costs, whereas the costs of medical services include very large elements for expensive buildings and equipment; hence medical costs are far higher.

3 As a result of this, medical costs which are not met by the state can be met (for people other than the very rich) only through insurance. This does not allow consumers much direct control over services.
4 In any case, because of the high status and monopoly professional power of doctors, individual patients have more limited opportunities to influence the kind of medical service they are given than the kind of care service.

So although I am arguing that there would be few if any benefits in providing a universal medical insurance element in a basic income scheme, I would contend that there is a strong case for paying all disabled people a sum to meet their costs of care, and allowing them to allocate it between informal, commercial and state services.

This sum could include an extra living costs allowance (to meet the extra costs associated with their handicap, including housing, fuel, diet, clothing, laundry and transport) and an allowance – related to their degree of handicap – to enable them to pay for the help they needed in doing tasks they could not do unaided. For those needing most help, this would be equivalent to the cost of 24-hour (residential) care; but it would give them the option of 'buying in' care in their own homes from commercial or state sources, or transferring their allowance to other members of the household who volunteered to provide this service. Carers might need to be protected by rules which guaranteed them a 'wage' out of the care allowance, where the disabled person nominated them as main providers of care.

This form of benefit would allow major shifts in the present boundaries of care. Instead of having to choose between state, commercial or informal care largely as *alternatives*, and often as substitutes for, rather than complements to, each other, it would allow each individual and household to construct a mixture of care from all three sources. Local authority officers would still be needed to advise about available options, to co-ordinate resources and to provide services for people who preferred their characteristic communal style; they might also provide expensive equipment (such as hoists and lifts), and buildings for use by groups. But they would not have a monopoly of services for any group, or the power to impose their definitions of welfare needs. Instead, they might be more involved in the strengthening of informal networks, including negotiations about financial transactions, such as payments to neighbours or local people for occasional assistance to handicapped individuals.

Some of the special needs of groups of dependent people will be discussed in the following sections. The assumption behind the proposal I have made is that the welfare of all such people requires a shift away from centralized management of services, with its inevitable emphasis on service outputs, towards a greater sensitivity to the personal projects and commitments of individuals, and to their actual networks of co-operation in families and neighbourhoods. This allows the needs of handicapped people and their associations to be treated the same as those of other members of society.

Elderly People

Elderly people are the most rapidly growing section of the population, and the very old are the fastest-growing group among these. In the original ten countries of the European Community the proportion of the population over 65 grew from 12.5 to 14.0 per cent between 1973 and 1982.[12] In Britain it has grown from 4.7 per cent in 1901 to 15.1 per cent in 1983 and is expected to rise to 15.3 per cent in 2001; but the proportion over 85 will rise from 1.1 per cent in 1983 to 1.9 per cent in 2001.[13] Between 4 and 5 per cent of the population aged 65 and over have been in residential care since the first decade of the century.[14]

The vast majority of retired people look after themselves or each other, but as age increases so does disability. Among people aged 75 and over in Britain, a third are moderately disabled and 18 per cent severely disabled. It is anticipated that by 2001 nearly 1.5 million people will be unable to walk down the road without help, and nearly a million will be unable to go up and down stairs without help.[15] It is also estimated that by that time the typical couple in their eighties will have only 11 female relatives, of whom 3 will not be in employment, compared with a similar couple today with 40 female relatives, 14 of whom will not be in paid work.[16]

Research shows that elderly people tend to lose their abilities to care for themselves in a certain order. First they cannot bath without help, then they cannot walk outdoors, then dress, then get in and out of bed, then sit down or stand up, then wash, and finally they cannot feed themselves without help.[17] In Britain, the 55,000 beds in geriatric wards contain the highest concentrations of severely disabled people; over half of them cannot get out of bed without help. Among elderly people living alone in the community, there are very few who are so disabled that they cannot dress themselves. Between these two populations are two other groups:- those in residential care, half of whom have only one or no disabilities but 17.5 per cent of whom cannot get in and out of bed without help, and those being cared for by relatives, many of whom are equally disabled.[18] There are about 100,000 elderly people in local authority residential homes in England and Wales, but the number is falling rapidly as financial constraints are forcing councils to close homes; there are about 55,000 elderly people in commercially provided homes, and their numbers rose by 82.5 per cent between 1980 and 1984 as more generous board and lodging allowances for elderly people on supplementary benefit became available (these have since been cut back).[19]

Research has shown that domiciliary services are the most cost-effective way of providing for the least disabled group, with residential care being the most cost-effective for the moderately disabled (family care is more cost-effective only if unpaid work is costed at zero) and hospital care for those with severe disabilities.[20]

However, that study was comparing traditional and rather standardized methods of delivering local authority and health services. A recent and ambitious study by the Personal Social Services Research Unit at the University of Kent has shown that different methods can produce different outcomes and costs.[21] In their experimental scheme, social workers were allowed to 'spend' the equivalent of two-thirds of the costs of residential care on 'packages' of care for elderly people who might otherwise have been admitted to residential homes, planned in consultation with each elderly person. These packages included both health service and local authority resources (which were given 'shadow prices' by the researchers) and the services of local 'helpers', who were hired on a short-term contract basis to do care tasks at frequent intervals or awkward hours, and hence to supplement the standard services. As a result, the elderly people in the experimental scheme had access to a much more flexible range of help, planned specifically for their individual need. When compared with a group of similar elderly people receiving traditionally organized services, in the first year twice as many in the experimental group had remained at home, and less than half as many had died. Because more severely disabled people in the experimental group lived into the third year of the research, more eventually needed *hospital* care, but only half the number entered residential care. The quality of life of the experimental group was assessed as better in respect of morale, depression, loneliness and capacity to cope, and that of their carers better in respect of subjective burdens, strain and mental health difficulties; they also continued to receive the same amount of informal care as those getting traditional services.

All this suggests that a more flexible approach to services for elderly people, using a greater number of part-time local contract workers (sometimes paying people already in the elderly person's network of neighbours or acquaintances), and more schemes that give allowances to families willing to provide respite or longer-term care, might well reduce the need for residential homes and improve the quality of life of elderly people. It suggests that there is a greater capacity to assist quite severely disabled people to live in the community than is at present mobilized by services consisting of full-time workers in centralized bases, or travelling from area offices.

Mentally Handicapped People

The change in the organization of services that is needed to allow mentally handicapped people to be cared for in the community is much greater than that required in services for elderly people. Until quite recently, a large proportion of babies born with mental handicaps were 'put away' in institutions soon after birth on medical advice; another large group were institutionalized when they reached the adolescent stage; and a third group when their parents died.[22] In order to provide care in the community, services have to help overcome fears among many people, especially concerning the dispersal of large numbers of ex-hospital patients who have spent most of their lives in institutions.

However, a new generation of mentally handicapped children is now reaching adulthood in Britain; many of these have had a better education and training for community living than in the past, and their parents also have received better advice and support.[23] They are demanding that similar services be made available for mentally handicapped adults, and that residential care, when this is needed, be closer to the person's home neighbourhood, often in ordinary houses. The best of new services, such as the scheme in eastern Nebraska, USA, illustrate that the skills needed for helping mentally handicapped people are mainly practical, educational and social, and that these can best be provided in ordinary settings.[24] The most important issue for the future, once old-style institutions have been closed, will be how to give sufficient respite care and day services to the families of severely mentally handicapped people to give them the chance of a normal life.

Children

Services which try to support parents in their care of children are faced with a range of contrasting problems. Young children are vulnerable to neglect and physical ill-treatment; children of primary school age are at risk of rejection, especially arising from the breakup of parents' marriages; and teenagers tend to evoke conflict, resist parental control or break the law. All this requires skilled and discriminating forms of help, directed both at parents and at children, both inside the family and away from it.

In Britain, families with children are now the main group among the bottom 20 per cent of income receivers.[25] Widespread poverty among families means that parents lack the basic resources – money, housing, access to amenities – to give their children a decent upbringing, even if they have the necessary skills. Services for families are heavily involved in the relief of poverty, and with advocacy on behalf of families with other state agencies. But they also have to identify children in need of care and protection, and parents who cannot be relied on to meet their children's needs, however much support they may get; they have to act purposefully and decisively to protect children from physical and emotional abuse. It is very difficult to do justice to one such broad and general task, and another that requires such sensitive assessment and communication. The sheer number of deprived families in need makes it difficult to distinguish between lack of material resources and the shortcomings that arise from emotional or psychological problems.

As a result of the death of several children with whom social services departments had been closely involved (many of whom were legally in the care of the local authority, but placed home 'on trial'), policy has moved in the direction of protecting services against public criticism. It is concerned primarily with identifying children who need to be compulsorily removed from their parents, and placing them in substitute families wherever possible. When children do come into care, this is seen as a last resort, as a sign of parental failure; parents tend to be excluded from the care given to their children.[26]

This approach severely limits the kinds of support that can be given to parents experiencing difficulties in bringing up their children. It means that work with families is often focused on keeping children out of care, rather than on providing a range of services to families; alternatively, it means that parents are 'monitored', waiting for an incident that can justify compulsory removal of children.[27] It is difficult to see how this can change without a fairly major redistribution of income and life-chances through changes in the major social services. If social services departments were to offer a much more open and supportive service for families, including easy access to generous care facilities (as has recently been recommended by an interdepartmental committee[28]) the demand for these services would be enormous; parents would use care resources as a substitute for the everyday income, housing and play resources they lacked. In the long run, this is clearly the direction in which policy should be moving. In the shorter term, the changes discussed in chapters 9 and 10 would probably have to be well under way before child care provision could be decisively shifted in these directions.

Social Work and Communities

The discussion in the last section of delicate negotiations between service-givers and parents over the needs of children raises the issue of how all these personal services can best be provided. In the case of elderly people, many of the services needed were practical, but here too there was scope for conflicts of interest between family members requiring tactful discussion. People turn to the social services not only for practical support; they also look for resolutions of clashes of interest, when their own processes of negotiation have broken down. Someone may protest that the rules of the household are unfair, or that one person is taking advantage of the rest, or that they are bearing too many burdens. As well as getting extra resources, they may be looking for a re-negotiation of roles, or a redefinition of household rights and responsibilities.

In this way, social workers are often invited into the informal systems of families or wider kinship groups, to mediate between individuals or groups about shares of welfare. This is an unusual, even privileged, situation for an official person; it is far more common for professionals and bureaucrats to represent formal systems in relation to the informal, or to be specialists with exclusive knowledge, power and control over resources. Social workers, although they have access to a range of resources for care and support, are seen mainly as being concerned in everyday relationships, and as being specially experienced in the ordinary problems of living, rather than being bearers of esoteric expertise.

But the social worker's role is not a comfortable one. To mediate over fairness and shares of welfare in households or kinship groups is to engage in a moral dialogue about fundamental, even ultimate, values. Even though the language of the informal system is usually direct, and the feelings are often raw, the intimacy and the pain in such negotiations for the participants is disturbing; to share in such a process risks something of the social worker as well as his or her clients. Perhaps because of this, or perhaps in search of more professional status, social workers often prefer to think of this work in terms of the social sciences – the psychology and sociology of human interaction – and of their role as that of a formal, professional person. Social work is apt to represent itself in terms of its scientific expertise in human relations, rather than its skills in informal negotiations about the stuff of ordinary life.

Yet social workers' potential strength lies in their ability to be effective mediators in situations where other officials would struggle. Precisely because they do not possess the characteristics of the higher-status professions (exclusive knowledge, awesome professional territory, exclusive decision-making power), they *have* to learn to work in unpromising situations – in natural (often chaotic) environments, making decisions over which they can be challenged by lay people or a number of other officials. They have to learn how families and neighbourhoods work, how informal decisions are negotiated and how welfare is shared out. They have to pay respect to people's values, life-plans and commitments; they usually cannot impose their own definitions of their clients' good, or predetermine the outcomes of their interventions.

In this way, social work, of all the processes by which the state provides social service, is in some ways best placed to mesh with informal systems for sharing welfare. It can engage directly in the processes that were described in the first part of the book, within people's own language, culture and networks. It should try to make use of this advantage as much as possible, and should avoid imposing its jargon, its organizational constraints and above all its statutory powers to coerce as much as possible.

Unfortunately, there are many pressures both within and outside social work to make it more formal, alien and compulsory, particularly from those who see problems such as child abuse, delinquency and family breakup as symptoms of a general social degeneracy, of which social work itself is sometimes suspected of being part. If it were possible to resolve problems of this kind by means of authoritative, imposed disciplinary interventions, there would be little point in providing social services through social work at all. Families and neighbourhoods would instead be policed by uniformed officials who reported to courts, which made orders requiring people to change their behaviour and removing incorrigible trouble-makers to structured institutions.

The justification for using social work in the provision of social services lies in the idea that some people need generous amounts of time and attention to discuss problems, to work out solutions and to link with available resources; and that many clashes of interest can be resolved through compromise and give and take. Social workers do not have any monopoly of the values and methods they employ, but they are trained and required to respond to very difficult human situations in a way which is contrary to most people's instincts – to approach such situations as family violence, bereavement, loss, cruelty, distress and despair, and to try to use human methods of resolving conflict or alleviating suffering. Social work assumes that, given goodwill and trust, co-operation and respect for shared moral values can be restored in situations where they have broken down, and that this can be done most effectively by discussion and the communication of feelings, rather than by medication or coercion. It also assumes that some social services resources – especially those needed for the care of difficult and dependent people – cannot be effectively used without relationships based on personal understanding and support; that simply dispensing them bureaucratically will mean that they are not used to the best advantage. It accepts that this ideal of service provision is not always appropriate. Some people prefer impersonally provided services; others are too disturbed, distracted, drunk or disorganized to discuss or negotiate; a few are too destructive to respond to anything but compulsory measures. But most of the time things can and should be done by negotiation and mediation, encouraging people to express their views and values, and to take full part in reaching solutions to their own life-problems.

The idea of social work that I have outlined is not well served by organizing it very bureaucratically, by office-based practice or by an ideology which is professionally precious and condescending. But in recent years there have been encouraging signs that the organization of social work services in Britain is moving in the direction of making social workers more available, visible and known to local people, by basing them in neighbourhoods and fairly informal settings rather than in large, purpose-built city centre offices. There has been a good deal of fairly grand theorizing about 'patch-based' social work,[29] but in essence it seems to me a sensible attempt to shift social workers towards a situation where they are more accessible to people, more in touch with the needs of their communities and more credible as welfare brokers.

Much more difficult is the question of wider issues of fairness in the distribution of welfare between communities. Locally based social workers are in a far better position to strengthen neighbourhood networks, by encouraging people with a lot to offer others in trouble (often people who themselves have had past bad patches) to help out. Informal fostering, informal group activities and ordinary neighbourly help can all be encouraged by social workers who really know their area, and make themselves aware of people's strengths as well as their problems. In this way they may actually do something to equalize welfare within small communities, sharing abilities to the benefit of people experiencing acute distress or conflict. But this limits the role of welfare broker to a small patch, and means that the human and material resources of some very deprived areas will be much less than those of more prosperous ones. This is only partly remedied by having other social services which are organized more centrally, and are available throughout the authority.

In the last resort, social work is rather like the family or the small group; it has the disadvantages as well as the advantages of the informal system. It can be good at negotiating fair shares and restoring co-operation (though like the family or the neighbourhood it can also be unforgiving and vindictive). But it can do little about the wider distribution of welfare; indeed, in constantly subdividing a diminishing share of resources and penalizing those who do not accept its own standards of fairness, it can even become a source of injustice in the wider context of a society which allows inequality and unmet basic need. Hence social work needs the background structure of major social services which meet basic needs and allow people to contribute to and benefit from all the spheres of social co-operation.

Conclusions

In a strange way, the wheel of social welfare has turned full circle. In olden times, communities cared for themselves; this tradition was continued among the working-class residents of cities after the industrial revolution. Trade unions, friendly societies and co-operatives were reluctant to concede their powers to care for their own. But first philanthropists, with their scientific charity, and then state agencies, with their institutions and their service-delivery, gradually created formal systems of organized benevolence. These formal systems defined acceptable standards of care, even though they often provided only for people who were not cared for to these standards by the informal system.

Both these processes of social care provided the backup support for industrial production – what in Marxian terms is referred to as the 'reproduction of labour power'. In the 1960s and 1970s the formal system began also to provide significant employment and earnings, as more married women joined the labour force of the social services and more tasks were done as paid work. Recently the whole process of change has gone a stage further. In Britain there are council estates (public housing) with 70 per cent unemployment rates, where people live on state benefits and also receive disproportionate amounts of state social care. It has become a sort of subsistence economy, but with no internal resources for subsistence – a state subsistence system.

Under these circumstances, it is not surprising that attention has refocused on the informal processes of social care, and on how these can be strengthened. For the new right, this often means reasserting the duty of families to care for their own, without reference to fairness in the distribution of burdens or resources. But the left, too, has become more interested in communities and their mobilization, in a rather belated recognition that services will be treated as 'theirs' only if people participate in shaping them, and have a share in the care they provide.

If the processes of industrial production in the advanced economies are going to use less and less human labour, and if the cost of formally provided services is going to go on rising in relation to the cost of goods, then there are important issues to be determined about the future balance between formal and informal social care. A basic income scheme would allow everyone to get enough money to finance their unpaid part-time caring for each other in households. But perhaps it should also be enhanced by additional payments for people who contribute to collective schemes for care in the community – those who help run groups or organize activities for difficult youngsters or disabled elderly people, or even those who help improve the local environment, run playgroups or food co-operatives. Perhaps there should be a range of different kinds of additional incomes, from these small supplements, through the fees paid to foster parents or families providing respite care, to the short-term contracts of the part-time helpers in schemes like the Kent University experiment, up to full-time earnings in social services employment. Perhaps this range should include care co-operatives which trade unpaid time, and systems of care-bartering, such as have been set up in parts of the United States.[30]

How significant are these small-scale contributions to fair shares in welfare? Does informal co-operation really provide a moral basis for fairness in wider society? Can these processes help bring social services and household need into some form of equilibrium? These will be the subject of the final chapter.

Notes

1 There is a long history of sociological theorizing about communities and the nature of community solidarity and interaction. For a lively debate about the relevance of past community organization and spirit to modern social care, see Philip Abrams, 'Social Change, Social Networks and Neighbourhood Care', *Social Work Services*, no. 22, 1980, pp. 12–23; Michael Bayley, 'Helping Care to Happen in the Community', in Alan Walker (ed.), *Community Care: The Family, the State and Social Policy*, Basil Blackwell and Martin Robertson, 1982; and the two appendices to the Barclay Report, *Social Workers: Their Role and Tasks*, National Institute of Social Work/Allen & Unwin, 1982.

2 R. M. Moroney, *The Family and the State: Considerations for Social Policy*, Longman, 1976.

3 See for instance Karel Williams, *From Pauperism to Poverty*, Routledge & Kegan Paul, 1981, and Kathleen Jones, *A History of the Mental Health Services*, Routledge & Kegan Paul, 1972.

4 Elizabeth Bott, 'Hospital and Society', *British Journal of Medical Psychology*, vol. 49, 1976, pp. 97–140.

5 A. D. Miller, L. E. Ohlin and R. B. Coates, *A Theory of Social Reform: Correctional Change Processes in Two States*, Ballinger, 1977.

6 E. Midlarsky and M. E. Hannah, 'Innovations in Mental Health: Case Studies in Community Intervention', *Journal of Psychiatric Treatment and Evaluation*, vol. 4, 1982.

7 Also people who are convinced that the only place for sick or bad people is an institution. See R. D. Scott, 'Cultural Frontiers in the Mental Health Service', *Schizophrenia Bulletin*, vol. 10, 1974, pp. 58–73.

8 Moroney, *The Family and the State*, pp. 47–80.

9 Equal Opportunities Commission, *Caring for the Elderly and Handicapped: Community Care Policies and Women's Lives*, March 1982.

10 Jean Martin and Ceridwen Roberts, *Women and Employment: A Lifetime Perspective*, Department of Employment and Office of Population Censuses and Surveys, 1984.

11 In 1900, 43 per cent of children between the ages of 3 and 5 were attending nursery schools, according to the Report of the Consultative Committee on

Infant and Nursery Schools (The Hadow Report), 1933. See Charlotte Stevens, 'The Politics of Day Care', Exeter University, dissertation for BPhil in Social Work (unpublished), 1981.

12 Eurostat, *Review 1973–1982*, Statistical Office of the European Communities, 1984, table 3.1, p. 105.

13 Alan Walker, *The Care Gap: How Can Local Authorities Meet the Needs of the Elderly?* Local Government Information Unit, 1986, table 1, p. 5.

14 Moroney, *The Family and the State*, p. 42.

15 Walker, *The Care Gap*, table 3, p. 10.

16 A. Charlesworth et al., *Carers and Services*, Equal Opportunities Commission, 1984, p. 31.

17 K. G. Wright, 'The Application of Cost–Benefit Analysis to the Care of Elderly People', University of York, unpublished paper.

18 Ibid.

19 DHSS, *Health and Personal Social Services Statistics, 1985*, HMSO, 1985, tables 6.1 and 7.2.

20 Wright, 'The Application of Cost–Benefit Analysis'.

21 David Challis and Bleddyn Davies, 'Long-term Care for the Elderly: The Community Care Scheme', Discussion Paper 386, Personal Social Services Research Unit, University of Kent, 1985.

22 Michael Bayley, *Mental Handicap and Community Care*, Routledge & Kegan Paul, 1973.

23 Alan Tyne, 'Community Care and Mentally Handicapped People', in Walker *Community Care*.

24 House of Commons Social Services Committee, *Community Care with Special Reference to Mentally Ill and Mentally Handicapped People*, HMSO, 1985.

25 DHSS, *Reform of Social Security* (The Fowler Report – Green Paper), Cmnd 9517, HMSO, 1985, vol. 3, p. 9.

26 Spencer Millham, Roger Bullock, Kenneth Hosie and Martin Haak, *Lost in Care: The Problems of Maintaining Links between Children in Care and their Families*, Gower, 1986.

27 Jean Packman, *Who Needs Care? Social Work Decisions about Children*, Basil Blackwell, 1986.

28 DHSS, *Review of Child Care Law: Report of Interdepartmental Committee*, HMSO, 1985.

29 See for instance Roger Hadley and Stephen Hatch, *Social Welfare and the Failure of the State: Centralised Social Services and Participatory Alternatives*, Allen & Unwin, 1981.

30 Edgar Cahn, 'Service Credit Systems', address to Basic Income Research Group Seminar, 2 May 1986.

13

Conclusions: A Hidden Hand
of Welfare?

In this book I have tried to show how individuals seeking their own wellbeing are able to associate co-operatively with each other. I started from small-scale, informal co-operation, and argued that it necessarily involved negotiations over fair shares of the benefits produced. I then went on to consider the problems of large-scale formal associations, and the measures necessary to achieve fairness in them.

My starting point was the subject view of welfare – that each individual seeks his or her wellbeing through chosen projects and commitments. But my main concern has been with distributive justice, with how it is possible to ensure that everyone gets a fair share of the benefits produced by social co-operation. This involves looking for general principles that can be applied to the terms and membership of associations, which allow fairness of outcomes. Ideally, it involves a single set of principles that can be consistently applied to society as a whole, allowing rules, roles and a distribution of resources which is recognizably fair.

But there is not much point in setting up a fair *structure* for social institutions if individuals do not seek fairness. For instance, if the principles of fairness demanded both a democratic constitution and a strongly redistributive welfare state, unless people actually wanted fairness they would use their democratic rights to change the system, by dismantling the welfare state. So it is very important to establish that, at the small-scale informal level of human associations, people do actually try to be fair to each other and to share out welfare between them, and that this, in turn, influences their attitudes towards participation in larger social systems.

Co-operation brings mutual gains in welfare whose sum is greater than the sum of individual advantages to be made from competition or isolation. So it does actually pay people to co-operate, but only if each gets a share of the benefits. The sharing of benefits entails standards of fairness, because the very idea of sharing is explicable only in terms of what is fair. Hence co-operation ultimately implies having some criteria of fairness for distribution. Again, this is of fundamental importance in understanding how maximizing personal welfare through co-operation necessarily entails a notion of fairness over sharing, and why sharing is therefore the 'natural law' of small-scale associations. It is this fundamental 'law of co-operation', working at the most humble level of society, which provides an unseen, universal process (rather like Adam Smith's 'invisible hand') that guides the distribution of welfare in the direction of fair shares. But the 'hidden hand' of welfare does not work, as Smith claimed the market does, without the conscious intention of human agents – it requires the perception of others as trustworthy potential co-operators with needs and aspirations which are different from, but comparable with, our own. It therefore works through people's beliefs, values and feelings about each other, and not (like Smith's process) in spite of them.

Co-operation therefore depends on a shared recognition – often implicit rather than explicit – that some kind of fairness in the distribution of social goods benefits everyone. Without this common belief in the value of fairness, co-operation would not get off the ground, and without informal co-operation formal structures would not work. Even the largest, most impersonal systems (like money markets) depend ultimately on the notions of mutual benefits and standards of fairness in the application of rules, even though they may involve very large individual gains and losses in the short run. Similarly, no political system can afford in the long run to ignore the notion that all its citizens should stand to gain from membership of society, because that is what membership of society is supposed to entail. So the informal system of co-operation underpins all formal systems in an unseen way.

Of course, this does not imply that unfairness is not universal also. Unfairness arises both through individual actions and omissions – people exploiting advantages or ignoring disadvantages opportunistically – and through the systematic exploitation that takes place when co-operation occurs on unequal terms. But the threat that constantly hangs over exploiters, cheats and free-riders is that others will withdraw from co-operation, and find other non-exploitative, trustworthy individuals or groups with whom to co-operate. This process may take many years, or even generations, but the threat is always there. For instance, even the most powerful capitalist faces the threat of the withdrawal of his workers' co-operation through strike action, through industrial sabotage, and ultimately through concerted political action (with other workers) against him and others of his class. While he may be able to take advantage of his power for long periods, he can expect in the long run that he and his descendants will lose it if they continue to be perceived as acting unfairly. Similarly, the South African government, which for many years never pretended to treat black people as citizens with claims to a fair share of the benefits of membership of that society, is now faced with a situation in which, if it continues to act blatantly unfairly, it will meet revolutionary resistance.

The whole of this book so far has been open to the criticism that it grossly overestimates people's capacity and willingness to co-operate and be fair, and underestimates their selfishness, greed, cruelty, rivalry and destructiveness. But this criticism would be misplaced. My intention has been to show how informal processes of co-operation based on fairness exist in every sphere of society, and how they interact with formal ones. This is not at all to deny that people often exploit, abuse, hurt or harm each other, or simply isolate themselves from others. It is just to point out that, if they *usually* did so in their day-to-day transactions, and particularly in their informal relationships, society would not be able to function.

Exploitation and cruelty exist on a vast scale in every human society. They are built into the structures of economic institutions, political systems, religious denominations, voluntary organizations and families. They are enshrined in the rules and roles of all of these, and many other systems. In addition, people endure arbitrary allocations of natural ability, fortuitous strokes of misfortune, illness or handicap, and so on. All these things work in the direction of unfairness. Yet beneath all this (or above it, or alongside it, or against it), people do work together, and do share out what they produce. The result is not fair shares, but without a concept of fairness no production or distribution would be possible. In the first place, people regard it as fair to stick to the rules, and to negotiate about exceptions. Second, people may co-operate conditionally on terms they perceive to be unfair, but sooner or later they will try to re-negotiate these terms, or to withdraw from co-operation, or to gain compensation in other spheres; in other words, they will seek fairness.

Political authority recognizes both exploitation and co-operation. It legitimates some social relationships and processes and proscribes others. It aims at achieving the maximum consent to the fairness of the processes it authorizes, and the unfairness of the ones it declares illegal. Successful forms of government achieve a high level of support for major social institutions as based on principles of fairness, and a high level of disapproval of lawbreaking as being unfair.

Liberal capitalist states, like Britain and the United States in the nineteenth century, rested heavily on the idea that fairness was achieved by a combination of the market and the household: both allowed voluntary exchange, the one commercial and the other customary, and each complemented the other. In this century support for these ideas has been eroded, and the state's role in providing social services has increased, in line with ideas that were already part of the continental tradition. It was recognized that market outcomes were not always fair, and required some readjustment; and that some people needed more care than they were able to get from families or other informal sources.

Once people came to perceive that the market did not share out welfare fairly, and that some households had unfair burdens of responsibility, it was logical that they should look to the state to achieve greater fairness. The social services of the welfare state were part of the postwar settlement in which new institutional arrangements, offering fairer terms of citizenship, were adopted in advanced capitalist countries. But, as I showed in chapter 6, these new social institutions still assumed that employment and the household unit would meet the basic needs of the vast majority of citizens, and that (except in the cases of health care and education) social service provision for welfare would be a compensatory redistribution after wages and salaries had been paid out and domestic services had been given.

In this book I have questioned the assumptions on which the postwar institutions of social welfare were based, in the light of subsequent social change and economic development. I have argued that they do not provide the social rights that individuals need to enter the labour market and the household on equal terms, and that in many cases they actually reinforce the inequalities inherent in traditional economic and domestic roles. My analysis of the direction of changes and developments in advanced capitalist societies led me to propose an entirely new basis for ensuring the equal freedom of all members of society, and new principles of distribution for the social services. The fundamental idea of my proposal was that individual citizens should have their basic needs guaranteed before they enter the labour market or the family, so that they have security of income support as well as health care as a precondition of co-operation and fairness. So, instead of trying to compensate individuals for economic or domestic disadvantages through redistribution, the state should provide a basis of equality for all spheres of co-operation, and allow people to enter them or withdraw from them as they choose, secure in the knowledge that in the long run they will seek fairness in sharing their product, at the same time as seeking their own individual welfare.

Far from undermining informal co-operation, self-care and mutual responsibility, this would – according to my analysis – enable these to be better meshed with formal systems for producing and distributing social goods. The duty which corresponds to the state's guarantee of all citizen's basic needs is that all citizens should care for themselves and each other, and co-operate for their mutual benefit. Because these activities are voluntary and informal, the state cannot enforce this duty; it can only enable it to be done.[1] I have argued for a structure of welfare services and social policies which I believe would be best to achieve this aim.

Formal and Informal Systems

The history of human society could be seen as a gradual incorporation of people once engaged in small-scale informal activities into large-scale formal ones. Once there was nothing but small groups producing for themselves ad exchanging mutual services; now there are political systems that include hundreds of millions of people, and international corporations producing enough hamburgers and motor cars to encircle the world. As people have been drawn into formal systems – by the promise of greater mutual benefits – they have given up some of their informal resources (their means of producing their own subsistence, their local networks for mutual care). But the informal system still absorbs most of our time and meets some of our most fundamental needs, even in the most advanced societies.

We are becoming more aware of some of the limitations of formal systems of all kinds. Technological advance in processes of production has allowed us to equip large numbers of people in the rich countries with refrigerators and televisions, but not with jobs. Services – whether provided through the market or through the state – are becoming very expensive. All this refocuses attention on the informal sector, and leads us to ask how we can evaluate its contribution, how we can promote its benefits, and how we can ensure fairness, both within it and between it and the formal sector. This interest in the household, the neighbourhood and the community – initially by the new political right, but increasingly by the new left also, as well as by the ecology movement – is a bit of an afterthought in the Progress of Humanity, but it should not be missed as an opportunity to reassert the claims of these neglected domains.

In any analysis of society, there is a strong case for starting from an account of the ways in which we care for ourselves and each other within these small-scale systems. Not only are they historically the oldest; they are also essential for the functioning of the economy and the political order. I have argued in this book that they provide the moral basis for all social interaction. The problem is that they are not easily susceptible to systematic analysis or measurement. They are *ad hoc*, sporadic, idiosyncratic and infinitely variable – in short, they are informal.

But we do know something about the sheer bulk of things that people do for themselves and each other,[2] and that, although some people do much more than others by way of unpaid caring, self-provisioning, helping their neighbours, doing voluntary work and so on, almost everyone does *something*. Even the most dependent members of households contribute by their presence, if only to the extra unpaid work that has to be done by someone else. So it is safe to assume that as households we are all engaged in self-care and in the care of others. I have also argued that within our own small informal systems we do try to give each person his or her due, according to principles of fairness.

If this is so, then a good starting point in the organization of society might be how to give everyone a fair share of resources with which to carry out their tasks of self-care and caring for others. If we can no longer assume that people have those resources at their disposal (as in the subsistence economy) or that they can get them through the labour market, then we should ensure that the state provides them, in the form of income and services. I have argued that the basic income principle, and the redistribution of housing, health and personal social services resources to meet basic needs, would be the fairest way of doing this.

The value of the resources distributed by the state to meet the basic needs of each individual citizen – the 'social wage' – would then provide a monetary equivalent to the value of self-care and mutual help that people provided for each other. If we recognized these benefits and services as being the resources counterpart to those activities (or the historical compensation for lost means of production, hunting and gathering rights, communal amenities, etc.), then we would have some way of measuring the contribution (and benefit) of the informal sector to the whole social system.

In the case of the basic income, this would mesh quite logically with the labour market. At present, in Britain a couple with two young children, average housing costs and a single earner on average male earnings get no benefits (apart from child benefit) when in work, and around £65 in unemployment benefit when out of work; so this couple's income from the state bears no relation to the amount of unpaid household work done, since this is approximately the same whether or not the man is in paid employment. If the man loses his job, he really has no options between staying unemployed and on benefits, and trying to get another full-time job which pays at least the equivalent of his benefit rate plus work expenses, after deducting tax and national insurance contributions. For the woman, since she gets nothing for her unpaid work, convenient and congenial part-time employment is advantageous to her to the extent that her wages (less work expenses) exceed the costs of paying a child-minder up to earnings of about £40 a week; after that she starts to pay income tax and national insurance contributions at nearly 40 per cent, so extra work becomes less advantageous, unless her wages are that much higher.

With a basic income, the calculation becomes rather different. If we regard this as the couple's state income for unpaid work, and put it at £25 per week each, plus £30 for the two children, then this can be represented as an hourly rate of income for the domestic and child-care work they do between them – say, £1.50 an hour. Since they now both face income tax at about 40 per cent on the first pound of their earnings, the wife will require higher pay to get her to join the labour market; if there are no such opportunities she will withdraw, as her after-tax earnings less her child-care expenses will amount to less than the hourly rate of her state (basic) income for caring for her own children. On the other hand, if both man and wife can earn at about the same wage rate, it would make sense for both to work up to the point where their marginal hourly net earnings are equal to their marginal hourly state income for their remaining domestic and child-care tasks. For instance, if they both worked for 30 hours a week, and their marginal hourly pay (after deducting tax, work and child-care expenses) was £2 per hour, it would not be worth either of them working an extra hour if they were left with 40 hours a week of domestic and child care tasks (i.e., a marginal hourly state income of £2 an hour).

In reality, of course, this calculation could seldom be so accurately made, since hours of unpaid work are variable and difficult to measure. My point is that under a basic income scheme there is a state income corresponding to unpaid work, and that choices about employment would be adjusted to average amounts of such work done. At present there is no such possibility of adjustment, since the choice for men is almost always between full-time employment and no employment, and women have no independent income to correspond with their domestic and child-care tasks.

In recognizing the contribution to social welfare made by self-care and mutual care, and in providing resources sufficient for people to meet their basic needs, the state would clearly be signalling that these activities formed the foundation on which all social relations were built, and to which all formal systems were related. By doing so according to the principles developed in this book, people would be encouraged to develop their own ways of sharing rights and responsibilities fairly, rather than having a rigid pattern imposed, according to inflexible rules. The result should be a much more dynamic and creative development of informal systems, and a much better fit between these and the formal spheres.

The principles of fairness embodied in the basic income approach to social policy are those of equal autonomy of members in all forms of co-operation, and in citizenship. The aim is to provide fairness through this form of equality, rather than by multiple, complex interventions to compensate for the unequal consequences of co-operation which takes place on unequal terms, between people who do not start from positions of equal automomy. The aim is to allow everyone the security of a guarantee of their basic needs, so as to enable them to withdraw from any form of co-operation that they perceive as unfair, without losing this security.

However, it is a matter for political decision which aspects of the individual's initial assets should be regarded as relevant for this calculation of equality. For instance, although many liberals might be persuaded of the case for a universal basic income, it would be much more difficult to convince them of the case for equalizing property holdings; socialists might be much more interested in tackling this issue (through inheritance taxes, for instance). Similarly, liberals would be likely to see basic housing needs as a policy issue to be tackled through income support, whereas socialists would favour direct intervention in the housing market, and possibly even the public ownership of houses or land.

Another important issue for political dispute would be the state's role in the planning and organizing production. Even if provision of employment were no longer an aim of economic policy, and public ownership for the sake of this or other aims were no longer a priority, socialists would favour a planned strategy over productive decisions and the overall balance of the economy at a national level, and an active approach to identifying and meeting social needs at a local level. This would produce different patterns of employment and output from the more market-orientated principles favoured by liberals. In this way, the formal organization of social co-operation would continue to provide the main issues for political conflict and competition.

Who is My Neighbour?

Informal systems are small-scale. They are limited to the number of people who can know each other personally, and can negotiate co-operative relationships face to face. The sense of fairness and negotiating skills that people learn from these encounters are carried over from one set of relationships to another, and allow informal co-operation to take place in any new situation – work groups in a large organization, or strangers in an emergency. But as a way of sharing welfare over time, informal systems can be relied upon to cover only a very small territory – often no larger than the household.

It can certainly be argued that the problem of modern advanced capitalist countries over fair shares of welfare lies in a tendency for society to fragment into rival competitive groups. The notion of social rights depends on a perception of common basic needs. It rests on an agreement that the state should protect people from the harm that would result from these needs not being met, as it protects them from external and internal attack. This in turn requires everyone in society to see themselves as sharing a common life as citizens, and to pool the risks of their society by contributing to a common fund.

The new right backlash against the welfare state consists in reasserting the free-rider problem.[3] Granting social rights to all rewards cheats and turns hard workers, wealth-creators and risk-takers into suckers; those who give nothing to the community are free to live off the efforts of others. Hence it emphasizes the duty to help ourselves and our own, and encourages a return to a narrower sense of mutual resonsibility. Its stress on family and community is part of this tendency.

This criticism is a self-fulfilling prophecy. The idea of fair shares (in large societies or small groups) depends on basic trust. If enough fear and resentment is generated, basic trust breaks down; it is far easier to destroy perceptions of common needs than it is to create them. We know how quickly people can return to behaviour based on stereotypes of blacks, foreigners, hooligans or scroungers if they are encouraged to do so. The next step from this is to organize in groups for self-protection and conflict.

We have seen this process in Britain under Margaret Thatcher. Her appeal was for both self-reliance and a strong state. By emphasizing conflicts of interest and pursuing divisive policies, her government has in fact reinforced the social strife that she won support for denouncing. The deprived are more resentful, more aware of their grievances, and less inhibited about taking direct (even lawless) action; the privileged are more insecure, more defensive and edgy. With each deterioration in social relationships comes a new pretext for stronger government, for more allocation to law and order, more drastic methods of control and tougher punishments.

Even so, and despite the British people's record of being more inclined to blame the poor than other European countries' inhabitants,[4] there is a good deal of evidence that people share an idea of an acceptable minimum standard of living, and see it as the state's duty to guarantee this standard.[5] The Thatcher government has suffered a decline in popularity as it has come to be seen as uncaring. Most people say that the government should do more about poverty, unemployment, health and education. This suggests that, even though people are critical about inefficiency or unfairness in the implementation of social policies, they retain a sense of the need to base policies on fairness to all citizens, and on a notion of universal social rights. Furthermore, the survey evidence suggests a considerable consensus about what are understood as basic needs.[6]

Where the new right has struck a chord with electorates all over Western Europe is in its insistence that the social services should not be the only sphere in which issues of fairness over shares of welfare are debated. Advanced capitalist societies can allow opportunities for moving between market, state and domestic spheres; and welfare shares depend on all of these, and on people's chances of combining their contributions to them and benefits from them effectively. The social services had become an obstacle to this kind of flexibility, because they were rigid, bureaucratic and paternalistic; they were also based on outmoded notions of people's roles in the market sector and in the domestic sphere. The radical new right stole a march on the complacent and conservative left by insisting that the boundaries of the spheres could and should be shifted, and their people would adjust their behaviour to new opportunities.

But the new right itself used ideas and categories which were even more archaic than those of the social services. They claimed that the market could by itself be the basis of fair shares in the formal sphere, at a time when it was quite visibly allowing a widening of the gap between rich and poor, employed and unemployed. They claimed that the family could meet people's need for care, at a time when there were more single-person and single-parent households than ever before, and when the proportion of disabled and handicapped members of the population was rising faster than ever. They argued for a far narrower view of the state's responsibilities when it was clear that it should be taking a new and wider role, and when they themselves (in government) were being reluctantly drawn into more interventions.

The welfare state was potentially unpopular when it could be presented as expanding inexorably and representing an obstacle to personal freedom and economic growth. But it is potentially popular when presented as an essential guarantor of basic needs, as the foundation for fair shares, and as allowing freedom and flexibility in access to all the spheres in which welfare is redistributed. But this is not simply a matter of presentation; the social services need to be radically restructured, and their rules and processes revised, for this version of their functions to be credible. This restructuring has to take account of the changes that have taken place both in the formal economy and in the household sphere.

I have argued to a view of fairness in society as a whole which starts from what all citizens have in common by way of basic needs, but which allows all equal access to the formal and informal spheres, to develop their individual and co-operative projects and commitments. This strategy tries to do justice to the two senses in which we are neighbours, and owe it to each other to co-operate and be fair, in modern advanced capitalist countries. On the one hand we are *all* interdependent, as part of the same highly integrated economy and the same complex political system; our society can satisfy our basic needs only in so far as it functions fairly and efficiently at this larger-scale level; and few of us could sustain ourselves, let alone pursue our life-plans, if these formal systems of which we are part were to break down.

On the other hand, our opportunities for active co-operation and for practising fairness are chiefly at the personal, small-scale and informal level. It is there that we negotiate with others about how to reconcile our individual projects and commitments with joint ones; it is there that we learn how to compare our welfare with theirs, and to design rules and roles that give fair shares. The welfare state must recognize this, must encourage it, and must enable these processes to mesh easily with its own distributions of benefits and services. In the long run, people's sense of common membership of wider society – their ability to treat someone from another region, race or religion as a neighbour – must depend on their experience of practising co-operation and sharing fairly with their small circle of personal friends and close relatives.

Both kinds of trust and co-operation are essential for modern advanced societies. The state must create a structure that enables both and links them together. The 'hidden hand' of welfare cannot make bricks without straw.

Economic development has deprived people of most of the resources they used for providing for themselves and caring for each other – land, tools, close-knit stable communities. It has given them much greater prosperity, but at a cost of far greater insecurity. This is a poor foundation for trust and co-operation. The state should provide security by meeting people's basic needs. Then they would be able to deal fairly with each other.

Notes

1 Clearly, the state can and should enforce people's duty to care for dependent people (children, elderly and handicapped) up to a basic standard, in the sense that it should substitute its own or someone else's care for theirs if they are being cruel or neglectful. But it cannot force people to be responsible for each other, or to treat each other fairly – it can only try to make this possible, and deal with the consequences when they do not.

2 See for instance Janet Finch and Dulcie Groves (eds), *A Labour of Love: Women and Caring*, Routledge & Kegan Paul, 1983.

3 Claus Offe, 'Democracy *versus* the Welfare State? Structural Foundations of a Neo-Conservative Argument', paper presented to a conference on Poverty, Charity and Welfare, New Orleans, February 1986.

4 Robert Walker, 'Resources, Welfare Expenditures and Poverty in European Countries', in Robert Walker, Roger Lawson and Peter Townsend (eds), *Responses to Poverty: Lessons from Europe*, Heinemann, 1984, table 2.19, p. 57 (based on European Community Survey, 1977).

5 See for instance Joanna Mack and Stewart Lansley, *Poor Britain*, Allen & Unwin, 1984.

6 Mack and Lansley found that there were five items on a list they presented to a very broad and large sample of British people which over 90 per cent agreed were necessities, essential for an acceptable standard of living in our society: heating, an indoor toilet (not shared), a damp-free house, a bath (not shared) and beds for everyone in the household. Over two-thirds agreed on the following eleven items: enough money for public transport, a warm waterproof coat, three meals a day for children, self-contained accommodation, two pairs of all-weather shoes, a bedroom for every child over 10 of different sex, a refrigerator, toys for children, carpets, celebrations on special occasions such as Christmas, a roast joint or its equivalent once a week, and a washing machine. Over half endorsed another six items: new rather than second-hand clothes, a hobby or leisure activity, two hot meals a day (for adults), meat or fish every other day, presents for friends or family once a year, and a holiday away from home one week a year.

Index